KU-053-362

Flying IFR

Also by Richard L. Collins

Air Crashes
Flight Level Flying
Flying Safely
Flying the Weather Map
Instrument Flying Refresher
(with Patrick E. Bradley)
Mastering the Systems
The Perfect Flight
Pilot Upgrade
(with Patrick E. Bradley)
Tips to Fly By
Thunderstorms and Airplanes

Third Edition

Flying IFR

Richard L. Collins

An Eleanor Friede Book
THOMASSON-GRANT
Charlottesville, Virginia

Published in 1993 by Thomasson-Grant
Copyright © 1993 by Richard L. Collins

All rights reserved. This book, or any portions
thereof, may not be reproduced in any form
without written permission of the publisher.

Any inquiries should be directed to:
Thomasson-Grant, Inc.
One Morton Drive
Charlottesville, Virginia 22903-6806
(804) 977-1780

Printed in the United States

00 99 98 97 96 95 94 93 5 4 3 2 1

Library of Congress
Cataloging-in-Publication Data

Collins, Richard L., 1933-
   Flying IFR/ Richard L. Collins. -- 3RD ED.
      p. cm.
   "An Eleanor Friede book."
   Includes index.
   ISBN 1-56566-043-9 : $29.95
   1. Instrument flying I. Title.
TL711.B6C64 1993   93-19594
                                        CIP

Contents

Preface vi

1 The Foundation 1

2 Basic Variations 12

3 Basics Plus 25

4 Actual Instruments 43

5 Preflight Action 48

6 In-Flight 60

7 The Points of Stress 78

8 Thunderstorms 88

9 Ice 111

10 Doing It in the Dark 126

11 Middle-Altitude IFR 139

12 IFR Emergencies and Glitches ... 161

13 The System 172

14 The Machines 180

15 The Risks and Rewards 198

16 Keeping it Together 218

Epilogue 225

Index 227

Preface

Flying IFR makes an airplane a reliable traveling machine. Where the VFR pilot is haunted by every cloud and visibility restriction, the current and proficient instrument pilot rarely has to cancel flights. Put another way, with IFR capability, we can really get our money's worth out of an airplane. But to accomplish this takes more than a canned FAA instrument rating. In most cases, the IFR rating is simply a license to learn. The process of preparing for the written and flight tests leaves many stones unturned. The excellent manuals on the theory of instrument flying don't always cover the practical aspects of IFR flying. That's why the original *Flying IFR* was written, revised once, and why this third edition is offered—to continue to explore the practical side of flying on instruments.

Since the last revision, many new IFR pilots have joined the ranks, many existing instrument pilots have increased their activity, and many things have changed. Turbocharging is a good example of equipment that really helps us in IFR flying. When the original *Flying IFR* was prepared, only four turbocharged singles were available, and none of them were pressurized. When the first revision was published, twelve turbocharged singles were being offered, two of them pressurized. Since that time the development of new airplanes has slowed dramatically, although an exciting new turboprop single, the

TBM 700, has come on the market. We have also seen the Piper Malibu go through extreme scrutiny after a series of accidents. It has become even more clear that while being able to utilize higher altitudes is an important capability, it is also something that requires a high level of proficiency and understanding. In this new edition of *Flying IFR* you'll find new coverage of light airplane operation in the Flight Levels, which begin at 18,000 feet. There is also increased coverage of the relationship between systems (including autopilots) and instrument flying.

A lot of new safety information is available today, thanks in many cases to the AOPA Air Safety Foundation, which has an extensive computerized database of general aviation accidents. Information from that source has been used throughout this revision as the risks as well as the rewards of instrument flying are explored.

Computers have come to aviation in droves since the last revision of this book; now many of us file our own flight plans through the DUAT system, obtain and interpret weather information, and use flight-planning software. A lot has changed. This book is up-to-date in its treatment of real-world instrument flying. It makes no effort to prepare the reader for tests other than the ones encountered on actual IFR flights. Regulations are covered only as they apply to practical situations and as they directly relate to IFR safety. *Flying IFR* is strictly about flying IFR in light airplanes. It will be helpful to both the student of instrument flying and the practicing instrument pilot, who will always continue to learn from experience. The real learning process is endless . . . and very enjoyable.

1. The Foundation

One of the primary tasks in instrument flying is to get priorities straight in your mind. I observed a good example of this one day as I followed another airplane on an ILS approach in VFR conditions. The pilot ahead was having a terrible time—swooping, dipping, and making what appeared to be rather mad lunges at the ILS course with his airplane. Clearly, this pilot had no business practicing ILS approaches. The effort was purely wasteful—he had the cart before the horse. From two miles behind, it was plain to see that the pilot didn't have a strong capability at basic instrument flying. He could not assimilate the data on the panel, he could not hold a heading, and he could not maintain a constant rate of descent. These problems are rather common; in these modern times, it is easy to forget the basics as we rush headlong into flight that seems related more to vast arrays of talented computers than to one person and one machine. Regardless of an airplane's sophistication, the basic ability to fly the airplane is first in importance. If you can't fly the airplane solely by reference to instruments, with a measure of precision and confidence, there is no way to utilize all the electronic wonders. Basic instrument flying is as important today as it was to Charles Lindbergh in 1927. It is top priority.

Many years ago, when the Aztec first came out, I had one around to fly for a few days. The first order of business was some simulated instrument flying under the hood, and the first thing I did was fly a VOR approach. The airplane didn't seem to want to come down quickly enough, so I put some flaps out when passing the station on the way to the airport. That was okay. On the missed approach, though, everything went wrong at the same time. I retracted the gear and then put the flap selector in the Up position. The nose on the early Aztecs becomes very heavy when the flaps are retracted; this is the reverse of what you usually find in a low-wing airplane, and it wasn't what I expected. Between reaching for the trim, pulling on the wheel, and wondering what in the devil was going on, I neglected the basic art of flying for a moment. The airplane began to go its own way. The safety pilot suggested I look up and fly visually to get things under control. It was embarrassing.

Lessons

The incident yielded more than one lesson. There was a clear message about learning something about a particular airplane before operating it on instruments. Delve into basics about trim changes with gear and flap retraction and extension, learn power settings for various phases of flight, and study the machine and its operating handbook, including all the supplements that cover items like the autopilot, for things that are different or less than obvious. I certainly should not have chosen a simulated instrument approach as the first chore in the airplane when flying it under the hood. Instead, I should have flown it around for a bit, developing a relationship between my mind, my hand, and the airplane's characteristics. Every pilot/airplane relationship starts out with the pilot a stranger to the machine, almost in the role of a passenger in the left front seat, and it evolves to the point where the pilot almost becomes a part of the machine. With the Aztec, I skipped the introduction and tried immediately to develop a complex relationship. The most important lesson is to heed messages from any such evidences of problems with basic instrument flying. Be a perfectionist about it. If you can't do an excellent job under the hood, the situation is surely not going to get any better in cloud.

A license to fly instruments is proof only that the pilot was capable on the day the license was obtained. After that, it is up to the pilot to stay current. When some weakness shows up in practice (or actual) instrument flying, don't pass it off with the thought that it couldn't have been too bad "because I made it." If the flying isn't something to be proud of, take it as a mandate to practice and polish basic instrument flying.

Two Ways

I think that we fly an airplane by reference to instruments in two distinctly separate ways. One way is natural, the other is purely mechanical. It is important to identify and use both methods to maximum advantage. You have probably observed what might be called a "natural pilot" at one time or another—someone who flies seemingly without effort. When VFR, little time is spent looking at the panel, yet the altimeter stays glued and the VOR or loran needle dead-centered. It's the same IFR. This is done with a keen awareness of the attitude of the airplane. In smooth air, if the nose is kept "right there" and the power is correct, the altitude of the airplane will not change. If the wings are kept level, with the ball in the center, the heading will not change. It is a relaxed way to fly, a result of the ability to perceive and respond without conscious, mechanical mental effort. In VFR conditions, the view out front and to the sides combines with the sound and feel of the airplane to tell the pilot what is happening. In IFR conditions, the expanse of the view outside is compressed into the artificial horizon. The information is there, and the sound and the readings of all the other instruments in the airplane verify that things are going well. The instrument cross-check, or scan, is talked of with reverence, but the natural pilot might not think in terms of a scan. The ability is in absorbing the big picture, in using all the human senses to fly the airplane.

Alert

This isn't to say that the natural pilot does not scan the panel. If asked for the oil pressure, the response might come in an instant. If a generator or vacuum pump were to fail, the pilot would catch it through the instrument indication in seconds. The pilot is simply able to operate with a single-mindedness of purpose, thinking of nothing but flying the airplane, and gathering all the data on the instrument panel in a relaxed and informal manner.

Mechanical

The instrument pilot flying mechanically might be the same person who was just (moments earlier) flying naturally, but on a different flight or a different portion of the same flight. There simply comes a time when it is necessary to fly with absolute procedural discipline. In the beginning of that early Aztec flight, I was probably flying the airplane rather naturally. I was moving along well and seeing everything. I was relaxed. Things were fine. Then, when the flaps were retracted, my mind jumped track. Instead of seeing everything, I saw nothing. I only wondered about the unexpected trim change. I did not make the required transition from natural to mechanical flying when a problem made this necessary.

At the first sign of something unusual, the clear call was for absolute attention to basic instrument flying. I should have disciplined myself to base eye and thought on the artificial horizon, and to put the airplane in a wings-level climb attitude regardless of the pitch forces required. Then I should have activated a mechanical and methodical check of the other instruments. Airspeed on the proper value. Altimeter indicating climb. Heading steady. Turn needle (or turn coordinator) steady and straight. Vertical speed indicating rate of climb. Discipline. Once that mechanical process was in place and working, I could have expanded to include missed approach procedures and navigational chores, and perhaps I could have allowed myself three seconds to ponder the reason for a trim change with flap retraction.

Some pilots never feel they have reached the point where they are flying instruments in a natural manner. There's nothing wrong with that. The mechanical way works just as well, and remember, the person who does it naturally much of the time still has to revert to mechanical means at certain times. And if you miss the cue, things are bound to get worse before they get better.

From the Start

The beginning of an instrument flight is a time when almost all pilots

fly mechanically and when the ability to concentrate on the basics is extremely important. An instrument pilot who flies infrequently might get the first dose of actual IFR as a climbing and accelerating airplane punches into the bottom of bumpy clouds. The key here is in concentrating only on flying the airplane until you are comfortable with it. A special consideration in the initial climb can be used to outline a couple of techniques.

The artificial horizon may not appear quite normal in the first phase of a climb. The depiction of nose-up attitude is accentuated by an acceleration error that makes the attitude appear more pronounced than it really is. The nose-up attitude in a Cherokee might, for a few moments, look more like what you would expect to see in a jet. A pilot might misinterpret this, lower the nose, and fly back into the ground if the indications of other instruments are not included in the deliberations. The period of initial climb into clouds is a demanding time, and a pilot must use everything available to verify that the flight is going well: pitch attitude set, wings level, positive rate of climb, airspeed correct, turn indicator correct.

First technique: A pilot can and should watch instruments during noncritical times VFR and relate the picture on the panel to the view out the windshield. As a result, any acceleration error in the artifical horizon, for example, will be a known quantity, and the pilot will know the indication when the pitch attitude is correct. That is what instrument flying is all about—knowing what it would look like if all the clouds went away.

Second technique: It is in the climb that we first put to the test the ability to look at the correct things at the proper time, get the message, and make the necessary control movements. What do we look at, and how do we demand proper performance? To begin, base on the artificial horizon, just as you would fly the correct attitude by referring to the real horizon in VFR conditions. Then grade the attitude being flown with a scan of the other instruments. When you are flying a standard instrument arrangement, a glance to the left will reveal that the airspeed is steady on the proper value; a glance to the right will show that the altimeter is moving upward. A glance down shows that the heading is steady on runway heading. The turn-and-bank or turn coordinator will verify that the airplane is indeed not turning, and the vertical speed is double verification that it is climbing.

Attitude

On the artificial horizon, the emphasis is on attitude. It is home base for the eyes, with the scan of the other instruments verifying that the selected attitude is producing the desired results. In the case of initial climb, the desired result is climbing while flying at a predetermined airspeed. But we still use the artificial horizon as a primary reference because it tells us about bank and pitch attitude simultaneously. No other instrument on the panel does that.

Scan

In these first moments of instrument flight, we must come to grips with some method of scanning the instrument panel. Some call it a "cross-check," a term borrowed from the military. When I worked at an Air Force contract school, much emphasis was placed on cross-checking. The emphasis was good, but nobody ever explained *how* it is done. The military did teach in terms of primary and supporting instruments—to put emphasis on the most important things at various times of flight, but there was no explanation of how much time should be spent with each instrument. In fact, the Air Force manual stated: "It has long been known that pilots do not use any specific method of cross-checking, but that they do use the instruments which give the best information for controlling the aircraft in any given maneuver. Most of the pilot's attention is devoted to checking these important instruments." That's rather like saying that most pilots don't plan a takeoff run longer than the available runway. The FAA is no more definite, in saying, in reference to scanning, "There are no set rules and no single method"—all of which leaves the reader wondering what the devil to look at and how much time to spend on it.

Experience

My experience has been, when flying instruments in smooth air, that I basically look at one thing—the most important thing (often it is the artificial horizon)—and check the rest with peripheral vision and furtive glances. Once a normal climb is established, I'm likely to look solely at the artificial horizon and satisfy the requirement of scanning with peripheral vision. The airspeed needle, on a correct value, can be seen out of the left corner of the eye; the altimeter reading, out of the right corner, is okay if it is increasing. I can see that the vertical speed is on a positive value, and the turn coordinator is visible to the lower left. At first I don't worry much about a precise heading. If the wings are level, it will remain close. The primary thing in my mind is establishing myself at the chore of flying instruments. The task is controlling the attitude of the airplane. This is done by looking at the artificial horizon. If a rate instrument suggests the need for a change in attitude, that change is made while I am looking at the artificial horizon. In short, I don't try to control the rate instruments directly.

Second Things Second

The initial IFR clearance often includes instructions to turn to a heading after takeoff and to contact departure control. The pilot must take first things first, though, and use the first minute of the climb in instrument conditions to make friends with the airplane, to settle in with the task, and to defeat any onset of spatial disorientation. If this isn't done, success is impossible. Once it is done, call departure control and then turn to the assigned heading.

As we progress through a flight, flying becomes easier. The airplane is more familiar, and if the flight remains in cloud for an extended period of time, the clouds and the water streaking back along the windows become friendlier. It is at this time that almost every instrument pilot lapses into more natural flying. Ease the seat back a notch and absorb all the messages from the panel. You can learn as you fly along, too, by monitoring what you look at and, if the results are good, storing this for future reference. For example, you'll note that peripheral vision works well so long as the air is smooth, but becomes more difficult to use when you're passing through turbulence. You just don't get a clear message out of the corner of an eye when the airplane is jiggling around. The call is for more glances to the other instruments, to verify that the attitude selected on the artificial horizon is doing the job.

You'll notice changes in pattern, too. For example, during a descent in smooth air, I noted that I was looking primarily at the directional gyro. The controller had assigned a heading, and that heading was occupying my attention. So long as it remained steady, I knew the wings were level. Peripheral vision verified this with the artificial horizon. I was descending to an altitude, and an occasional glance at the altimeter gave the progress on that. The airspeed was easy to interpret with peripheral vision because the needle was close to the top of the green sector on the indicator.

Hand-Fly

You can't learn much about basic instrument flying with the autopilot doing the work, so hand-fly the airplane when in cloud. This is a fine time to practice precision instrument flying. Hold the heading and altitude precisely. Keep the navigation needles centered. Work at the division of time between instrument flying and chores such as frequency changes, consulting charts, and writing down revised clearances. Fly it perfectly for thirty minutes or an hour, and then turn on the autopilot if you wish. Begin by earning the rest.

Basic Maneuvers

The various elements of the basic flying tasks are things that can and should be practiced. There is really nothing to instrument flying other than climbs, climbing turns, level flight, level turns, descents, and descending turns. Those are the things to work on until they are well in hand. The rest is pointless until you can fly with precision. Grade every flight, and work at the basics methodically.

Touch

Control touch is an important part of instrument flying. For a demonstration, trim the airplane, release the controls, and then "don't touch" except as necessary to correct an instrument reading. Touch with only one finger. Nothing is likely to get far off, and you'll soon see that you could fly all the way across the country using just one finger. The airplane requires very little "flying"; it is more a matter of a pound of pressure here and a pound of pressure there—at the correct time. Contrast this with the oft-noted jut of a pilot's jaw when heading into instrument conditions. Some pilots look as if they face an instrument *fight* instead of an instrument *flight*. Back to our pilot who was having trouble with the ILS: from another airplane, it was obvious that he was making abrupt and gross corrections—and that he was fighting with his airplane.

Fixation

Mental and visual fixation is an acknowledged scuttler of instrument pilots. Building a guard against this is part of the basic art of flying. It is often tempting to hang on one instrument—to stare. If the airplane is a hundred feet low, a pilot might look at the altimeter, add a bit of back pressure, and wait for the altitude to come up a hundred feet. All the while, the bank attitude of the airplane might be going to pot. The correct way to fly is to note the excursions and trends of instruments and then use the artificial horizon to change the attitude of the airplane in a manner that will nudge any wayward instruments toward a proper value. Don't move a control without consulting the artificial horizon, and keep an eye on the horizon during the control input. Then check results on the other instruments. This keeps the eye and mind active. It does the job.

Fixation can take many forms. We can, for example, lapse into daydreaming. The eyes are on the instruments but the brain is on the note at the bank. Or, in time of trouble, the mind might be virtually paralyzed by a problem such as turbulence or mechanical malfunction. I've found that the best cure for fixation is a thorough tongue lashing. I speak to myself frequently at such times, and rather sternly. The admonition is usually to settle down and fly the airplane. The reward offered is that all bad things will pass if the airplane is flown properly.

Power versus Elevator

Power is a flight control that we use in basic instrument flying. The use of power is both very important and very simple. In a basic airplane, you really only need five settings to cover most of the things that are done, but you need to memorize them so that power can be quickly set for what you want to do. Then attention can go to the proper pitch attitude. The basic power settings are: climb, normal cruise, cruise in turbulence (maneuvering speed), normal descent, and descent in turbulence. In faster airplanes and retractables, a few more settings are needed for instrument approaches. They would be for level maneuvering or holding at reduced speed, and for final approach descents with the wheels down, in the case of the retractable.

One additional thing must be considered in relation to power. There has long been disagreement about whether power controls airspeed or altitude. The same argument is applied to the elevator control. Hopefully the instrument pilot is too savvy to fall victim to an argument on this score.

In certain situations, it is best to think of power as a primary influence on altitude, and in other situations, it is best to think of the elevator as a primary influence on altitude. For example, if you are flying level at 120 knots and the time comes to start down, you don't want to think of the elevator as the control to use. Power would be the thing then. Reduce the power to begin the descent and maintain the airspeed with the elevator. By the same token, if you're running just a tad high on the glideslope, lowering the nose a hair would be a perfectly acceptable way to make that altitude correction. Or you could back off the power a bit. Anyone who would argue with either would be nitpicking. The business about what controls what is critical only when the airplane is being flown near some extreme. Extremes are unnecessary in light airplane instrument flying and should be avoided. Just for the record, though, remember that in low-speed situations where the chips are down, using the elevator to control airspeed is what will save your tail.

Self-Taught

One recurring thought about the basics of instrument flying is that they are not things that anyone can teach a pilot; they are things the pilot must learn through experimentation and experience. No instructor can tell exactly where you are experiencing a touch of disorientation or when there is fixation on some instrument or subject. The pilot must practice enough to work these things out and to determine where the eyes need to look at given times. What an instructor can do is give you helpful hints, such as recommending fifteen inches of manifold pressure here and thirteen inches there, but even that must be subjected to a measure of self-discovery. The instructor also can critique your basic instrument flying, but if you can be objective, you can do an even better job there; only you know where your mind and eyes were when a mistake was made. If you don't know what you were thinking about or looking at when something went wrong, then your mind was apparently in gridlock. That means that work must be done before basic instrument flying can be successful. The thinking process must be developed. The instructor can always pinpoint the result; only the pilot knows the cause.

2. Basic Variations

Now that we are proficient and current on the basics, can we spend all our time on those exciting (and required) instrument approaches? Patience. In instrument flying, patience is the only virtue and impatience the only sin. There are variations on basic gauge flying, and mastery of these can be a real life preserver in time of need.

Partial panel is the primary variation. Flying takes on a new challenge when one or more instruments is no longer operative. This is highly pertinent in single-engine airplanes, because there's sometimes no system or instrument redundancy, so that a vacuum, electrical, or instrument failure can leave the pilot flying with less than a full deck. The newer the airplane, the more likely it is to have dual vacuum and/or electrics.

Very definite limits should be set on what will be attempted when flying partial panel in an actual situation. Back in the good old days, it was all partial panel, and indeed you can do anything with a needle and ball (or turn coordinator) that you can do with an artificial horizon and directional gyro. In fact, in recoveries from some unusual attitudes, the basic partial-panel instruments become primary. But regardless of the degree of emphasis placed on partial-panel in training and whether any attention was given to it in proficiency flying, a partial-panel situation must be treated with care. The transition from everything to a little can be tedious.

In an actual situation, the loss of any instruments or equipment should be treated as an emergency, or at least a possible emergency, with the air traffic controller notified so that he can render as much assistance as necessary and cut some corners for you. Maneuvering should be limited as much as possible. Standard-rate turns and gentle descents should be all that would be required to fly an approach. (A climb would seldom be required, except on a missed approach.) The turning should be separated from the descending or climbing to the extent possible—one thing at a time.

Vacuum-source failure is the most often addressed problem—for good reason. Vacuum pumps are not the most reliable things on the airplane, and when a pump fails, it results in the almost immediate loss of the artificial horizon and DG as well as the autopilot in most airplanes. The horizon is the cornerstone of full-panel flying, so this is quite a blow. And the DG (when properly set) is the primary heading indication, so its loss is also quite serious. One must be optimistic; when flying partial panel, there are fewer instruments to demand attention. Only the turn-and-bank (or turn coordinator), airspeed, altimeter, and vertical speed require attention. The basic requirements of flight are unchanged, and the controls do the same things.

My P210 (Pressurized Centurion) had a strong tendency toward vacuum pump failures when I first got it. At the 1,600-hour mark, there had been six. In the process, I learned quite a bit about failures and how to deal with them. The first occurred while I was flying on top of clouds. I was IFR and didn't mention the failure to the controller. I didn't even think about it. There was a cloud deck below, but the destination had good ceilings and I motored on in without incident. The number two failure was at a slightly less opportune time. I was about to penetrate a warm front but was still in VFR conditions. Nothing to do but return to base on that one. The third pump failed during an IFR descent. I continued on to the destination, where the ceiling was good. The fourth occurred in IFR conditions at 19,000 feet. The airplane was immersed in icy clouds, and the descent to VFR conditions was through about 15,000 feet of cloud with some showers to dodge. The fifth pump failed as I was scooting along just under an overcast and right after I had asked for clearance to a lower altitude because of turbulence. The flight was continued in visual conditions to the destination, where I flew an ADF approach. The sixth failed on a local test flight—no problem.

The first thing I learned was that what happens first after a vacuum failure is (at least on my airplane) that the pitch indication on the artificial horizon becomes inaccurate. This was easy enough to catch in the cases where I didn't see the vacuum gauge on zero before the instrument went awry. The altimeter, airspeed, and vertical speed told me quickly that the artificial horizon was telling a fib. That raised suspicion, and I looked over at the vacuum gauge—zero.

The second thing I learned was that things were much easier for me if I covered the artificial horizon and DG: I slipped business cards under the false panel; this eliminated them from the scan and reminded me that this was no longer a routine operation. More importantly, it hid the incorrect readings on the dead instruments. Another pilot related to me a situation in which he didn't cover the instruments; after being on partial panel for a while, he instinctively (and absent-mindedly) latched onto an artificial horizon that was parked in a 30-degree bank and tried to level the wings. By the time he got his brain unscrambled and figured out what was going on, he thought he heard an angel whispering his name. But he managed to get back to the operative instruments and recover from the unusual attitude.

The third thing I learned was to carry on as planned unless there was a good reason not to do so. On the second failure, I elected to reverse course and return home because I was in VFR conditions about to enter IFR. That wouldn't have been smart. In the others, everything (save the vacuum pump) was going okay, and things were better, not worse, ahead. To change things and attempt an immediate instrument approach seemed unwise to me. I learned to minimize cloud time as much as possible and do everything gently. In most cases I did remember to tell the controller that I was on partial panel. He couldn't help me fly the airplane, but he did get some weather information and save me the trouble of switching over to the Flight Service Station.

The fourth thing I learned was that I really wanted some redundancy of instrumentation. After a couple of failures I had added an electric DG, and an electric artificial horizon later on, along with a standby vacuum pump to add suspenders to the belt. Then I swapped the primary vacuum DG for an HSI, so I made the standby DG the vacuum.

Scan Patterns

Before exploring some of the techniques of partial-panel flying, I want to pass along an observation on scan patterns and their relationship to the placement of instruments. At the time of this incident, my electric gyros were side by side at the lower right of the pilot's panel. The rest of the instruments were in their normal locations. On one trip, the vacuum artifical horizon shot craps. I covered it, leaving the vacuum DG and the full set of electric instruments. Our son was working on his instrument rating at the time and was flying the trip under the hood. He was doing a better job of holding a heading than usual, and I finally asked him what he was using as his primary bank attitude reference, given the failed vacuum horizon. He was using the turn coordinator. He felt that the electric gyros were too far out of his normal scan and that it was easier just to use the TC and directional gyro. The former is very sensitive to any turning, and it was making him do a more precise job of flying the airplane. I still like having those standby gyros—even though I originally learned to fly instruments on partial panel.

If that dissertation on failures tells us anything, it is that systems and instruments do fail, and we'd best have a plan when they do. To begin, make friends with the instrument that gives information that can be related to the bank attitude of the airplane. The airplane can be trimmed to a stable pitch situation, but roll stability absolutely must be handled by the pilot. Either the turn-and-bank, with a needle, or the turn coordinator tells the tale. For general discussion, both will be referred to as turn indicators, and think of them as simply telling whether the airplane is or is not turning, the direction of the turn, and the rate of turn. There is no direct bank-attitude information there, but the bank attitude can be envisioned with the information from a turn indicator. Fly with a mental picture of bank, and use bank (ailerons) to control the instrument.

Three primary bank-attitude tasks must be mastered. A straight-ahead condition comes first. If the turn needle is kept centered, or if the turn coordinator is kept level, the heading will not change. As noted earlier, being able to hold a heading is a most important basic. If the ball is in the center, the airplane will also be in level, coordinated flight, but don't worry a lot about the ball. If you hold the heading, who cares if the ball is a tad off, one way or the other? If it is off more than a tad, do something about it with the rudder or rudder trim applied in the direction of ball deflection.

Next come the turns, one in each direction, first at a standard rate and then at half a standard rate. Three degrees per second is the standard, and both types of turn indicator have an index for this rate of turn. The rate of turn is important if the directional gyro is gone, because the magnetic compass is difficult to use in turning to headings. So we use the beginning heading and combine it with time and the rate of turn to tell us when we have reached a new heading.

The Vision

How much bank on a standard-rate or half-standard-rate turn? If you are looking at the needle of a turn-and-bank, nothing gives a mental image; the pilot must interpret. The bank required for a standard-rate turn is determined by airspeed, and you should know a couple of values for your airplane—the angle of bank for a standard-rate turn at normal cruise and the angle of bank for a standard-rate turn at a reduced maneuvering speed. Roughly, the airspeed less the last zero and plus seven is what it takes. For example, at 100 knots, a standard-rate turn requires about 17 degrees of bank; at 140 knots, it would be 21 degrees. Half standard rates would be half that. The turn coordinator shows turn by the banking of the symbolic airplane, and the variation in bank angle with speed is one reason I do not like this instrument as well as a turn-and-bank. Remember, it shows rate of turn, not bank, even though the presentation purports to do the latter. Going to an extreme, for illustration, it shows an indication of what appears to be the same angle of bank when an airplane is actually banked 15 degrees at 80 knots or banked almost 30 degrees at 200 knots. This can be misleading if a pilot hasn't put some effort into understanding the characteristics of this instrument.

Experiment

As you experiment with partial panel, you'll probably note that the turn indicator requires the most attention, and if you give it that attention, the airplane is rather easy to fly. If the airplane is properly trimmed, pitch control is going to involve only a pound of pressure here and a pound of pressure there as the airplane is maneuvered. The real task is managing bank attitude. When pilots become spatially disoriented and lose control of an airplane, bank is what they have lost control of. Keep the wings of a properly trimmed airplane level and nothing much happens. Bank the airplane, or let it bank unintentionally, and everything starts to go awry.

Try a little experiment the next time you fly. With the airplane trimmed and the wings level, as shown by a centered turn indicator, note that things are stable in pitch. Then bank until a standard-rate turn is indicated and release the controls for a moment. Only bank attitude was changed, but it affects a lot of other indications. The airspeed, vertical speed, and altimeter will all make a move very quickly.

Pitch

There are three good pitch-attitude references on partial panel, and any one of the three can be used to visualize pitch attitude. They are most commonly used together, with one assuming somewhat more importance than the others during various phases of flight. For example, in level flight, the altimeter tells of a constant altitude or of the need for a correction. If 100 feet needs to be lost, for example, lower the nose slightly, note descent on the vertical speed, and as the altitude approaches the correct value, level off. There is lag in the standard vertical speed indicator, but if all corrections are gradual, the instrument is quite useful. A little practice will teach its lag properties.

Added Attraction

Fly straight and level now, with the eye perched mainly on the turn indicator while cross-checking the airspeed, altimeter, and vertical speed. Next, we'll add a task. Bring the nav instrument into the picture. It is reasonably difficult to get somewhere in the clouds without navigating, and the VOR needle can be used in some basic partial panel flying even though it is not directly sensitive to heading. What you'll learn rather quickly is that, given some talent with the turn indicator, it is surprisingly easy to fly to, and right over, a VOR station without continually referring to the compass. This is based on being able to hold a heading, and those who are both proficient and motivated often do as good a job of holding a precise heading with the turn indicator as they do with the DG. When flying with the horizon and DG, it's common to not even look at the turn indicator. Who needs it? It's also common to weave a little bit—a few degrees to the left and a few degrees to the right. In partial-panel flying, turn indication gets so much attention that the pilot tends not to let the heading stray much. For instance, if the airplane banks slightly and the turn indicator deflects half a standard-rate indication to the right for one second before it is caught, the heading will have changed only one-and-a-half degrees. You can hardly see a degree and a half on a DG.

Track

In tracking to a VOR station, it is true that the compass must be referred to quite often when you are a considerable distance from the station. The VOR isn't heading-sensitive—it only gives information about the airplane's position relative to the station and desired track—so if you are, say, thirty miles from a station, the needle really won't let you know that your heading is incorrect very quickly, and if you don't know what heading resulted in the deviation, it is difficult to decide on a correction. As the airplane gets closer to the station, though, tracking can be done very accurately with just the turn indicator and the VOR needle. How?

The key is to be able to hold a constant heading with the turn indicator, and to be able to make accurate five-degree heading changes. These small turns are best made at half standard rate, with the turn held for a count. Practice with the DG uncovered, to make perfect. With the airplane stabilized on an approximate inbound heading—for example, 180 degrees—and with the VOR showing 180 "To" with the navigation needle centered, maintain a constant heading with the turn indicator and keep an eye on the VOR needle so that any movement will be promptly noted. If the needle starts to drift to the left, for example, make a mini-turn (five degrees) to the left. Then nail that turn indicator back to the center and watch the nav needle. If it persists in a drift to the left, make another mini-turn to the left. If it remains steady, good, unless it's more than half-scale out, in which case another mini-turn to the left would be dictated, to start the needle back toward center. Then, as it approaches center, some of the correction should be taken off.

Success is found in being on an approximately correct heading to begin with, so that any needle movement won't be drastic, in making all corrections small turns of a known value, and in holding a heading between corrections. As the station gets closer, excursions of the VOR needle will be at a more rapid rate. And if it moves out to one side and stays there, the limit would be a couple or three little turns toward the needle and then a steady heading to await a "To" to "From" switch at station passage. After you try this under the hood a few times, you'll find that the turn indicator is very trusty in tracking the VOR.

Localizer/ADF

The localizer works the same way. Except here there's a wild card if you have an ADF, which gives positive relation to a point on the localizer course—the compass locator. Any time the localizer needle is in the center and the ADF (tuned to the outer locator) needle is on zero, the aircraft heading matches the localizer; the ADF is pointing directly through the nose of the airplane at another point on the localizer. When off the localizer, the ADF provides orientation to a point on the localizer—the outer compass locator. An example of how useful the ADF can be is in intercepting the final approach course.

Position the aircraft outside the outer locator, either just completing a procedure turn or in the process of intercepting the localizer for a straight-in. Suppose that the localizer being intercepted runs northeast and that the airplane is south of the localizer, headed approximately north. So long as the ADF needle is to the right of zero and the localizer needle is to the left, we know we will intercept the localizer outside the outer locator. It's like flying into a funnel.

Now, what happens if the ADF is actually used for heading information and the needle is kept, say, thirty degrees to the right of the nose? Simple. We intercept the localizer outside the outer locator at a thirty-degree angle. When the localizer needle starts to center, turn right until the ADF needle is on zero. Presto. The airplane is on or at least near the center line of the localizer inbound, and the heading is approximately the same as the inbound localizer heading. From here the localizer is flown just as the VOR was flown when close to the station—using mini-turns to correct for drift and the turn indicator to hold a heading precisely between adjustments.

The ADF can be used like this when approaching the localizer from either side; the headings and position at the beginning of the discussion were just to give a mental picture of an approach. Practice using the ADF in this manner, because it is an important tool in basic partial-panel instrument flying.

Glideslope

Flying glideslope on partial panel is a worthy subject in a discussion of basics, because it can seem a difficult thing to do at a crucial time. The concentration required to track the localizer doesn't leave an abundance of eye-and-mind time for tracking something else. A patch on normal procedures can thus be in order. To insure getting down after passing the outer marker, descend below the glideslope to the point where the no-glideslope minimum descent altitude is reached, then level off at that altitude. When the glideslope is intercepted again, from below, more feet can come off; you can even go on down to the full ILS decision height, depending on how good the glideslope interception and tracking proves to be. If the airplane doesn't have a glideslope, you can forget that problem. The key thing is that the localizer needle is of vital importance all the way in. If it ever drifts away to a full-scale deflection, the approach must be abandoned.

As long as you don't go below the no-glideslope minimum descent altitude, the glideslope isn't quite so important. What the use of the glideslope does in most cases is lower the minimum from 300 feet and ¾-mile visibility (or 4,000 runway visual range, if you will, and 300 feet minimum descent altitude) to 200 feet and ½-mile. And we trust that the day your vacuum system or gyros flunk out, you will have the good fortune to find a place with a little better weather than 200 and ½ for your grand arrival. Better yet, get a no-gyro approach from a terminal radar approach control facility.

Practice

Practicing partial panel can be quite challenging. First work at the basics, and then apply the basics to getting down. You might say to yourself, "The localizer intercept is strictly no sweat using the ADF on the outer marker. I'm going to try to fly the glideslope all the way in. When the marker is reached inbound, the localizer is reasonably well tied down. Put the landing gear down to start the airplane on a rate of descent that will approximate the glideslope. The communication with the tower while I was passing the marker cost a localizer excursion. A couple of mini-turns got that in shape, but it should not have happened. I must learn to communicate and fly at the same time. If I can't, let the communication wait. The pressure builds on something like this, even though it's just under the hood. Maybe that's because it would be embarrassing to completely botch it in front of a trusting safety pilot. On this first one, the control movements are a little stiff. Calling the tower at the river (when the safety pilot says we are there) results in another excursion, this time of both the localizer and the glideslope. The localizer is tied back down before the middle marker, but the glideslope needle stays down, showing the airplane to be high. High is okay. When the marker beeps through the sweaty atmosphere in the cabin, the altimeter shows 300 feet above the touchdown zone instead of the proper 200. A missed approach is executed from this point, without looking up."

Going Around

"The sensations on the first partial-panel go-around in a long time, or the first ever, are pretty spectacular. There is no trusty artificial horizon information about attitude. It is still quite flyable, though. The airspeed was on 100 knots when the go-around was started, so it can be the primary reference for pitch attitude with no change in value. Apply full power and hold airspeed constant. As soon as the vertical speed shows a positive climb indication, retract the landing gear. The trim change is momentarily disturbing. The turn indicator has been approximately in the center all this time, but the localizer is long gone, full scale.

"The next approach is a little better, with less sweat. Don't really fly the glideslope. Rather, gradually descend below the glideslope to the no-glideslope minimum descent altitude and level there. Then, if everything else is just right, descend on the glideslope to the ILS decision height after intercepting the glideslope from below."

If such a practice flight doesn't reveal plenty of skill, go back to the practice area and polish up the basics in need. I find the most difficult time to be toward the end of the approach, when needles are moving faster and the temptation is to make larger corrections. I work to master that by practicing simultaneous half-standard-rate turns and changes in descent rate of about 200 feet per minute. The objective is to do them smoothly and to consider these values as maximums.

Another good partial-panel practice is a simultaneous standard-rate turn and 500-foot-per-minute rate of descent that reverses at the end of one minute and then continues for one additional minute. If this is done perfectly, the airplane will descend 500 feet and turn 180 degrees, then climb 500 feet while turning 180 degrees in the opposite direction. After exactly two minutes, the airplane will be right back where it started. There's more discipline in that than you might imagine, and the exercise will provide quite an education in what to look at in order to juggle two balls at once. Don't practice it only in smooth air—try it in the bumps.

Autopilots

A lot of us fly with autopilots, and if not completely understood and carefully monitored, these can present us with a split-second demand for perfectly flawless performance. It can even be demanding when they *are* completely understood and monitored.

There should be a supplement to the Airplane Flight Manual for any autopilot installed, and until it is read and completely understood, the autopilot should be left off. For example, the supplement for a Bendix/King system in a Cessna 210R specifies that the autopilot will automatically disengage when roll rate exceeds twelve degrees per second or when pitch change rate exceeds five degrees per second—except when the control wheel steering switch is depressed. If accelerations exceed 0.4 to 1.7 *g*, the autopilot will disengage whether or not the control wheel steering switch is depressed. These parameters suggest that the autopilot would disengage in anything greater than moderate turbulence. In other words, the autopilot would say, "Here, Ace. I've had enough. You fly."

The autopilot will also disengage because of failures within the system. Among the autopilot-on limitations is a requirement for a belted pilot in the left front seat and a maximum indicated airspeed of 180 knots and a minimum of 80. The maximum allowable flaps extension is ten degrees with the autopilot on.

Another autopilot approved in the same airplane has an entirely different set of parameters for automatic disengagement, and on some other airplanes autopilots are approved that disengage only for a failure within the autopilot. That is why you have to read and understand the flight manual supplement for the specific airplane and autopilot.

Electric Trim

Most autopilots include an electric trim system that, when the autopilot is on, automatically keeps the airplane in trim. Because of this and the nature of the autopilot, it is imperative to understand that only one pilot can fly the airplane at a time. Never touch the wheel when the autopilot is on. If, for example, you decide to help the autopilot level off, you have just begun to tread in dangerous territory. With the autopilot on, if you apply back pressure to the elevator control, the autopilot will think there is a need for opposite trim—remember, it keeps the airplane in trim—and will trim nose down to couteract the nose-up force you are applying. As long as you pull back, it will trim nose down—until the nose-down trim limit is reached. Because there is no requirement that an airplane be controllable with full nose-down trim, this can lead to real problems. If you are very strong, you might be able to hold it—and you might not.

When autopilot and electric trim systems are certified, the test pilot has to determine what happens in case of a failure—a berserk autopilot or runaway trim. The failure has to be induced and then the test pilot has to wait three seconds and recover. The time is one second in maneuvering and approach flight. The parameters that may not be exceeded are aerobatic in nature: the roll limit is 60 degrees; pitch is ±30. No accelerations outside the 0 g to +2 g are allowed except under certain circumstances, but in no event may the limit load factor of the aircraft be exceeded.

It goes without saying that a pilot would be under considerable stress after an autopilot failure. The demand for quick thinking and fancy footwork would definitely be there, and you would want to be able to reach each thing that disables the autopilot and trim without having to look at it. Do be aware that, on most airplanes, the button on the control that disconnects the autopilot usually only interrupts the electric trim. The trim would have to be disabled through a circuit breaker or other means.

It is very easy to lapse into a feeling of false security when flying instruments and to rely on everything in the airplane on every flight. Using everything is fine. That's what it's all there for, and a pilot should certainly have everything going for him at all times. But we had better be ready, willing, and able to get the airplane safely to the ground regardless of what mechanical or electronic device fails.

3. Basics Plus

Whether flying with all the instruments on the panel working or only some of them, the basics of instrument flying must be adeptly and methodically applied to all situations for the result to be a smooth and safe flight. There's no way to do this on a helter-skelter basis. All aspects of the things we do in instrument flying must be examined; the result of the examination is a knowledge of the best way to do each particular thing.

For example, the pilot's knowledge of power settings for various phases of flight is acknowledged as important, but the application of that basic is not always simple. What if the pilot is descending at a speed in excess of the landing-gear extension and/or approach-flaps speed and he's still a thousand feet above the glideslope-interception altitude, and the controller calls with word that the airplane is five miles from the marker and cleared for the ILS approach? If all our practice and search for understanding have been on the basis of decelerating to the gear speed while flying level, we are likely to experience some confusion when faced with a combination of descending and a need to slow down.

The message is to look carefully at all situations in practice. If your airplane takes four miles to slow from a normal letdown speed to landing-gear-extension speed in level flight with the power set on 15 inches and 2,200 rpm, you would know that in the example given there would be no way to arrive at the outer marker at the proper speed while following the accepted procedure. An unprepared pilot would have only blank thoughts; a prepared pilot would know there exists a choice between asking the controller for a 360 (which, in a busy area, can really clog the works) and pulling the power back below 15 inches, accepting the increase in wear that results from rapid engine cooling. And if the decision is to throttle back, that should have been done at least once in practice so you could note the trim changes, sensations, and sounds associated with the maneuver. The purpose of practice is to do all the things that might be expected in actual operations. So look for situations like this and work on them. Don't practice only the easy and routine things.

Turbulence

Turbulence is another area where the application of basics is very important. Bumps can shatter calm and destroy a pilot's ability to perform—unless he possesses an understanding of the effects of turbulence and confidence in his ability to manage the basics (wings level and a reasonable pitch attitude), regardless of the level of turbulence.

Keep Cool

What do we worry about when the airplane starts lurching around in wet and bumpy clouds? The controllability of the airplane, the structural strength of the airplane, and our ability to fly instruments in turbulence are the three primary concerns. The first item, controllability, is not really a question. The necessary control power to handle expected levels of turbulence is built into every airplane. Structural strength is adequate as long as the pilot does his part by maintaining a proper airspeed and doesn't fly into a roll cloud on the lee of the mountains or into a strong thunderstorm. The key is in keeping the wings level and the airspeed close to the desired value— in other words, maintaining control of the airplane. Our ability to fly instruments in the tougher times is something to be introspective about.

There is no question that turbulence on instruments is an uncomfortable experience, whether in a large or a small airplane. Nothing else is quite like it. There is no way to see what comes next, no way to avoid the bumps, and really, no way to tell when the turbulence will stop. I'll never forget the worst, most turbulent ride I've had in an airplane. I wasn't flying; I was a passenger in the back of an airline 727. The captain elected to penetrate an area of weather as he was starting a descent into Washington. About 30 minutes of flying was involved; it seemed an eternity. With no instruments to look at, I was completely disoriented throughout the experience, but I rather enjoyed the sensations of the turbulence. I spent the entire time trying to imagine how it would have been in my airplane. There was little question in my mind that I would have badly wanted to get out. I think the captain of the 727 felt the same; after landing, he apologized for the rough ride.

Some years later, I had another 727 ride through a thunderstorm, only this time I was in the jump seat. I was watching the radar. The captain carefully interpreted what was there and selected the best path, avoiding the red return that signifies heavy rain. But we were in the rain and clouds of the storm, and the airplane was taking a pounding. The crew was working hard, too, and we soon flew out on the other side.

My primary thoughts during these flights related to how I would have flown the airplane. On one hand, I would have had something to do other than contemplate the bumps. On the other hand, there's no question that I would have been tense, to say the least. The thought that there's nothing between you and very deep trouble but immediate and continuing eye/mind/hand coordination is not a settling one when that coordination has to be matched against the twisted and tortured currents of air within convective clouds. On the other hand, if you can relax and convince yourself that there are bumps in every road and that the airplane is controllable and strong as a horse as long as you do your job, it becomes easier. We have to recognize also that we often make turbulence worse by our very own actions. On those 727 rides, I thought that some characteristic of the airplane must have caused the rather slow-motion pitch-up and pitch-down action in turbulence, but a long-time 727 captain told me that wasn't the case. He chuckled and said those lads were probably just overcontrolling—chasing the airspeed or something. We all do that.

I was watching another pilot fly my 210 in turbulence one day and started wondering why he was moving the wheel so much. I took it and held it stock still for a bit. The airplane's motions lessened. Often we do respond more quickly and with more control movement than is necessary. The airplane moves too far in the direction opposite the original displacement, the one that prompted the correction. So we provide another correction that might or might not be overdone. Add turbulence to the equation and you see that the airplane can move around a lot, and in the process, the pilot can lose track of what motion comes from turbulence and what motion comes from overcontrolling. The way to separate the two is to slow down on wiggling the wheel for a moment.

Real Turbulence

There is no question that pilots occasionally fly into turbulence that induces rolling moments strong enough to require large and immediate control inputs to counter the effect of the turbulence. Don't be bashful in such a situation. But remember that such turbulence is more than likely related to wind shear—that is, the interaction between air moving in one direction and air moving in the other—and will thus be transitory. It'll go away. But it might come back, too. If, for example, the initial effect of shear is to make the airplane roll rapidly to the right, it won't last. The next little bit might have a neutral effect, or might induce a left roll. So, in a particularly wild situation, you can counter a roll to the right with a lot of control motion to the left that for a split second seems ineffective. Then you can find yourself riding in an airplane that is rolling rapidly to the left with the wheel (or stick) to the left. That prompts a wild jerking of the wheel back to the right. I think it's always a good idea to at least pause at the neutral control position in such a situation, to see what, if any, rolling moment there is with no control input. This should be done when the wings are level, as indicated on the attitude indicator, or when the airplane is not turning as per the turn needle or turn coordinator.

Pitch

We know that in smooth-air instrument flying, the pitch attitude will take care of itself if the airplane is properly trimmed and the wings are kept level. And we also know that a loss of roll control almost always precedes a loss of pitch control, the latter being the one that gets you to the ground at a spot not of your own choosing. There are exceptions here, and they should be understood.

The stall is one exception, but if the wings of an airplane are kept level and the airplane is trimmed for a safe airspeed, the pilot has to pull back on the wheel with some force to stall the airplane. The pilot has to provide the control input to increase the angle attack to the stall. If the airplane is trimmed for and flying at a relatively slow speed, wind shear can cause a momentary drop in airspeed, bringing the airplane close to the stall, but the nose will want to lower of its own accord as the machine seeks its trim speed. To stall, the pilot still has to pull back on the wheel. True, the airplane might fly into the ground if the pilot doesn't pull back on the wheel, but it wouldn't likely stall.

Also, if the airplane is flying at a relatively low but normally safe speed and encounters turbulence that causes an increase in g-loading, it might stall. In this case, the stall would be momentary. The attitude and power setting were for a normal airspeed, and the airplane will likely move out of the g-producing bit of turbulence and on to something else. If the stalled condition lasts for more than a second or so, it could result in a loss of longitudinal and lateral control—this is one of the reasons we don't want to fly too slowly in turbulence. (Another reason is the lessening of control effectiveness at slower speeds.)

Pitch Upset

Another form of pitch upset is related to jet aircraft operating at high altitudes, but there are lessons in it for all pilots.

When a subsonic jet is flying at high altitude, its safe speed envelope becomes smaller. On the low side is the buffet of an impending stall; on the high side is the buffeting that occurs as the air flowing over the top of the wing goes supersonic (because in passing over the wing it has to travel farther than the air passing beneath the wing) and as shock waves form and move aft on the wing. This results in a phenomenon called "Mach tuck," or a nose-down pitching moment at a speed around Mach 0.8, plus or minus a bit, depending on the airplane. Some airplanes have automatic systems to compensate for the onset of Mach tuck; in others it's hardly noticeable. And as a subsonic airplane gets too close to Mach 1, elevator effectiveness diminishes and other interesting things begin to occur.

In some models of the Learjet, for example, an aileron buzz develops (at well over the airplane's limit speed) and becomes more pronounced as the airplane accelerates. The nose also pitches down. This in turn results in more speed and a compounding of the problem. G-load accentuates the aileron buzz, so the pilot has to retard the power and bring the nose up to reduce airspeed while imposing as little g-load on the airplane as possible. It's a rather delicate act. The stick forces are relatively high in this case, but, as in all airplanes, elevator trim (or especially the stabilizer trim in airplanes so equipped) should be used carefully when dealing with any sort of upset or potential upset. The airplane should have been correctly trimmed before the upset; that baseline trim might best be left untouched.

In jets operating at high altitude, use of the stabilizer trim can actually result in an absolute loss of longitudinal control. The nose has pitched down, perhaps because of a "too fast" situation, and elevator effectiveness is reduced because of excessive speed. Trimming "nose up" on an adjustable stabilizer reduces elevator effectiveness even more as it trims the leading edge of the stabilizer in a downward direction. Given full nose-up trim, the pilot might face a situation where the airplane is headed down and accelerating, even though the wheel is all the way back. At least one jetliner made a smoking hole back in the days before this phenomenon was fully understood. A contributing factor might be that an airplane may feel and even act as though it is having a low-speed stall problem when it is actually going too fast. The airplane shakes and the nose pitches down. When it does that in a stall, the drill is to add power and reduce the angle of attack—actions that would only aggravate the situation in a jet with a high-speed problem.

Turbulence is a factor in many high-altitude upsets. If an airplane is moving along in undisturbed air and moves into an area of rising air (an updraft), the latter will cause the nose to pitch down because an airplane wants to weathervane into the relative wind. The airspeed would start to increase, and the airplane might quickly move into the area where there would be further pitch down for aerodynamic reasons. Or, in horizontal as opposed to vertical wind shear, increasing wind from ahead might result in an airspeed increase (to above the limit) that would result in the aerodynamic pitch down, which would in turn result in a further airspeed increase.

Most of us don't fly airplanes in such critical situations, but we do see pitch excursions in turbulence. Vertical wind shear that results in our passing into an increasing updraft (wind component from below) will cause the airplane to pitch nose down. When the process reverses, the airplane might pitch nose up. One thing we learn from the high altitude problems is to leave the trim alone while dealing with pitch excursions. And the airplane should be flown gently, to avoid pilot-induced *g*-loading to the extent possible. The objective should be to maintain a level attitude—in pitch and bank—until the worst of the turbulence is cleared. Altitude and airspeed excursions are to be expected. In heavy airplanes, the admonishment is always to set power to the value that will result in the airplane's flying at the proper turbulent-air-penetration speed in a level pitch attitude in undisturbed air, and not to change the power. In light airplanes, where power response, acceleration, and deceleration are much quicker, power adjustments are more acceptable, but still probably not necessary. Once control of any airplane is completely lost, reducing power to idle is usually an integral part of the recovery. Whether it's an airplane in a spin, an airplane that a pilot has lost control of in instrument conditions, or a jet overspeeding at high altitude, retarding the power enhances the potential for an effective recovery.

Approach

Turbulence behind, let's move on to some of the more sophisticated applications of our basic instrument-flying ability. In the discussion of partial panel in the preceding chapter, we worked through an approach with the least in gauges. That is an emergency procedure for time of need. Apply the basics to normal approaches, too. The interface between the basics and radio procedures is what converts instrument flying into a complete IFR flight. One thing that must constantly be kept in mind in every situation is that the pilot's most important job is controlling the aircraft. If control is in jeopardy and the pilot tries to reach for the microphone or look at the chart to check a heading or do anything other than fly, the trouble is multiplied. So while we have to plan around navigational problems during an instrument approach, any indication that control is problematic is a clear call to fly the airplane first and work on radio procedures when there is time. A constant awareness of position and what comes next is key: "I am here, at this altitude, and the next thing that happens is . . . ."

Let's study an ILS approach first. When we come to the outer marker outbound or get close to the final approach course under radar guidance, we know that x number of things are going to have to be done to and with the airplane before we can walk into the airport office and tell the troops about the tight approach we just flew. First, we have to slow the airplane down. When to do this? The important thing is to have a definite time and to accomplish the chore at that time—or, as an alternative, to have a procedure for flying an approach at a higher-than-normal speed, following it with a normal landing. If it is a straight-in ILS with radar vectors, the controller should tell us when we are getting close to the outer marker. The flight is usually transferred over to the tower frequency a few miles outside of the marker, and this is a logical time and place to reduce speed. Or, if your airplane is so equipped, the DME, loran or the RNAV would suggest a time.

Each airplane is different; slowing down and descending is strictly an airplane control item; it is up to the pilot to develop a procedure that will result in the right thing happening in advance of the eleventh hour and on a methodical basis. In some cases, around busy airports with jets behind, you might need to keep that speed quite high on final. This can be done, and it's an item to practice. Certainly you wouldn't want to comply with a "130 knots on final" request for the first time while flying a tight one to Washington National.

How Slow?

How much should we slow down for a normal approach? There are several schools of thought on this. Some like to fly them fast; some like to slow-fly the approach unless requested to do otherwise. I like them fast. The instrument runways are seldom short, and most light airplanes are easy to slow down for a normal landing once you are contact at the published instrument minimums. On a Twin Comanche I used to fly, I used 120 knots with the gear down as a normal speed for an ILS final approach. The controls were very effective at that speed, and application of full power for a missed approach didn't produce an airplane that was badly out of trim. In the twin, if an engine should fail (that always comes up), even during the first stages of a go-around, there would be no question about good directional control. And the higher speed got me down and out of the way quicker so the next fellow could have his turn. In my Cessna Skyhawk, I flew the ILS at 105 knots indicated, which is close to its normal cruise. Why not? It didn't have to be slowed down or trimmed, control response remained as it had been through the flight, and a go-around was exceptionally easy. I used 120 knots in the Cardinal RG, because that speed is okay with the gear down. And when flying any other airplane, I try to look for a comfortable approach speed that is high enough to get the airplane down and out of the way quickly yet slow enough to allow extension of the landing gear at a normal time of my choosing. In a fixed gear, I just let the airplane seek a comfortable speed on final.

Hustle That Approach

Maybe it's because of subtle changes in the ATC system and the traffic mix, but I've found it desirable to develop a system for a very fast approach in my Cessna 210. Crossing the outer marker and intercepting the glideslope at 160 knots indicated, I select 15 inches of manifold pressure and track the localizer and glideslope. This results in a slow decay in airspeed, but it's still enough to keep a 727 from gaining much. Then, when I am 1,000 feet above field elevation, I extend the landing gear and approach flaps, leaving the power untouched at 15 inches. This causes the airspeed to decay to 115 knots, the speed for further extension of the flaps, by the time the airplane is at or near the decision height. Then I have the option of extending more flaps or landing in the approach configuration. I almost always do the latter, unless there is reason for a short landing. It only adds ten knots to the speed across the fence. That's a good example of using the "here I am, here's what I do next" method of managing a flight.

"I'm over the marker at 160 knots, I reduce power to 15 inches and fly on, tracking the ILS. The next event comes at 1,000 feet above field elevation. Here I am, 1,000 feet above field elevation; I extend the landing gear and approach flaps and fly on, tracking the ILS. Here I am, at the decision height. I do/do not see the runway, and it's in a proper position for a normal landing. I have the option to add additional flaps. If the runway is there, I fly on, tracking the ILS to the touchdown zone. If it's not there, I go into the published missed approach."

That really is quite easy, and using one power setting helps make it work. There might be times with a strong headwind on final when I'd use a little more power, or with a strong tailwind when I'd use a little less power, or with a potential for turbulence when I'd use a little more power, but on virtually all approaches I never touch the power. Slight glideslope excursions are handled with pitch changes. If there's a major glideslope excursion, I make a power adjustment along with the pitch change, but the occasion seldom presents itself. If the option of extending further flaps is exercised, I know that the airplane balloons and that a lot of forward pressure is required to keep it from going above the glideslope. That procedure, developed for those instances where the controller requests good speed on final, works so well that I use it almost all the time. The exception is on a relatively short runway with a tailwind component for landing. There I like to stablize it on a 100-knot, full-flaps approach at the outer marker inbound and then slow to 80 knots crossing the fence. If the runway is that short and there's a tailwind, there's not likely to be a faster airplane following.

When Push Comes to Shove

When any airplane is sliding along on the approach, I've always been impressed with how every instrument on the panel must be watched closely, and how the navigational instruments add a little mental push and shove by taking on added importance and demanding a lot of the pilot's time. For a basic example, let's talk about airplane control on a localizer (no-glideslope) approach.

Pick up the approach after the procedure turn is completed or after you've been vectored to the final approach course. The airplane is flying level on the inbound heading for the localizer, toward the outer marker. There is where we really start learning about the actual winds aloft. And when starting down after passing the outer marker, remember that the wind will likely change during the descent. If the localizer needle indicates the airplane is drifting to one side or the other while maintaining altitude, with the heading steady on the inbound, a correction is taken toward the needle. About 15 degrees is a good initial correction if the needle has moved away from center at a moderate rate. (If it crept away, use 10; if it sailed away use 20.) After taking this 15-degree cut toward the wayward needle, an active instrument scan between the localizer needle (to see if the correction is bringing it back toward the center, if it just arrested its departure from center, or if the needle is still moving away), the artificial horizon (wings level, pitch attitude correct for level flight), and the DG (steady on the correction heading selected) is necessary.

The scan needs to be active, because if the correction heading brings the localizer needle back toward center, it is important to be aware of the rate at which the needle moves. If it comes back in very slowly, then when it reaches center it would be best to take off, say, only 5 degrees of a 15-degree correction and fly with a 10-degree correction for drift. If it comes back very quickly, the message would be to take off most of the correction as the needle centers. This all accentuates the basics of holding a heading. If you don't hold the predetermined heading, you don't know what causes the needle to move.

Outer Marker, Inbound

The balls that have to be juggled at the marker include noting passage of the compass locator on the ADF and noting the 75-mc marker receiver indication by ear or eye, calling the tower to report the marker inbound, establishing a rate of descent by changing power and attitude (or lowering the gear and changing attitude), and, in some cases, turning the audio off on the marker receiver to restore a little peace and quiet. What did I forget? The most important thing: keeping the wings level so the heading won't change. Heading, again, is what gets the airplane to the airport. It's good to know an airplane well enough to be able to change power to the letdown setting almost by ear—at least to the point where you can set the power approximately and then glance at the power instruments and airspeed momentarily to verify that all is in order. The call to the tower while passing the marker is a very low-priority item, to be accomplished after everything else is in good shape. If the marker beacon receiver is so loud that you want it off, it should be something that you can turn off without looking at the switch. Eye time is at a premium at this critical moment, and the artificial horizon needs a lot of it. Many an approach has been ruined because the pilot became preoccupied with all the other stuff and let the airplane bank and the heading stray, with the result that the localizer needle sailed away from center at a good clip. That begins the final part of the approach on an offbeat note.

Final Approach Heading

Here I made a note to myself to once again stress the importance of determining the heading required to track the final approach course and of maintaining that heading. Then I backed away from that thought, at least a little, because the heading seldom remains constant in a perfectly tracked approach during instrument weather, as the conditions associated with inclement weather often result in a shift in wind direction and/or velocity between 2,000 feet above the surface and the surface. When this happens, the heading cannot remain the same all the way in if the airplane is to maintain the desired track. The emphasis is still on heading; keep it steady on a known value so that you can catch a wind shift quickly during the descent. Then any correction can be made on the basis of what the navigation needle did in relation to a known heading, rather than on the ignorance that is bred by flying along with the heading varying 10 or 15 degrees either side of center. Don't use the likelihood of a required change in heading during the final approach as an excuse for large heading excursions or for letting the navigation needle stray far from center. If the nav needle gets more than a couple or three dots away, it is time to abandon the approach and try again. It will not get far from center if the scan is active and your mind keeps a running tab on the situation.

Fly an approach. "There, 040 is tracking the localizer. Good. Now the needle is moving to the right slowly. Not much. Turn right to 055. That is moving the needle rather rapidly. Let it come back almost to center. Okay, all but centered, back left to 045 to track." Note that the heading is always related to what it does to the nav needle. If you don't hold the heading, there's no way to develop a picture of the relationship between the two things. As you get closer to the airport, the maximum acceptable heading change should become smaller. If at any time it seems that a big turn is necessary, or if the heading strays so far from where it is supposed to be that the nav needle starts to move rapidly from center, then it is time to call that approach a miss and start over.

The Straight and Narrow

Heading management must tighten up toward the last, because the localizer course gets progressively narrower as the runway gets closer. It's like flying into a funnel. Localizer courses have a total width of from three to six degrees. The total course width of a typical localizer might be about a half mile at the outer marker. So if you are a quarter of a mile (1,320 feet) to one side of the center of the localizer course at the outer marker, the nav needle will show a full-scale deflection. At the approach end of the runway (the localizer transmitter is at the other end) the total width of the localizer is about 700 feet, so if you are only 350 feet from the centerline, you'll have a full-scale needle deflection. The necessity for maintaining a heading is clear when an incorrect heading is applied to a localizer. If you are halfway from the outer marker to the runway threshold and at 105 knots groundspeed, a heading 10 degrees away from that which will keep the localizer needle centered will result in a full-scale deflection in only about 25 seconds. It is a precise business, and a little heading change goes a long way.

A Fine Point

On heading changes, a fine point is determined by what kind of airplane you fly. In some airplanes you can turn five degrees with the rudder and not disturb the bank attitude of the airplane much. That is, the wings can be kept level with little if any cross-control. In others, a little rudder at approach speed seems not to have much effect, and you have to bank for even the slightest correction. Try your airplane to see how it comes out. I think that airplanes in which you can make a small heading adjustment with rudder are the easiest in which to track a localizer. When the localizer needle strays just a little from center, you can move the DG five degrees with the rudder and have everything else remain relatively undisturbed. Airplanes you have to bank to get a small correction aren't as easy to keep on the localizer, because the pitch-attitude status quo is more likely to be upset when you make a bank correction.

I have flown all the way down the localizer course without mentioning the airspeed and the altimeter. The airspeed will be okay if the power is right and the pitch attitude is correct. The altimeter, though, is a very important reference instrument, as it defines the minimum descent altitude if you don't have a glideslope and the decision height if you do. We'll be talking more about altitude later on.

Missed Approach

Next comes the toughest moment of the approach, especially when you are doing it without a copilot, as most of us do. At minimums the pilot must look up, away from the instruments, and make a decision. If a runway is there and in the proper location, the message is to go on in for the landing. If a runway is not there, it's back to the instruments and square one. Climb power has to be added for the missed approach, and then there's that big change in pitch attitude to get the airplane into a climb. The gear has to come up, if applicable, and the airplane probably has to be trimmed. All this while you're wondering "what next?" The published missed approach—that's what comes next. Forget about other things such as missed appointments and ground arrangements. There shouldn't be much acceleration error in the artificial horizon when you're changing to a missed approach, so you can just look at the horizon and bring the nose smoothly up to a normal climb attitude while adding power. Check the altimeter and vertical speed regularly to make certain a climb has been established, and also to verify the correctness of attitude and power (a glance at the airspeed indicator).

The things that probably make a missed approach the most difficult are the look away from the instruments to see if the runway is there, the disappointment if it is not, and the thought that the ground is so close and you are still on instruments and faced with a difficult task. It's a good thing to practice to perfection. And to keep practicing. Most of us don't fly a lot of instrument approaches. We fly even fewer when the reported weather is at or below minimums. So our chance for actual experience at missed approaches isn't too great, and we have to be satisfied that practice does indeed make perfect. Missed approach perfection begins with not going even one foot below the minimum descent altitude or decision height unless the runway is in sight.

A pilot has to be wary of visual illusions here, too. At night, lights can often be seen directly below when there is little or no forward visibility. In the daytime, the ground or forms on the ground might be seen speeding by in the murk below when it is impossible to see ahead. I had an interesting missed approach session at Auburn, Alabama, one summer morning. The weather at Columbus, Georgia, and Montgomery, Alabama—the two nearest reporting stations—was okay. Auburn, with a VOR approach, was in between, and would logically have minimums. I forgot one thing—elevation. Auburn's airport is on higher ground, and simple arithmetic would have revealed that a 500-foot ceiling at Columbus might be near the ground at Auburn. The Unicom operator said the weather was lousy, but I thought it would be worthwhile to try the approach anyway. I was observing an aspiring instrument pilot (he was in the left seat), and the opportunity for real missed-approach exposure was too good to pass up.

On the first approach, there was no question about the miss. Flying at the MDA, there was absolutely no view of anything, even straight down. On the second, there was visibility down, and when we passed across the airport, I saw the runway. There is no way, though, that a normal approach and landing can be made to a runway visible only straight down. On the third approach, I spotted the airport and the hangars from about a mile away. The pilot flying would have missed the approach because he didn't see the runway. That was okay. I made the landing.

The pilot did a good job of executing the approaches and following the missed approach procedure. If there was a flaw, it was in power application for the missed approach. In retrospect, I think this was caused by sound. We had been holding at greatly reduced power, and then descending for the approach. It was very quiet in the airplane. The noise level increased dramatically when the throttle was applied for the climb, and I noticed that he quit advancing power at about the 75-percent point. That's not the way to do it. A missed approach calls for maximum power and a prompt transition to a climb.

Next

Flying good ILS approaches should be considered in steps. First, the localizer needs to be mastered. It's not even bad practice to fly the localizer up high, level, without worrying about the descent. That way it's possible to learn the increase in sensitivity of the needle as you get closer without having the added distraction of the letdown. After the localizer is mastered, the descent at a given rate to the no-glideslope minimums can be added. Then can come the glideslope.

The Letdown

On a nonprecision approach—one without the benefit of a glideslope—the letdown is quite simply a matter of basic airplane control and discipline. A good rate of descent, at the proper airspeed, to the minimum descent altitude is all that's required. Not one foot lower than MDA, either, unless the runway is in sight. The glideslope, though, adds another localizer-type task to the approach. The descent must be made to correspond with the electronic path. The principles that worked on the localizer are applicable to the letdown on a gildeslope, except that we will be talking of different instruments. Just as a heading will track a localizer, a rate of descent will track a glideslope. The heading required is affected by wind direction and velocity, which are apt to change as the airplane descends. The rate of descent required is determined by the airplane's groundspeed (not airspeed), so the rate is also likely to change as the airplane descends and the wind aloft changes. Thus, while we can go at a glideslope with a predetermined configuration (gear and approach flaps down, for example) and power setting, there is certainly no guarantee that this will track the glideslope at an unchanging airspeed. And there is no guarantee that what tracks the glideslope as the approach begins will continue tracking the glideslope as the approach continues. What is true is that there is a proper attitude and power setting that will work well and that this combination doesn't vary a whole lot. Too, just as we must know the relationship between a given heading and the reaction of the localizer needle, we must know the relationship between a given situation—power, attitude, airspeed, and rate of descent—and the glideslope. Swooping and dipping just don't work.

One other glideslope item: the altitude at which the glideslope crosses the outer marker is shown on the approach chart. This gives a good double check between the altimeter and the glideslope.

Nothing Major

It is important to guard against gross corrections, big control movements, and other dramatics on any approach. Smooth and basic flying is what gets the airplane to the runway. This is perhaps best illustrated on a clear day. Fly the airplane visually to the outer marker of an ILS. There, with the needles centered, set the airplane up in the rate of descent that should track the glideslope and fly the published heading of the localizer. Maintain both the descent rate and the heading until at the decision height (unless the airplane drifts far off and it would be hazardous to continue down to DH), and then note the airplane's position with relation to the end of the runway. Unless the wind is strong, the airplane will likely be close. Thus relatively minor corrections, ones that could have been made with your pinky, would have resulted in the airplane's flying out the small end of the funnel and onto the runway at the appointed moment. Remember this if you are ever tempted to make a wrestling match out of an instrument approach. Remember that simply holding a heading and maintaining a rate of descent will almost do it. True, in situations with strong wind shear, some rather large changes will be required, but these are the exception rather than the rule, and the changes should be made smoothly when necessary.

Don't Crash

A very important glideslope-related moment comes when the runway or the approach lights are sighted and the decision is made that the flight is visual. Most pilots will, at such times, fly below the electronic glideslope in establishing a visual approach to the runway. There seems to be a compelling urge to do something—to make some motion to mark the transition from instrument to visual flight. That something is usually a power reduction or a pitch-attitude change in the nose-down direction. This is unfortunate, because the electronic glideslope gives little clearance over obstacles, and there is certainly no reason to go below it once the runway is in sight. When a pilot sees the approach lights and the runway, the best thing is to just continue flying the glideslope. The power, pitch attitude, and descent rate should remain at what was necessary to track the glideslope. It got you that far, and the glideslope will lead you on to a good landing point.

As an illustration of how pilots go below the glideslope, the National Transportation Safety Board noted that most IFR-approach accidents happen after the airplane is clear of cloud and on the visual part of the approach. It is only logical that the airplane would usually break out at some time before an accident; the point of the NTSB observation is that the visual part of an instrument approach is critical, and pilots tend to disregard guidance at this time. At least they do have to go below a glideslope to crash. If it's an ILS, the message is to stay on the glideslope after becoming visual; on a nonprecision approach, the minimum descent altitude should be maintained until it is absolutely necessary to leave that altitude to land.

As we move from basic flying by reference to instruments to actual IFR operation, the primary thing to remember is that basics come first. There is a lot to contemplate about planning, weather, the system, and other facets of IFR flying, but we must always remember the basics and spend ample time critiquing our basic ability and practicing to make it as perfect as possible. Too, when things go well on an approach, think in terms of its being a reward for a good job of heading and descent management. Those items, and those items alone, are what keep the needles crossed.

4. Actual Instruments

An important step in learning instrument flying is using the rating after it has been earned. And sometimes it seems as if the rating is a lot easier to get than it is to use, primarily because the training system seems prone to avoiding actual situations. For example, one day I noticed a fellow waiting for the weather to improve before starting from New Jersey to the Bahamas in a Cherokee Six. He had started from Long Island and was en route with his wife to pick up another couple in Washington and then to flee from winter. The forecasts had been good, but the weather wasn't living up to the forecasts. What was supposed to have been good VFR was actually at IFR minimums. The pilot was in a quandary. He kept saying to his wife that they could file IFR and be out of the small bad-weather zone in just a few minutes' flying, but I could sense a lack of conviction in his voice. The pilot never did file and go, and at the time it seemed questionable that he really had an instrument rating.

Finally, one of the local pilots offered to take them home for the night. They accepted, and left the next morning in CAVU weather. The pilot's overnight host later said that the man did indeed have an instrument rating, but that it was brand new and had never been used. The proposed flight would actually have been as easy as they come, but the pilot just wasn't ready, willing, or truly able to tackle an actual IFR. It was of great credit to him that he realized this and decided not to make the flight. It was of discredit to the training system that he wasn't ready, willing, and able to tackle actual IFR when rated. There has to be a first time, and someday this pilot will complete his instrument training by actually using the rating. Perhaps he would have done so that day if his wife had not been along. She didn't seem keen on the instrument flight, and some of her hesitation probably rubbed off. Or maybe he'll never use the rating. Too bad, and if that is the case, I hope his instructor has a guilty conscience.

Acknowledged Hurdle

There is no question that the first actual instrument flight, or the first instrument flight in a while, is a hurdle. For many pilots, the first actual IFR is as memorable as the first solo. I know that I remember mine as at least being equal. It was a short IFR flight in a Piper Pacer. The date was October 19, 1955. The purpose was to get through a bit of a front that was draped across the Allegheny Mountains. I had flown quite a distance in VFR conditions, and I had landed because VFR flying had become impossible. A check of the weather revealed it to be cloudy but benign. I'm sure my hand trembled a bit as I filed that first IFR flight plan.

In 1955, light-airplane IFR just wasn't the great outdoor sport that it is today, and I was doing what nobody else was doing that cloudy day. There were a lot of light-airplane pilots waiting at the airport for improvement in the weather; all eyes were on the fuzzy-faced kid in the Pacer. I had gotten my instrument rating without ever penetrating a cloud, and my mind was awash with questions about IFR as I walked to the Pacer to commit my hide and the Pacer's Grade-A fabric to the mercy of the clouds. The unknowns outnumbered the knowns by a commanding margin. The only rationale I could muster was that conditions did have the appearance of being rather ideal for the venture. Besides, I knew that I would never learn how to fly IFR by watching from the sidelines.

The flight was an anticlimax. I was both nervous and excited to begin with, but when the airplane didn't melt as it entered cloud, I felt some measure of relief. The air was smooth, and the temperature stayed comfortably above freezing. The Pacer ran like a top, and in a short time I was over the cloud-draped mountains and in VFR conditions on the other side. I felt the exhilaration that one might feel after parting with virginity. The mystery was gone.

The dramatics shouldn't have been part of that first flight; it should have been more routine. The fact that it was so special meant that if I had faced it at another time in life—later on, with family responsibilities and other considerations—I might not have flown, much like the nervous Cherokee Six pilot. About 30 years passed before I landed again at Morgantown, but when I did, I enjoyed taking a few minutes to relive that flight.

The Obvious Things

How might we make actual instrument flying easier and more natural? The question is applicable both to new IFR pilots and to infrequent ones. It isn't a good idea to use a brand-new or a rusty rating when there is strong pressure to deliver. The fellow in the Cherokee, for example, felt pressed by the fact that he had told people in Washington he would be along that afternoon. There was also perhaps some pressure from his wife. Even though she didn't appear overly eager to go, her husband probably knew that she was aware that the instrument rating and all those transistorized marvels in the panel represented quite an investment, and there would be some natural wonder about why it wouldn't serve as intended at the appointed time. In my case, it was a matter of getting to New York on time or joining the ramp-walkers waiting for VFR conditions. The latter would have been easier. But there was some pressure to go. I had to get there. Had I picked a more relaxed atmosphere for my first actual IFR flight, perhaps I might have approached it with aplomb.

Relaxed Atmosphere

Rather than going for a command performance on a first actual IFR flight, or when breaking the ice after a period of inactivity, it is far better to fly with as little pressure as possible. Do it as if the day is a beautiful one for floating about the countryside and the flight is for the purpose of learning skills as well as for enjoyment and the basic challenge of flight. If possible, pick a time when there isn't much traffic and when conditions are thoroughly IFR but reasonably stable. Don't fly with a destination; just file a round-robin IFR and fly a few actual approaches at the end of the flight if it's an airport where multiple approaches are practical. I've often gone out on a Sunday morning, moved around IFR in cloud for a while, and then returned to fly every approach in the book for my airport. With radar vectoring, it doesn't take long, and the practice is fine—much better than hood practice. As I noted earlier, it's a shame that actual instrument operation isn't conducted in all training, and any time a training institution avoids it, perhaps the pilot would be better off finding another place to fly.

Familiarity

A measure of familiarity with the environment inside cloud and/or rain is also important. The sensations in cloud can be special. The cloud form passing by can give a visual feeling of great speed. The water streaking the windshield and side windows gives a sensation not found when flying on a CAVU day. On the other side of the coin, there are some actual instrument situations where the airplane almost seems suspended, with little or no sense of motion. Whatever the conditions, the IFR pilot's world is inside. Don't let cloud or rain pull your vision or thought away from the gauges. Rain can be quite a diversion. Sound tends to draw the eye, and rain beating on the windshield is no exception. There is a strong tendency to look at the source of sound, especially when it changes. There is no time for that in actual IFR. A pilot must develop the discipline necessary to refuse to respond to any distraction. Another example of a distracting time is when flying in and out of cloud. It takes a bit of concentration to stay with the instruments and not be drawn to an examination of the wisps of cloud whipping by outside or the cloud formation into which you are about to fly.

Hard to Take

I have heard reluctant instrument pilots say that it's difficult to accept the fact that it's normal to be in a situation where a handful of gyros and concentration on the instrument panel are the only things that stand between them and deep trouble. Perhaps that is so, but when flying VFR, there's very little other than personal concentration and ability keeping the old devil at arm's length. And there are many other fields of endeavor where similar situations exist: a lot rides on one tire of a car when you're negotiating a curve at maximum allowable speed, and when boating, only a half inch of fiberglass might separate sailor and shark.

The Object

When moving into actual instrument flying, confidence finally comes when we learn to approach IFR in the same manner as VFR flying. Some experience is necessary for this. The fact that there are clouds means little or nothing to the airplane, unless those clouds are hostile, as in the case of icy or cumulonimbus formations. The pilot needs the same attitude toward cloud as the airplane has, and only actual instrument time will create that attitude. Another beginning helper might be to fly the first few actual IFR flights solo. Certainly passengers can be a diversion, and it goes without saying that a pilot is more relaxed solo than with two or more eyes eagerly watching every move.

Picking Weather

Once a pilot feels comfortable with the airplane in cloud, it is still wise to bite off small chunks. Try to pick stable weather for the first few flights. Do be aware, though, that weather forecasting is an inexact science, and that you had better be prepared to fly every instrument flight in cloud and in turbulence all the way. Accept the fact that the destination might be at minimums, as might the alternate, regardless of the forecast. That is the maximum task that one might be called upon to perform, and it is always best to be prepared to do the most. If the weather is better, it is a pleasant surprise. And pleasant surprises are the only kind that should be allowed in instrument flying.

5. Preflight Action

As we move into the real use of an instrument rating, acknowledge right off the bat that IFR flying is challenging. In fact, there is nothing more demanding or challenging in flying than the production of a smooth and precise actual instrument flight. A good foundation is absolutely necessary. The quality of preflight planning can actually make or break a flight.

A common conception of preflight work is that it is nothing more than dull drudgery. The image that pops to mind might be of a sea of pilot applicants locked in a testing room, anxiously punching buttons on electronic computers, trying to find the best answer in a multiple-choice exam that was designed to harass instead of teach, and filling in torturous little forms with headings and anticipated groundspeeds.

But try not to think of IFR preflight planning as drudgery. Instead, try to consider it a stimulating exercise that makes the flight easier. A proper amount of planning will help avoid any number of booby traps that can foul up your basic instrument flying and make an adventure out of a trip that should have been routine. Pilots who use computers have progressed to making an art form out of flight planning by using much of the excellent software that is available. The important thing to remember here is that time en route and fuel required are only as accurate as the winds aloft forecast. The importance of planning can be easily emphasized if we follow the good practice of grading all flights. The poor grades most likely come when the unexpected creates a diversion. If the event had been properly planned, the unexpected would have at least been anticipated and would not have derailed the mind and caused so much trouble.

The Machine

Much of the preflight of our airplane is continuous. For example, I know that my airplane has all the required paperwork on board. The required VOR check is done and recorded on a regular basis, so the VORs are always ready for IFR. The transponder, altimeters, and static system are always kept current. The avionic equipment is kept in perfect order. No squawks are ever left over. The same goes for the condition of the instruments and of the airplane in general. If something isn't 100 percent at the completion of a flight, it gets fixed before the next flight. Instrument planning begins with knowledge that the airplane was put in top shape after last being flown and should be ready to go with only a verification of conditions required before takeoff.

The Pilot

We will look at special IFR-related items for the airplane more thoroughly in Chapter 14, but it needs to be said here that just as the airplane should give a little extra for IFR, so should the pilot. I personally feel that there are times when a pilot is okay to fly in good VFR conditions but should not fly in IFR conditions. For example, if I have a bit of a head cold, I don't mind flying on a pretty day when climbs and descents can be gradual and at whatever rate my ears will allow. But it is difficult to impose a 200-foot-per-minute rate of descent on the IFR system, and it shouldn't even be attempted. Nor should uncomfortable rates of descent that might cause ear problems and create a throbbing diversion from the primary chores. Any general feeling of malaise, whether from overindulgence at a party or just general blahs, is a sign to steer clear of real IFR. When you punch into bumpy clouds just before daybreak and face the task of managing the instruments while the airplane bounces up and down, the message is plain that this activity is reserved for people who are awake and alert. Don't read this as a statement that IFR is reserved for superpeople flying four-engine Boeings. All it suggests is that you fly IFR in a good airplane and when feeling reasonably chipper.

The Environment

The next step is to check the weather. This involves organization, discipline, and a basic knowledge of meteorology. A pilot who keeps up with general weather trends all the time is far ahead of the pack when preparing to fly. If you know that there was a cold front to the west last night, and if you look out the window this morning and note rather low clouds moving quickly from the south, you can begin putting things together before calling the FSS or using your computer for a DUAT briefing. The cold front is still to the west, moist flow ahead of it. Strong flow? Look again. The trees are swaying—strong flow. The television weather map will give some hint of the big picture expected for the day, and, if you have cable, The Weather Channel can expand the briefing. Many times, I have gotten a heads-up on potential serious weather problems from looking outside and watching TV. While it is possible to go into a weather briefing without any preparation, the pilot who skips the preliminary effort is swinging with a short bat.

The Plan

If there is to be a call to the FSS, determine what information is needed unless you want a full route briefing. I usually let the picture I get from looking out the window and at the TV dictate which way to go on a phone briefing. If the weather looks generally good, I might ask for the actual weather, the terminal forecasts, the wind at the desired cruising level, and any pertinent sigmets, notams, and the radar summary, if there is any chance of precipitation. If there is any question at all, I get the full route briefing.

Hello, My Number is. . .

It is important to get the telephone briefing off to a good start. "Good morning, Four Zero Romeo Charlie, a Cessna 210 slant

Romeo, IFR from India Six Niner to Whiskey Five Four at one seven thousand, leaving at 1500 Z." That gives the briefer what he needs to know to call up a briefing for you on the computer, and it gets a full route briefing. After the briefer gives you what he has, then ask for any additional information you feel you need. The usual need is for an alternate airport; hopefully, by the time you read this, they will have a program in the computer that will display, at the touch of a button, all legal alternates within a specified distance of the destination. Until then, it's a guessing game. You tell the specialist what stations will be in alternate range and he calls them up to see if they will work.

The next business is to file the flight plan. Three flight-plan items probably can't be completed before the call—the altitude request, time en route, and alternate—but these can be added at the last minute. Somehow using one call for a briefing and then calling back to file a flight plan seems wasteful. Also, it means sitting through all the recorded messages twice (not to mention the business about all briefers being busy).

Roll Your Own

The DUAT system added a new element to preflight weather briefings and flight planning, and it is used by a lot of pilots. With it you can get a route briefing or selected weather products just as you can on the phone. While some pilots feel that the route briefings are too much, I like them. I can be doing something else while the briefing prints, or I can read the high spots as it prints. If the weather situation is complex, I can scroll back through the information, see what I need as an alternate, and call those forecasts as selected weather products. Then I can complete the flight plan. Filing flight plans with DUAT is simple, and, knock on wood, I have not lost one as of this writing.

Wait a Minute

Did I miss something? Well, that much-heralded and holy savior of pilots, the go/no-go decision, was not fully explored, and it might be argued that it should have been. I find, though, that the best way to plan IFR operations is to think only in terms of "go." The reason it is best to plan only for go is that you can't make an intelligent decision while talking with someone on the telephone or watching your computer printer go as fast as it can. The object is to gather the information and file the flight plan. Any decision is best made in a quiet and reflective moment, after all the available information has been recorded and assimilated.

If a pilot starts trying to make a decision on the phone, often as not the pilot will wind up mumbling in parables and virtually asking the briefer to help make the decision. A briefer can always find at least one reason for you not to fly on a given day, and some of them have made an art form out of terrifying pilots who seem reluctant.

Consider the briefer as an information source, just like the computer. You can file the flight plan and study the information and then modify the flight plan if weather conditions dictate. In fact, I always thought the flight plan should be filed first. Then the briefer or computer would know what you want to do and could tell you about it. If a change was needed after the briefing, it could be made.

The pilot is responsible, and only the pilot can make intelligent decisions about the conduct of a flight. And if a pilot hasn't had the wisdom to develop more than a basic knowledge of meteorology, heaven help him or her in IFR or VFR flying.

Start/Continue

Over the years, I've come to dislike the "go/no-go" terminology used in relation to weather decisions. In fact, if a pilot charges his mind with "go/no-go," it can be dangerous. Maybe the forecasts are all pretty good and the decision is to go. That carries with it the implication that the flight will be flown as planned. If the weather is worse than forecast, the pilot might have trouble bringing himself to an alteration of the plan. If, instead, the decision is thought of as "start/continue," then the pilot is charged only with determining that the weather is okay to start out and knows that a continuous in-flight decision-making process is required to ascertain that it is okay to continue.

The two most frequently found reasons to delay, alter, or cancel an IFR flight are thunderstorms and ice. These will be explored in Chapters 8 and 9. For the purposes of this chapter and the next, we'll assume that neither is an operational consideration along the route of flight.

When a flight is of any length, start/continue decisions have to be tempered with respect for the fickle nature of weather and the potential inaccuracy of forecasts. Experience will suggest, perhaps later rather than sooner, that reliability comes from making the initial start/continue based on the conditions to be expected over the territory covered in the first half hour of flight. The decision that is made before flying is that it is okay to start out. After takeoff, the start/continue decision is continuously examined, and the flight is extended, terminated, or diverted to an alternate based on actual conditions ahead. A pilot should never feel bound to continue by a decision to start. An instrument pilot simply must be mature enough to play the game by flying it a mile at a time while keeping a wary eye on the miles ahead.

Gassed

Another item to complete before flying has to do with fuel. If you know enough about the airplane to be flying it, you should be able to make an accurate determination of the fuel that will be required for a flight of any given duration. Once the calculation has been made for the flight to the destination and the alternate, make sure there will be an hour's fuel on board at the completion. That is 15 minutes over the legal requirement, but every pilot owes himself an extra 15 minutes. The tanks might not be quite full to begin with, there might be a delay in getting off or some vectoring, or some other factor might increase consumption slightly.

Once the fuel calculations have been made, make a mental or written note of groundspeed required to complete the flight on this amount of fuel. This is the magic number. Any indication that the groundspeed is below the magic number is a demand that the fuel reserve be recalculated. Any deterioration of groundspeed later on means the same thing. If, on recalculation, it appears that landing at the alternate will be with less than an hour's fuel on board, the flight must have a new plan and a new destination and/or alternate.

When my hour's reserve is going to be close, I always write the necessary groundspeed on the flight-plan form in rather big numbers, as a reminder of its importance. If you consider the consequences of a forced landing on an IFR flight, as we all should, you'll always carry extra fuel and manage it well, because the number-one cause of engine failure is fuel starvation or exhaustion.

Remember, too, when using published information in planning flights, that the data given on range in miles are absolutely useless unless the wind happens to be calm. That is highly unlikely, and what counts on every flight is time. The fuel runs through the pipe by the clock, not by the mile. Don't be suckered into thinking that a 500-nautical-mile flight will be comfortable because the book shows a 750 nautical-mile range at the chosen power setting and altitude. Planning must be based on endurance, with a generous allowance for taxi, takeoff, and climb as well as for variations in fuel flow and any other contingencies that come to mind.

There's a good way to calculate fuel required for a flight. It's to use one value for the first thirty minutes, which includes the taxi and take-off and climb, and then a per-hour value for the rest of the flight. On my P210, for example, with the wing tanks chock full (something I assume only if I put the fuel in myself or climb a ladder and make sure they are brimfull with the wings level in a left-right sense), I figure that after 30 minutes, 85 pounds of fuel have been used and I have 449 pounds left. If I'm running 90 pounds an hour at cruise, that means there's an absolute 5 hours left in the tanks, or, 4 hours for the trip to the destination and alternate. I'll hit within a couple of gallons on the estimated fuel for any flight using this method—but only if the tanks were indeed brimfull. We'll again consider fuel in the next chapter, which is on in-flight planning. Just remember that it's important that there is no kidding allowed. Kidding leads to dry tanks, to silence.

Flight Log

What about preparing a detailed flight log in advance? There is certainly more than one way to keep books on a flight. Some pilots like elaborate logs, including distance flown, distance to go, the bearing of each airway segment, and other items. These can be done by computer or by hand. Some pilots keep up with their en route business on a blank piece of paper. Either way is fine. Just make sure you have a system. I think pilots enjoy inventing their own forms, and the jiffy printing services of the world make it easy for each of us to be in the IFR-form-printing business at a nominal cost. Others delight in using the product of one or more software programs for flight planning. And then there's the widespread use of good loran sets that keep up with almost everything for you. Whatever you use, be prepared in case something happens to it. If your loran goes out, have a plan. If you drop your computerized plan and can't retrieve it, have something to take its place.

SID?

Sid who? Standard Instrument Departure, that's who, and while you're still planning the flight, don't fail to look at departure procedure for the airport in question. If there are published SIDs, the flight plan should have been filed along one of them. If not, chances are the clearance won't come back as filed and there will be a moment of silent confusion when the clearance is received. Equally important, the approach chart for the departure airport should be scoured for any instructions on how to leave the area, and this should be studied and understood in advance.

The departure procedures on an approach chart are usually for terrain or obstruction avoidance, and not heeding the printed word could lead to a rock-strewn hillside. At this writing, Jeppesen includes these procedures, where applicable, on the chart with the airport diagram, at the bottom, in rather small type. NOS warns that there is a procedure with a "T" dropped out of an inverted triangle on the lower left information box on the chart. The procedures are in the front of the book. I keep a complete set of WAC charts, and when a question about high terrain or obstructions is raised by something on the approach plate or en route chart—a special departure procedure or high-minimum en route altitude, for example—I study the WAC chart for an understanding of the reasons. And at times I've noted that a different airway, involving only a few extra miles, will take a flight over lower and more friendly terrain than the primary and direct airway between two points. That's always worth a few miles.

Route Survey

A little route survey is a good wind-up and is quite useful in setting the mind for the task ahead. Trace the flight on the chart from start to finish with your finger. Mentally position your weather information on the chart as you go, and visualize what it should be like along the way. If MEAs are high, check why. Note the availability of alternate landing sites. If the weather is really grungy, the airports with a full ILS take on special importance. They might well be the only true havens. A route survey is especially important when you're flying in an area that is not familiar.

The Airplane

Some items of the preflight inspection become extra important when you're checking the airplane before an IFR flight. In addition to the usual good things, take extra care in looking at the static port or ports, because these affect the pressure instruments. Peer into the pitot tube and check the radio antennas. As things are stowed, make certain the baggage door is closed securely. If it comes open in flight, you'll almost surely have to land to close it. That might mean an extra instrument approach. Other things that might prompt a return in VFR conditions—coattails hanging out the door, opened oil-access doors, loose and banging gas caps, for example—can become major projects on an IFR flight. It is quite accurate to say that you are placing more faith in the machine for an IFR flight than for a VFR flight, and that faith calls for an extra measure of attention during the preflight inspection.

On Board

There's no question that a light airplane isn't an ideal place to do the type of work that is necessary during an IFR flight. Ideally, we would have a large table on which to spread the charts. Actually, that large table must be compressed to the size of a kneepad or lap-held clipboard in the airplane. A little organization is necessary to make the most of this confined work space.

We all know that it is easier to fly any flight without passengers than it is with passengers. This phenomenon is even more pronounced when flying IFR. The empty seat to the right that can be so handy for books and charts is full, and there never seems to be a place to put anything. We thus need to devise a system for getting pilot, passenger, and charts neatly in place, with charts readily available. If possible, the system should not involve the passenger at all. Unless he is an active pilot or at least a person who frequently rides with you, a passenger is best left completely in that role.

Most high-wing airplanes have an advantage over low-wing airplanes when you're arranging stuff for an IFR flight. In a high-wing with a door on each side, I get the passenger(s) in place and belted, and then stand outside the airplane and arrange all my little charts and papers before boarding. The Jeppesen books are stowed or stacked on the floor between and under seats. The proper en route charts are folded and placed in the clipboard, which is put atop the panel while I get into the airplane. In a low-wing, my system is to stack things on top of the panel (if it is large enough) while I board, and then get everything organized after everyone is in and strapped. The main thing is to have a plan, to do as much as possible in advance, and to completely assume the role of aviator (as opposed to flight attendant) once any passengers are buckled up and settled.

Hush in the Gallery

One other word about passengers. They must understand that IFR flying requires a certain degree of concentration and that they should speak only when spoken to. Give some advance word on the methodical nature of IFR flying so they won't automatically assume that the pilot isn't quite with it because of continuous references to checklists and charts. After that, retreat into a shell and care not what the passengers think. Every IFR pilot should use a headset, and many of us fly with intercoms. It's fine for a passenger to wear a headset and listen in, but again, be sure the passenger understands that chatting is allowed only when instituted by the pilot. If another pilot is on board, the good policy is to discuss nothing but the flight and the flying except in the en route phase of flight.

The Object

The object of prestart and pretakeoff work in the cockpit is to get as much done as possible before flying away. Make certain that everything that can be put in place is in place. The whole purpose of a checklist is to command the discipline necessary for the pilot to know that everything is just right when the throttle is advanced for takeoff. Checklists aren't for sissies, either. They should be used religiously in IFR operations.

Some checklists don't specifically cover all the IFR items, or they don't cover things in a logical sequence. In this event, make your own. The list should include everything on the original checklist plus every item specific to an IFR flight. Include things like setting the transponder and turning it on, putting the heading bug on the first heading to fly, setting the navigation radios, setting the departure-control frequency in the number-two radio or on the flip-flop, and turning the pitot heat on. Get everything that you might need turned on in advance. The checklist should be arranged so that as many items as possible are handled before taxiing, with only the last-minute things left for the runup position.

The Clearance

Many different forms of clearance shorthand have seen the light of day. Clearance shorthand is like the flight log—to each his own. If a pilot gets all hung up over memorizing and using some specific form of clearance shorthand, he or she might well draw a blank over what symbol to use for one thing that is said and thus miss the rest of the clearance. Just write it naturally, using whatever abbreviations come to mind. Also, when copying a clearance, do not try to make sense of the instructions as they come to you. If it is an involved clearance, that means it won't be as you filed the flight plan. That, in turn, means you will mentally question it. Resist the temptation to think of questions during the reading. Write it down, putting all the mental effort into catching the spoken words and making a record of them. Then read it back. Then read it again and make sense out of what it says.

Make sure you understand a clearance before flying, and make any necessary changes in navigational radio settings before takeoff. If, for example, your filed route was over Yardley and then outbound on the 276 radial, but your actual clearance is to intercept the 152 of Yardley and fly that to the Gdork intersection, get it all straight before takeoff. Set the radios in accordance with the clearance. If this isn't done, that difficult period in basic instrument flying immediately after takeoff is likely to be confusing as well as difficult as you try to fly and figure out a routing at the same time.

I read a while back of an IFR accident in which a pilot flew in exactly the wrong direction, 180 degrees out of phase, and finally lost control of the airplane in the confusion that ensued. Perhaps he was turned around to begin with, and once this was called to his attention, he fixated on the navigation problem and forgot all about flying the airplane.

Ready for Takeoff

If the preflight effort is effective, everything will truly be ready for take-off as the airplane moves out onto the runway. The airplane has been checked and is in good shape, the pilot is okay, every setting that can be made in advance has been made, the charts are at hand and are understood (and the approach chart for the point of departure is readily available in case the need to return and land should arise), the clearance is on paper and is understood, and the weather is suitable for the launching. Something to watch: many of us do well at all this planning for the first flight of the day but regress as the day wears on. It shouldn't be this way. The second leg (and any subsequent leg) of a day's flying should be planned just as carefully as the first. Take off, too, with the thought that planning does not end when the airplane leaves the ground. That is actually when the planning challenge really begins. Up to this point, time has been expandable as necessary to accommodate planning. Once you are airborne, there is a fixed amount of time available to do all the necessary things.

6. In-Flight

This first item isn't quite off-the-ground, but it's close enough, and it is first. After the engine spins up at the beginning of the takeoff roll, I always check a few things. If there's time, I look at the rpm, manifold pressure, fuel flow (if applicable), exhaust gas or turbine inlet temperature, vacuum reading, and alternator output. And I usually find time. My theory is that if the engine and accessories accept the acceleration to full power, and if all the readings are normal, they are likely to keep on working for a while. And if something in there is weak and looking for a time to malfunction, perhaps the increase to full power will expose that weak link. Needless to say, an indication of anything short of perfection would be a mandate to abort the takeoff and seek mechanical aid and comfort.

Punching In

In speaking of basics earlier, I stressed the importance of concentrating on flying during the first few moments. Have a plan for the way it will be done, and things will go extra smoothly. Unless there is a compelling reason not to do so, I like to climb on runway heading at full power to at least 500 feet above the ground (1,000 feet is even better) and then go to cruise climb before making any turn. If flaps are used for takeoff, they are left extended to this transition altitude. Any local noise rules or considerations could modify this slightly, but none that I know of would require much turning. The gear is retracted normally, but I avoid doing anything else. It is my time with the airplane, a time of introduction.

There could be one variation on normal procedures, too. If there is a strong pitch change or a marked sinking spell with flaps retraction on a particular airplane, it is good to take a hard look at the necessity for flaps on takeoff. Unless they are called for on an absolute basis, it might well be best to start out flapless and avoid any pitch change and sinking spell in those important first minutes on instruments.

Once in cruise climb with the initial communications out of the way, it is time to start gathering information to use in the planning process. In the weather briefing, you should have gotten temperature-aloft forecasts along with the wind forecasts. Check their accuracy on climb. A really bad temperature forecast would suggest that all other forecasts might also be off by a good measure. Note the rate at which the temperature drops as you climb, too. If the temperature drops rapidly with altitude, that is a sign of unstable air. In the summertime this could suggest thunderstorm activity later in the day if yours is a morning flight. If the temperature increases with altitude, that's a sign of stability. There is not likely to be much bumpy action, but the surface wind and the wind aloft are probably far apart, and the ceiling and visibility might well have been low. Keep a continuous tab on those temperatures to gauge the accuracy of the forecast and also to know where warm air is located in the event that ice should become a problem during a flight.

Winds

You can get some feel for winds aloft in a climb, even without loran or DME. If the airplane climbs better than usual at some time during the ascent, perhaps it is climbing into an increasing headwind at that point. This situation does result in a momentary boost in airspeed and climb until the airplane adjusts to the new flow. Remember the altitude at which it happens; above it you might go very slowly, but if you could fly below that altitude, the headwind might not be so bad. On the other hand, pronounced sagging in climb might indicate an increasing tailwind. If there are mountains around, flow over these could be the cause for better- or worse-than-usual climb, as could cumulus development, so any variation in a climb can't be taken as absolute word on anything, but it is surprising how often it portends groundspeeds to come.

The clouds tell some tales as we climb. If there was any indication of layers or tops during the briefing, be curious about the accuracy of the prediction. Continuous turbulence in clouds means they are cumulus types, unless there is some wind-related turbulence from terrain or from wind shear. Was the forecast such that cumulus clouds or wind shear might be expected? All this curiosity about the elements shouldn't be allowed to detract from the flying, but try not to neglect it. Once the airplane is off the ground, it becomes a much better weather sensor than anything offered by the National Weather Service, and the pilot should be keenly interested in the airplane's surroundings.

All the information gathered before takeoff was for the purpose of deciding that it was okay to start the flight. By the time the flight is over, a wise instrument pilot will have collected a few more complete sets of data. What is actually happening along the route and at the destination and alternate is a lot more important than what was happening or what was forecast to happen. Whenever there is new information, get it. It isn't necessary to neglect basic instrument flying to do this. Just budget time properly.

Keeping Busy

When you're moving along en route on a routine IFR flight, things don't jump at you and demand attention as they do in other phases of IFR flying. Someone prone to be a touch on the lazy side might even while away the hours immersed in boredom and idle thoughts. That is survivable some of the time on some flights, but the time often comes when such apparently mundane busywork as checking groundspeed in relation to the plan and studying charts can help avoid thrills and adventure.

Groundspeed

The preflight deliberations included the calculation of an estimated groundspeed. If the speed goes below the estimate, the fuel reserve will have to be recalculated. This is an important chore throughout the flight, but it is especially important when you level off for cruise. There, you get the first grade on the wind forecast. If you don't have DME or a loran or GPS, add the estimated time en route to the time off for an estimated time of arrival at the first fix, and then keep a running tab on how things are going as you progress toward that fix. If there's groundspeed information on board, fine. Use it. If not, a second VOR can be used for intersections along the way. Certainly intersections are not precise, and you wouldn't want to change an ETA based on the time over one intersection, but you can surely become suspicious of a gross error in the winds aloft forecast if times over intersections are far off what was estimated based on the winds aloft forecast.

If you have to figure it yourself, the ADF can be very useful in these initial groundspeed deliberations as well as at other times. Nondirectional beacons have proliferated, and if there's one on or along an airway, use it as a fix. These positions would be at least as precise as anything you'd get with VOR cross bearings, so long as the station is close to the airway. The greater the distance to the first VOR along the airway, the more important it is to work at an initial groundspeed verification before reaching that fix.

When I had a Skyhawk, first legs from my home base were almost all over 100 nautical miles. If the wind was 40 knots instead of 20, I needed to know all about that before the first VOR was reached, because an extra 20 knots on the nose was the difference between possible and impossible on a lot of trips. It is less critical with a faster airplane or with a lot of fuel, but the sooner you know the groundspeed the better—in any airplane.

Wind, Weather

Another reason for nailing down groundspeed early is to get a reading on the accuracy of the synopsis. If the wind forecast is badly in error, that means they didn't have the pressure systems correctly evaluated and the real weather map is probably somewhat different from the one you have in mind. A badly missed winds aloft forecast should be a clear signal to dig carefully into all available weather information to see if the switch is going to have any pronounced effect on flight conditions. It'll likely mean a recalculation of fuel reserves, too, because, alas, the unforecast wind always seems to be from ahead. The wind is unlikely to stay the same during a trip of any length, and we have to keep up with it all the way. It is true that the wind strength usually increases as you fly toward a front or low-pressure system and it tends to decrease as you fly away. The forecasts are averages for a given period of time and, on a trip where the wind was forecast to be the same all the way, you can see wide variations if there is a frontal zone or low on the route.

Traffic

Most of our IFR hours are actually flown clear of cloud. This brings with it a total responsibility to look for, see, and avoid other traffic. It is a serious mistake to let the IFR busy-work ruin the scan for other airplanes, and it certainly isn't necessary. The way to look for airplanes is with a methodical search pattern, and this can easily be maintained while flying the radials and altitudes and doing the necessary bookkeeping. This is a good time to use an autopilot, too. Let it track the radial and hold altitude (if equipped with that feature) while you divide time between looking for traffic and taking care of other IFR chores. Controllers will call traffic for IFR flights, but this is done only on a workload-permitting basis, and it is nothing to depend on. Sometimes they have time to call the traffic and sometimes they don't.

Talking and Listening

Much IFR communicating is done en route, so this is a good time to examine the techniques of talking and listening. The words we say as we fly along are hardly conversational; they are more a series of grunts and acknowledgments. This becomes quite obvious when someone, pilot or controller, says something out of the ordinary on the frequency. It is difficult to understand words other than the magic ones that are used routinely.

An example came one day—a pro-football play-off day—when I was flying over Texas. The Dallas Cowboys were playing, and pilots seemed to think controllers would be listening on their transistor radios, while controllers seemed to think that pilots would have the game on the ADF. In the course of flying for several hours in the area, I must have heard the question "What's the score?" asked a half dozen times. Not once was it understood on the first asking. Not even in Texas, with the Cowboys playing.

What this tells us is to speak in a predictable fashion. Use the magic words. This is easy to learn just by listening to how others do it, especially airline crews. They fly more than most of us, and they have learned better than anyone the art of communicating with the controller. Their transmissions are very brief—no excess verbiage—and they speak more effectively than general aviation pilots. Example: When cleared to descend from 6,000 to 4,000 feet, a general aviation pilot might say: "Roger, Cessna 40RC will descend to 4,000, ah, I'm out of six." The airline pilot might say: "American 330 out of six for four." The airline version uses fewer words, and when we study alleged airspace saturation, we find that it's not really airspace saturation, but word saturation combined with limited runway availability. If everybody would conserve words, things would be a lot better.

The use of call signs is very important, too. Air traffic controllers complain that more and more pilots acknowledge clearances and instructions with "okay" or "roger" without including the aircraft call sign. This can only breed confusion. Controllers can sort some things out by voice recognition, but we owe it to them to use the call sign. Put it at the first of the transmission so the controller knows who is talking: "40RC is out of six for four" instead of "out of six for four, 40RC."

Think

If what you are about to say is not routine in nature, compose a little speech in advance. You call a controller because you want something, and the more clearly and concisely the request is stated, the better. For example, they generally expect pilots to stay at one altitude for the en route portion of a trip. They do not expect you to call and request a different altitude halfway between here and there. So there is no anticipation of what you are about to say, and if you say it in a confusing way, you might well expect to draw a blank.

I heard the following exchange one day:

"Ah, Center, ah, this is 40 Romeo Charlie, I'd, ah, like either a higher or a lower altitude."

"Say again, 40RC."

What is a controller supposed to do with something like that? The person on the other end of the line is supposed to be pilot in command of the aircraft, he seems to want to fly at a different level, and yet he doesn't know whether he wants to go up or down. Some command! If the pilot had only thought, a more concise request could have been phrased:

"Center, 40RC requesting higher altitude due to turbulence." Less-than-concise communications can come from the ground, too, with controllers using different phraseology in different parts of the country. For example, a controller once transmitted the following to me:

"Zero three zero is cleared to Woodstown only, maintain 7,000."

I thought he said "cleared to Woodstown holding," because I had never before been cleared to somewhere only. After listening to the controller clear a couple of other airplanes in a similar manner, I caught on: what he was saying meant that Woodstown was the clearance limit.

Basically, the air traffic controller either clears us to do as we wish (as filed), gives an alternative, or tells us to do something. Relatively few words are used for a high percentage of communications. Cleared, turn, right, left, climb, descend, cross, hold, approach, the terminology for airways and facilities plus numbers and place names account for a large portion of the words they say to us. There is certainly nothing complicated about that limited vocabulary, but at times we still tend to misunderstand or misinterpret the word from the ground.

Managing thought processes helps in understanding the other person. Consider anything the controller says in the same manner that you consider a clearance. Listen to the entire message, then decide whether or not it was understandable and made sense. If, for example, the controller says: "November 34030 is cleared to the Aramb intersection, to hold northwest, left turns, one minute legs, maintain 6,000," don't stumble over "Aramb" and miss the rest of the message. Get all you can and then ask for a repeat of the intersection name. That is a lot better than becoming derailed right off the bat and having to do the whole thing over again. Thinking of a communication as a total message, with the finished product contemplated for a moment before acceptance or rejection, is a good practice. By that I don't mean to give the controller a fast "roger" and keep on flying whether the message was understood or not. Rather, consider the transmission for a moment, in context, because if there is confusion in one part there might be clarification in another. This can be very helpful when a controller happens to use a bit of nonstandard terminology. "Cleared to Woodstown only" was understandable after a moment of thought. If one said "cleared into position and hold for release," the word *cleared* might charge the mind with *taking off*, as in "cleared for takeoff," but the rest of the message certainly clarifies and shows that what he really means is for you to taxi into position and hold.

Too, if you have trouble getting the message, consider the possibility that it might be caused by your questioning things in the transmission before the controller is finished. There is just no way to hear and interpret a message when the mind is charged with a question. It is a cinch, too, that audio quality in some airplanes leaves a lot to be desired if you depend on the cabin speaker. I flew for years fumbling with microphones and trying to hear speakers. Then I retreated inside good headsets and never intend to emerge. Now, flying an airplane without a headset is something I would do only VFR on a clear day with no requirement to talk with anyone. Flying for years without a headset did save me a lot of money: a $59.95 tape player from Radio Shack sounds as good to me as the finest Bose sound system.

As you fly around the country, there will be some inevitable clashes with accents or even colloquialisms and different regional procedures. The key is always to get it straight. Never fly on with doubt about what the controller said. Communication should be an easy and natural thing. It takes very few words to get through an entire IFR flight. Brevity is of the essence. The airline crews are aviation's best communicators. Listen, and imitate them.

Checking Weather

As the flight progresses, get each hour's weather reports along the way. It is pure foolishness not to do this. It takes but a few minutes, and current weather information is all you have to use to avoid surprises. The decision to continue is based only on aeronautical factors, too. The IFR flight must be conducted in an isolated context, free of wishful thinking. If the fuel reserve is in danger of compromise or if the destination isn't up to minimums when you are a couple of hundred miles away and the alternate is looking shaky, the importance of "being there" deserves not a thought. What counts is conducting the flight within the framework of conservative IFR principles. The greater part of the framework is defined by weather conditions, and there's no way to stay in bounds if you don't continually check the weather and heed the messages.

Remember, too, that a very important part of your mental weather picture is knowledge of where the weather is good. If a problem should arise, where could you take the problem for solution in the best possible conditions?

What If?

Time now for some en route puzzles. Two hundred miles to go and the destination weather is 100 feet overcast and ¼-mile visibility two hours after it was forecast to lift to 500 and 5. The alternate is just barely hanging in there with 200 and ½ even though it is forecast to be 800 and 5. What to do? It is tempting to respond to such a situation by asking for a "new" forecast, without giving much thought to the fact that the new forecast will come from the same place that produced the old, bad forecast.

When things unfold in that manner, it is clearly not the time to bet on forecasts. It's time to study actual conditions and put together a picture of what is really happening. In such a case, I'd start looking for a place between myself and the destination that had decent enough weather for an approach and make a pit stop there—especially if the original fuel calculation was at all tight. Continuing toward weather that is worse than forecast, regardless of what it is supposed to do next, is a bad deal unless the airplane is literally awash with fuel. Have enough to go to the destination, accept the busted forecast, go to the alternate, accept the busted forecast there, and then go somewhere that has weather that you know is good enough for an approach.

Alternate

We give a lot of thought to selecting alternates, and I suppose we do this because the alternate is part of the regulations. We must consider one for the flight plan, and it must be done according to the rules and forecasts. Given the potential inaccuracies of weather forecasting, though, alternates are best filed with a grain of salt. I certainly never consider that the filed alternate is cast in stone, and on a touchy day, the true alternate in my mind might change half a dozen times during the course of a flight. One of my favorite alternates is the last airport with an ILS approach before the destination. Such a place is more likely to have minimums than an airport served by a VOR or NDB approach, and before passing that last ILS, I like to recalculate reserves, recheck weather, and make sure continuation to the destination really is a viable proposition.

Often as not, the IFR situation is one of flying from relatively good weather into inclement weather. Keeping a close tab on that bad weather as we move toward it is important, and if things are really on edge, the best of all deals might be a fuel stop before flying into the area of bad weather. With plenty of fuel, the pilot has time to think and plan. And act. With minimum fuel, decisions are as likely to be influenced by the fuel gauges as by aeronautical and meteorological considerations.

Getting Closer

As the distance to the destination grows short, it is customary to listen to the automatic terminal information service, if the airport has such. ATIS gives word on the approach and runway in use, in addition to meteorological data. It also tells all the horror stories about such things as 75-foot cranes operating in the vicinity of the airport. When is the best time to listen? I always tune it in when in range, but before things start to get busy. Some pilots wait until the center controller hands the flight off to the approach controller and then listen before calling on the new frequency. This does insure getting the current information, but it doesn't give a lot of time for contemplating the approach. Listen early, and you'll have time to plan the arrival. If the approach in use changes before you get there, you won't be any worse off than if you had checked it later rather than sooner.

The current weather is important only as a point of reference. If conditions are above minimums, you are probably going to fly the approach anyway, and the operation should be conducted with the same concentration regardless of weather. It sure doesn't hurt to have the current weather, but don't bet on its being correct. I've anticipated good weather from an ATIS only to wind up flying a really tight approach more than once.

One weather item that is important is surface wind. Make special note if it is markedly different than the winds aloft. This means there will be some wind shear on approach. More important to planning than weather is the word on which approach and runway is in use. Good preflight preparation included a look at the big picture, but the real final details can't be planned until the actual approach in use is known. Then study the appropriate approach chart. If it is a non-ATIS airport with more than one approach, ask the controller which approach will be used before flying into the last phase of the flight.

AWOS

There are a lot of AWOS (automatic weather observing station) facilities now and their number is increasing, as are new developments in this area. These are excellent facilities to have, but my experience with their accuracy has been mixed. One day I was taxiing for departure with about a 400-foot ceiling, and the AWOS said there were no clouds below 10,000 feet. At another time the one at home base reported surface wind 180 degrees opposite the actual direction. Automatic weather observing equipment will become an increasing source of weather information. Just remember that it can make a mistake.

What's Important

The approach chart is littered with information, and you can't memorize it all. And, really, only one item must be absolutely committed to memory: the minimum altitude to which you will descend on the approach. This is the minimum descent altitude for a nonprecision approach (no glideslope) or the decision height for a precision approach. This is a critical value, and disregard (or misinterpretation) of it is closely related to a majority of the serious accidents that occur in instrument flying. Descending below the MDA or DH without the runway in sight has proved to be the most hazardous thing the general aviation pilot does in IFR flying. The MDA or DH should be etched in your mind before starting an approach, and it should be taken as an absolute discipline.

The bearing of the final approach course is also a primary approach item, but we have crutches here and don't really have to rely on memory except perhaps during an ADF approach. On a VOR approach, the number is set on the omni bearing selector or horizontal situation indicator, and there is plenty of time to compare the setting with the chart and to double-check it. On an ILS, the bearing is published, and for reference it can be set on the omni bearing selector. (When using an HSI, it must be set.) On an ADF approach, the bearing can be set if the directional gyro or horizontal situation indicator has a heading bug. Otherwise it must be remembered.

The missed approach is also an item to note and remember. Keep the basics in mind: "climb straight ahead to 2,000," for example. If the missed approach involves a turn, memorizing the direction of turn becomes very important, because it is often away from some obstructions. Turn the wrong way and you'll be going toward those obstructions. It has been done, with disastrous results at times.

I also like to position obstacles or high terrain in my mind. The route survey before takeoff should have provided an overview of terrain, so we fly with basic knowledge of where the high stuff is. In looking at the approach chart to be used, the question is where the highest obstacles are around the specific approach and around the airport.

Two Ways

Here we'll consider the planning of nonradar and radar approaches separately. When making a nonradar approach—one in which the controller is issuing clearances without vectoring the flight—the only protection is in flying published routes and altitudes. When you learn of the approach in use at an airport that is bereft of radar services, note the available published route carefully and plan the arrival accordingly. If the controller clears you for an approach when you are forty miles away, don't be in a hurry to descend.

First, determine that any descent will be on a route on the chart and then descend only to the altitude shown on the chart for that route. Fly it methodically and don't cut any corners. When you are in radar contact, the trip to the final approach course will likely be vectored, with altitudes assigned by the controller. The altitude given to you will be the minimum vectoring altitude or higher; MVA provides the legal minimum above the terrain or obstructions.

At first glance this vectoring business seems by far the easiest way to maneuver in preparation for the approach; someone else tells you which way to point the airplane and the altitude to fly. You shouldn't turn into a vegetable during such an approach, though. Keep up with position, and make note of high terrain or obstructions and the airplane's position in relation to them. The pilot is responsible for the flight, and the pilot who completely relaxes about position and altitude when being vectored is hardly reflecting much command ability.

I at least like to have World Aeronautical Charts on board to use in noting position in relation to other things when being vectored. If the country is flat and there are no TV towers, no sweat. A glance at the chart shows that all is well. If it is mountainous, or if there are big towers, it's nice to confirm that the vectoring is being done away from or above these items.

This is not always easy to do and at times it seems impossible to keep up with position in relation to terrain. A place that I often go— Asheville, North Carolina—is especially difficult. Most of the approaches I've made there are to runway 34, and I know the lay of the land on the paths to that runway pretty well. There's an ILS to runway 16 now, and I don't know it as well. Also, on the 16 approach there is a hill off to the right that you pass by on the approach, as a reminder to keep those needles in the center.

We always have to know what to do in case of radio failure, and if this were to occur, you would know the location of the briar patch if you had been keeping up with your position.

Hazards of the Wake

When approaching a large airport, make note of any airline jet aircraft ahead if you are between layers or on top. Wake turbulence set-

tles, and we do operate at a disadvantage because procedures usually bring jets in above light aircraft; controllers clear the jets to descend after they have passed us. Thus, the big airplane will lay its wake right through our altitude. If you see a big jet and have an idea for wake avoidance, tell the controller. A heading 10 degrees either side of that assigned might be just the ticket. If there is any question in your mind about being in the vicinity of the wake of one that passed through recently, at least slow your airplane to maneuvering speed. I've had two wake encounters in busy terminal areas. Both were at a right angle, and there was quite a bump.

Jets almost always make ILS approaches, so we get some help on wake turbulence avoidance from the glideslope. The fact that the wake settles means you should be able to follow a jet with standard separation without encountering its wake. I always add just a little more in my favor by staying one dot high on the glideslope when following a large airplane.

A Breath of Oxygen

Here, you might do something for the old brain and bod before tackling the approach, especially if the day has been a long one. Fifteen minutes of oxygen can help sharpen the mind for the task ahead. If the flight has been at moderately high altitude (above 8,000 feet), 30 minutes' worth of oxygen might be a better deal. If you'll analyze the performance you expect from yourself during an approach, the wisdom of using oxygen for a refresher is quite apparent.

Into the Funnel

The airplane is now moving into the funnel. If the pilot remains one step ahead of the airplane and is confident of the proceedings, things should go well. If the airplane is flown by a pilot with a blank mind, the machine will soon move ahead of the mind and things won't go very well. Catching up once you realize that flying has outrun the thinking is difficult, and the mark of success is in staying ahead. If you do get behind, there should be a plan for that too, even though such a plan can only provide some time to be used with more discipline than was found up to that point. This might mean a missed approach, but a missed one is better than a botched one every time.

Organization puts work load items in the idle time slots, when they can be best handled. It also helps to identify points in the arrival and to key items to these points. The first point might mark a time by which you'll want to have studied the approach plate and charged the mind with the task that is ahead. Good discipline is to do this right after listening to ATIS or learning of the approach in use. Don't procrastinate—do it.

The next collection of things is an "in-range" checklist. This would include final positioning of the fuel selector or selectors, if applicable, turning on boost pumps, asking the passengers to be quiet for the remainder of the flight, and every other item from the landing checklist that can be handled at this time, as applicable. This in-range check might be prompted by being told to contact approach control, or by being cleared to descend below 6,000 feet above field elevation in the case of an arrival where no approach control facility is involved. Time or distance can also be used as a key. Just don't fail to have a plan.

Getting those items out of the way early means that the final landing checklist is minimized and that the items on the final check can be used as helpers in the approach itself. In a retractable, the landing gear is best extended over the point at which the descent to MDA or DH begins. That gives it a dual role. The first is obvious: wheels to land on. The second is to establish the descent. Flaps use varies from airplane to airplane, and the objective should be to use flaps consistently if possible, and to have a plan for flaps extension.

Throughout all this, keep a running inventory of the situation. "Here I am, here's what I am doing, and this is what happens next." Key things to position. Mandatory altitude callouts are an example. I like to use 1,000 feet, 500 feet, and 100 feet above the MDA or DH, plus the altitude itself. The call at 1,000 feet is a reminder of the minimum altitude, plus a reminder to verify that the airplane is indeed 1,000 feet above that altitude, plus a final reminder to have things set for landing. In a light airplane, it is basically a two-minute warning. I'd hopefully catch any misinterpretation of the altimeter or approach plate at that time. Five hundred above is about a one-minute warning for the final event. One hundred above is the reminder to be cocked and ready, and the MDA or DH call signifies the end of the descent. In the case of the DH, it is the absolute time to miss the approach if the runway isn't in sight. In the case of MDA, timing or some other factor might be the determinant of the time to start a missed approach, but it has always been my experience that not having good ground contact at the MDA means it'll be a missed approach.

The Approach

Let's consider the thinking and planning done on a sample approach. I'll use a P210 as an airplane of reference, because that's what I happen to be flying as this is written. Adjust as necessary to fit your particular airplane. "Fifty miles out now. ATIS says it'll be an ILS to Runway 4. The weather is 200 overcast and a half a mile, runway visual range to be given by approach control. Alternate weather, checked a few minutes ago, is good and holding. Altimeter 29.72, set. The surface wind is calm. The wind aloft has been strong southwesterly. That means a decreasing tailwind on approach, which makes the airplane trend toward high on the glideslope through the altitude range where the wind goes from southwesterly to calm.

"Cleared to 5,000 feet. Through 10,000, do as much pre-landing check work as possible. Fuel is on fullest, strobes are on unless it's night and the airplane is in cloud. Prop, windshield, and pitot anti-ice on if appropriate.

"The localizer frequency is 111.3. Set it on number one and identify. The locator at the outer is 369; set it in the ADF and identify. The marker beacon receiver is on. DME was held on the Vortac frequency; the Vortac is 2.5 from the marker, so this gives a good indication of distance to fly to the marker. It shows 30 miles. The loran backs it up. So, here I am 27.5 miles from the marker, descending to 5,000 feet, flying a heading of 100 degrees to intercept the localizer. The next event is to level off at 5,000 feet. Final approach course is 041, the decision height is 455, 200 above the touchdown zone. There's a 501-foot obstruction beneath the glideslope, not far from the middle marker. Missed approach is straight ahead to 2,000. There is a 2,272- foot obstruction 15 south of the airport.

"Clearance to 3,000. Vector heading is now 130, 90 degrees to the localizer. The ADF needle is 45 off to the left and moving slowly, so I've got distance to go to the localizer. DME is on 20. Leave the speed at 160 knots.

"Closer, level at 3,000. Put the number-two nav on the localizer frequency. (Some would put it on the VOR as a double check on the outer marker, but I like them both on the localizer. If they don't agree, it's time to become suspicious.) The nav-one audio is left open, with the ident playing softly in the background. I like to hear the ident of any station used for an approach on a continuing basis.

"Left to 090, 50 degrees to the localizer. DME shows 12, or about 9.5 from the marker. Still at 3,000, 1,000 feet above the glideslope intercept altitude at the marker. Tower frequency is set in the other comm radio. The speed is stable on 160 knots, so the gear can go out at any time. It looks like it'll be a turn on final close to the marker, and the descent from 3,000 to 2,000 will come later rather than sooner. Next big events are intercepting the localizer, descending from 3,000 to 2,000, and intercepting the glideslope.

"Cleared from three to two, left to 070, intercept the localizer at two, cleared for the approach, tower at the marker. Looks like intercept will be a couple of miles outside the marker. Go to the all-purpose 15-inch power setting now. Shouldn't have to touch power again. Runway visual range is 3,000 feet, good, and no heavy airplane ahead so no sweat on wake turbulence. Final prelanding check. Mixture rich, everything done but the gear and approach flaps. Do that at the marker.

"Southerly wind at this level. ADF is now pointing at the locator almost straight ahead. I'll intercept right at the marker, at best, right to 080 to improve on that. Glideslope is starting down, DME is on 3.5, localizer is starting in. Localizer is in, left to 040, glideslope is there; gear down, marker, ADF reversal. Approach flaps. Power is still on 15 inches. Get settled down in the descent and then call the tower.

"Okay, cleared to land. Trending high on the glideslope. Diminishing tailwind. Power back to 14 inches, be ready to put it back to 15 when out of the wind shear zone. Light turbulence. Localizer moved to the right slowly on 040. Flying 050 now, when it centers will try 045. At some point will be down out of the wind and will probably have to go back to 040. Decision height is 455, now at 1,455, 1,000 feet above. Everything checks. Needles crossed, heading 045, airspeed on 115. The runway is long so the landing will be with approach flaps.

"There's 955, 500 above DH. Needles not quite crossed but within two dots. Slightly low on glideslope. Power to 15 inches and nose up slightly. Heading between 40 and 45. Airspeed is good, rate of sink is 500 feet per minute. Air is smooth.

"Hundred feet above DH, ready for a missed approach.

"DH, look up. Lights, runway. Do not change anything. Keep flying the localizer and glideslope. They lead to a safe place on the runway.

"Landing was only tolerable. Four on the Richter scale. Take the first left, cowl flaps open and wing flaps up after clearing. Call ground control. Cleared to the ramp.

"Parked and secured. The planning of that flight has now been completed."

No joke—the planning of a flight is never completed until the airplane has been parked. Flying is the mechanical part, planning is the thinking part. Operations on the gauges requires both, and both continue until the airplane is parked.

7. The Points of Stress

Every pilot has stress points, some have more than others, and instrument flying tends to involve more of them than other types of flying. To the mind, there's a substantial difference between operating an airplane when you can see Mother Earth and when you can't. If you ask a hundred pilots what's hard about IFR flying and what's easy about IFR flying, you might well get a hundred different answers, too. The person with maximum cool, good training, and recent experience will insist that it's all a piece of cake, except of course when cumulonimbus menace the flight path, when ice coats the wings, or when every airport within fuel range is below minimums. The nervous sort who doesn't have much actual experience and who trained in good weather under the hood might break out in a cold sweat at the thought of flying through any cloud, much less a bumpy, frosty, or low one.

Looking Inward

It is easy to identify the stressful moments in an instrument flight. Right off the bat, it is common to find tension at the beginning of a flight—especially if there is some doubt about the weather or if the pilot hasn't flown in actual instrument conditions for quite some time. The careful checking of weather and the deliberate process of deciding that it is okay to start the flight can help on the weather question, but often nothing will eliminate all initial queasiness. Somehow we seem to forget from one time to the next that clouds are not solid and that the airplane will fly through them perfectly well. Instrument flying can seem almost contrary to the laws of nature. The best way to combat this hang-up is to recognize that it exists. A lack of recent actual instrument time can also contribute to initial reluctance. A salve to use on this is enough practice to know that you can fly the airplane, plus that deliberate preparation for flight that insures that everything is in its place before launch and that the flight will get off to a smooth start.

The importance of the first minute or two of flight is obvious here, too. If the pilot is properly psyched to settle in with the gauges, taking first things first, it is possible to brush away the doubts and cobwebs rather quickly. A lot of factors accentuate the first stress point in a flight. The airplane is at its noisiest and the atmosphere is more charged than at almost any other time in a flight. The defying of gravity is much more apparent when leaving the ground than it is when cruising level or descending. The sound and feel of the machine (and of flight) is less familiar at the beginning than later on.

Discipline is the key, and with it the initial stress point can even be turned into an advantage. If the stress can be put in perspective and allowed to serve as a mandate for methodical operation and awareness, things will go well.

Next Point

The next point of stress likely comes with any indication that things are not going exactly according to plan. Anticipate such an event, because there is at least one in virtually every flight. One mark of a good pilot is the ability to accept whatever comes along and to move forward with a methodical plan to handle any glitches. A good example can be found in our dealings with the air traffic control system. Perhaps the original clearance is as filed, but later in the flight the controllers decide that a more circuitous routing is necessary or more to their liking. This is aggravating, and whereas composure and concentration might have been the norm before, the pilot is likely unhappy and not concentrating on anything properly after the issuance of an undesirable new clearance. Many will argue with the controller. In you have a difference of opinion with air traffic control, there is nothing wrong with a request to return to the original route or whatever you desire when and if possible. Then, to move away from the stress, the only thing to do is move enthusiastically into the task of following the new clearance and replanning the rest of the flight. A new fuel calculation will have to be made, and if the change involves a substantially different routing, there will be new weather to obtain. Apply yourself to the chores, and the stress of the moment will go away.

Do You Read?

Difficulty in communicating can create stressful moments if it isn't handled properly. Pilots (or controllers) sound very calm and matter-of-fact on the first call. If there is no answer, the second call is made with a slight sense of urgency in the voice. The third carries still more urgency, and you can hear composure crumble in repeated and unanswered calls.

Why be bugged about communications difficulty? There is always a procedure or a plan by which you are expected to continue the flight if communications become impossible for any reason. Have confidence in Plan B and any aberration in Plan A won't be so bothersome. Too, probably 99.9 percent of the communications difficulties are resolved before a pilot has to resort to radio-failure procedures, simply because a high percentage are caused by some error in the cockpit. The squelch might be improperly adjusted, the incorrect frequency might have been selected, a switch in the audio panel might not be in the right position, or the volume might be down.

The first question during time of communications difficulty should be, "What have I done wrong?" If it is determined that you have not done anything wrong, then study the situation. We fly general aviation airplanes at relatively low altitudes; perhaps the communications site we are trying to reach is simply out of range. Perhaps the controller is busy with something else and can't answer immediately. When the pilot has done everything correctly, these two items are the cause of almost all the rest of communications problems.

Finally, if things remain silent, just remember that communications difficulty in no way affects the laws of aerodynamics. The certificate we carry is a pilot's certificate, not a communicator's certificate. Always concentrate on flying first, and handle any communications problem as time allows. Above all, don't let a communications problem cause a level of stress that creates problems in the area of aircraft control or navigation.

Turbulence

Turbulence is a great cause of stress, and we learn early that there is a lot of turbulence in instrument flying, even if we never get within five miles of a thunderstorm. A primary reason that turbulence induces stress is that it makes us wonder if we have miscalculated. "Is this the beginning of a thunderstorm that I somehow missed and the controller did not mention? Will it get worse? Isn't that rain heavy? Will it get heavier? Should I slow the airplane to maneuvering speed? How long will it last? Sure is getting dark outside."

One's gut can tighten and the taste in one's mouth can become quite bad in such a situation. Those are two of the best indicators of stress, so recognize them in such a situation and try to generate a little inner peace. Settle down. Fly the airplane. That's what counts. Flying the airplane gets it through. Worrying about it does not. With the best possible information, there should be nothing there that will really bite. Relax and analyze the situation. Perhaps a different altitude would be better. A few bumps don't signal the end of the world. Hang on, fly, and plan.

Often we make turbulence stressful by fighting the controls. The bumps probably wouldn't be bothersome when we are clear of cloud, but they become our almost consuming interest when we are in the cloud. In such a situation, I note the airspeed and vertical-speed excursions that are resulting from the turbulence. They are often rather minor, and this tends to classify the level of turbulence and put the mind somewhat at ease.

The Leans

Any pilot who professes never to have had a touch of spatial disorientation—often called "the leans"—either hasn't flown much or doesn't recognize a problem that affects all pilots sooner or later. The leans can come at the oddest times. I vividly recall flying in the Houston area one hazy day and getting such a bad case of the leans that it took intense concentration on the instruments for quite a long while to overcome the malady. I was not really on instruments in the sense that the airplane was continuously in cloud. But with the wings level and the ball in the center, I felt that the wings were not level and the ball was not in the center. I almost knew the instruments were telling falsehoods, and I'd have very certainly moved the controls in a manner contrary to that which was proper if I had allowed anything other than the instrument indications to hold sway in my mind.

In this case the trouble was caused by differential lighting, among other things. There was an immense thunderstorm off to my left. It was very dark in that direction, and the very hazy sky was brighter in other directions. Too, I was flying through the tops of little building cumulus of varying heights. I had visual cues, but they were misleading, and even as I concentrated on the instruments, my peripheral vision was still feeding those confusing visual cues to my mind.

The influence of visual cues can be seen in many other instances. One comes when flying below the level of the tops of building cumulus. There is certainly no natural horizon to use for reference, but there is still always a strong temptation to use the visual cues. You can see, so look. Trouble is, there is vertical motion in the visual cues, and you'll almost always climb when trying to fly level in such a situation. The remedy is to fly the gauges.

Sloping cloud tops can also create some wild sensations. There once was a collision between two airliners that resulted from one pilot's perceiving a conflict that actually did not exist. The airplanes had the required vertical separation to begin with, but they were on top of a sloping cloud layer, and an evasive maneuver prompted by the illusion led to the tangle.

Another version of the leans can come when you divert from the primary task of flying instruments at the wrong time. It is bad practice in a turn to try to do anything other than fly the airplane. You shouldn't try to copy a clearance when turning. Trying to read a chart in a turn is bad news. And even communicating when in a turn can be distracting. For one thing, moving your head around can be spatially disorienting. For another, when an airplane is turning, it's just that much closer to a lateral upset than when in level flight. Both are good reasons to concentrate on the gauges when in a turn. If you don't, you can have stressful moments.

Picture yourself in a 20-degree banked turn when the controller calls with clearance to the Bltzf intersection. Write it down. To the chart for location of the intersection. The wheel gets moved a little bit. The bank steepens, the airspeed increases. You perceive that something is awry, either through a change in the sound level or through a glance at the instruments. To restore full vision to the panel you have to move your head, which in itself is a promoter of disorientation. Now comes the crucial and immediate need to interpret the instruments correctly and take action. A very stressful moment, as well as a likely time for the leans. There is a 50 percent chance of moving the wheel in an incorrect direction, and in this situation you might well come up with the wrong answer.

Again, any diversion from the instruments when turning is bad. It is much better to ask the controller to stand by or to request a repeat of the clearance after the turn is completed. Even when you are straight and level, certain techniques need to be used to minimize problems when writing things down or consulting charts. The primary point is to have the airplane trimmed and to release the control wheel when looking at something besides the panel. That precludes the inevitable inadvertent slight movement of the controls that comes when your mind is in one place and your hands are on something else. On most airplanes, you can glance at the artificial horizon as you write and make any required small correction with the rudder.

Confusion

Stress also enters the picture whenever we have a feeling of being behind the workload curve. In planning an arrival, doing things in advance is for the purpose of avoiding moments of ignorance or indecision, things that lead to stress. If you forget to listen to the ATIS information and the controller tells you to let him know when you have it, the flight is punctuated at a point where you didn't want or anticipate a pause for information. If you don't study the chart in advance and have to find the decision height on the chart after passing the marker inbound, that diversion will move the thought process from keeping the needles crossed to interpretation of the chart, and the result can only be harmful.

Anticipate

When moving into the arrival phase of a flight, try to avoid stress by anticipating any special information needs. For example, when flying light airplanes, we don't have to give a lot of thought to wind and runway lengths for ILS approaches, but in nonprecision approaches to small airports these can become critical items. I recall two approaches that illustrate this point very clearly.

On the first VOR approach, the straight-in minimums were quite a bit lower than the circling minimums. As I moved toward the MDA, it was quite apparent that it would have to be a straight-in approach. I continued and was about to give up on even a straight-in, when the end of the runway became visible not too far ahead. I was at MDA for the straight-in and below the circling MDA. The decision had to be made in an instant: straight-in or missed approach? My decision was that the airplane was in a position from which a normal landing could be made. I chopped the power, extended full flaps, and headed for the runway. Trouble was, I didn't know either the wind or the runway length. I could easily have had both—the runway length by looking at the chart and the wind by asking—but I had neither, and I was conducting the important final portion of my flight based on eyeball and ignorance. The runway was probably around 3,000 feet long, I thought, and the southerly flow wasn't too strong, I hoped. I landed and stopped, thankful for good brakes. There were a few stressful moments along the way.

A similar approach was later flown to home base. The runway appeared a little to the right and ahead at the straight-in MDA. I wanted to circle to land into the wind, which I knew was from the south at ten knots, but there was no way. The ceiling was just too low. Again, it was a straight-in or a missed approach. The difference was that my mind was filled with information this time. I remembered that the pilot's operating handbook gives a number for down-wind landings with up to 10 knots, and I had once figured that it would take at least 1,200 feet to stop with a 10-knot downwind after a normal touchdown. I knew the runway length, and I knew there would be 1,700 feet left if I landed just before reaching the taxiway. That left 500 to spare. So I continued and landed. I used just as much brake in stopping as on the previous approach, but there was less stress, or doubt, or whatever you want to call it, because I was operating with a set of known quantities that all suggested success.

Single Pilot

I have heard some general aviation instrument pilots say that it is dumb to fly with just one pilot in the airplane in areas with a lot of IFR traffic. Or they at least insist on a good operative autopilot when flying to such a place. This feeling is no doubt related to some feeling of stress that has been encountered when going to and from a big terminal.

In reality, there is no valid reason why any pilot should find it stressful to operate a light airplane IFR in the busiest terminal area in the world. All the rules are the same, and the only true difference in the operation is in the number of other aircraft the controller is talking to at the same time. If there are enough, the informal and chatty patter we find at some smaller terminals goes away and is replaced by very crisp and businesslike talk. If just hearing that induces stress, the pilot probably needs more help than is available from another pilot or an autopilot.

In light airplanes, we have the advantage of flying rather slowly through procedures that are designed for faster airplanes at the busy terminals. So instead of letting the busy spots bug you, just remember that while the Learjet pilot might indeed have a copilot to help with the chores, the Cherokee pilot has twice as much time in which to do them.

The amount of work at hand, or the amount of information coming in, can have a definite bearing on stress, too. In fact, studies have shown that overloading the brain can all but cause it to cease functioning. Given too many things to think about or sort out, a pilot won't be able to make sense of anything. Brain management at such a time is critical. You have to pause, regroup, and all but start over at the beginning.

Air traffic control personnel use the phrase "stand by" rather freely; pilots should do the same. If a clearance is incomprehensible, it could well be because there was enough there to paralyze your thinking process. This is often your fault—for going in cold without studying charts in advance to know the lay of the airways and the names of intersections and vortacs likely to be used in clearances. But while it is happening, the drill is to improve the situation, not to lay blame. If the brain has a severe overload from some new instruction, it certainly would be in order to ask for a pause with "stand by" and then request that the new clearance be read more slowly.

Rusty

There is another time of stress that we often face. Maybe all the squares on instrument proficiency are checked, maybe they are checked twice, but that does not mean that an approach like the one at hand had been flown in the past six months. Instrument flying has so many variables—weather accounting for most of them—that we can face flying an approach that, at the moment, seems to have some unknown. There can be wind shear, there might be a steeper-than-normal glideslope, and the vectoring procedures might resemble a dive bomber attack if the airport is in the mountains.

When faced with this, it is natural to let the stress level build. "Boy," you might say to yourself, "do I really have to perform on this one!" The stress level might go even higher if the weather was forecast to be pretty good but the ATIS reads the minimums on the chart as the current weather. The only way this stress can be relieved is with confidence in your proficiency. There is no way you can properly fly an approach unless you are confident that you can do a good job of flying it, so relax and enjoy whatever is there.

Educational

We can learn a great deal from our moments of stress. They should be remembered for study and future reference, because they tell us a lot about our weaknesses in creating bad situations and our ability to recover from a burst of stupidity by handling the situation. Whenever there is a bad moment, spend some time reflecting on it later, in a quieter time. Dissect the event and your response, and think both of ways to avoid such situations and of ways to handle them with aplomb when avoidance procedures are unsuccessful. Don't ever pass off a bad moment with the thought that it couldn't have been too bad because the flight did end in a successful landing. There is a very fine line between an airplane parked on the line and one crumpled in a heap, and any event that is the least suggestive of the latter must be considered serious.

Some of our most stressful times come in the special IFR moments when we become involved with thunderstorms or ice. Night IFR is a different league, too, and each of these is worthy of a separate chapter. These follow next.

8. Thunderstorms!

By some estimates there are as many as 40,000 thunderstorms a day in the world. Pair this with the fact that forecasters are likely to include the chance of thunderstorms if conditions are the least bit ripe, and you can see why general aviation pilots spend so much time thinking about thunderstorms. It's a broad subject, too—broad enough for this author to have written a book entitled *Thunderstorms and Airplanes*, which explores in depth the relationship between our relatively small aircraft and nature's really big storms. Here we will cover some of the basics of the subject.

Most of what is written stresses thunderstorm avoidance. Don't fly into a thunderstorm. Preachy, and it often seems easier said than done. But they can be avoided. Through a combination of information gleaned before flying and what is seen out the windshield, what is learned from the air traffic controller, what is depicted on airborne weather radar or a Stormscope (if the airplane is so equipped), and from updated information from the Flight Service Station, a pilot has plenty of tools available to use in keeping out of thunderstorms. True, not every method works every time. But in studying thunderstorm-related accidents, it is pretty clear that in every instance the pilot had at least one means of being aware that he was trespassing. In most instances there were several indications of thunderstorm activity in the area.

Of all the tools available, the forecast is the most difficult to use. Why? Because forecasts are prepared well in advance, relatively old information is used in preparing them, there's some delay in amending them, and they are prepared to cover every eventuality. Forecasts should be taken as educated guesses only. It's the responsibility of the pilot to add in all the current factors to see if the forecasts are correct. The best National Weather Service product to use here is the convective sigmet. This is a statement of fact that tracks thunderstorm activity that has already developed. It includes a two-hour trend forecast for the activity, and in some cases a convective sigmet is issued to cover the expected development of significant thunderstorm activity. Even here, they are occasionally a little slow on the draw, and airplanes have been lost to thunderstorms in areas not covered by convective sigmets—but it doesn't happen often.

Precip/Turbulence

When flying, most pilots relate precipitation to thunderstorm turbulence. This is because radar shows precipitation, we talk to controllers who have radar that display precipitation, and more and more aircraft have on-board radar to display precipitation. A lot of aircraft now have a Stormscope that displays electrical activity—another thunderstorm-related phenomenon. In either case—precipitation or electricity—it is true that there is a relationship between the phenomenon and thunderstorms. But it is also true that severe thunderstorm-related turbulence can be found away from precipitation or the site of electrical activity.

A thunderstorm exists at an airport from the time thunder can first be heard until fifteen minutes after it is last heard. The reason for this is that wind shear from an approaching or departing storm stirs up the air near the surface away from the rainfall of the storm. All the clouds and all the precipitation—even the light precipitation—associated with the storm are part of the storm.

Finally, from the Airman's Information Manual: "No flight path through an area of strong or very strong radar echoes separated by 20-30 miles or less may be considered free of severe turbulence." That means you might well not stay out of the thunderstorm simply by avoiding the red return on the radar that signifies the heaviest rain.

The key is in understanding the thunderstorm condition and then staying an appropriate distance away from it. This is quite a challenge, because if our airplanes are to be useful, we must operate them in thunderstorm areas but must avoid the storms and the airspace affected by the inflow and outflow of the storm. Knowledge of how a storm is built is important, so let's look at one.

Three Requirements

There are three basic requirements for thunderstorm formation: unstable air, lifting action, and a high moisture content in the atmosphere.

Stability, or instability in this case, refers to the atmosphere's resistance to vertical motion. In very general terms, if the rate at which air cools with altitude is more rapid than normal, then the air tends to be unstable. If, in unstable conditions, a particle of air is given a little upward shove, it will tend to keep going up and even accelerate. This makes turbulence, and if there is moisture around, it gathers it up and uses it to make clouds.

A hot summer afternoon provides the best example of instability. As the surface heats, the warm air rises. The rising air cools, and puffy cumulus clouds form at the level where the rising air cools to the dewpoint. Lifting continues where the clouds form, and they billow on upward. If there is enough of everything, nature can get it all together and create a thunderstorm.

On the other hand, in stable conditions, a piece of air that gets a little vertical nudge tends to just move up an amount about equal to the nudge and stop. It can even settle back to where it was. So no vertical development is possible. If there is warm air above cool air it's called an *inversion*, and things are really stable. The lifting action that gets things started in unstable conditions can come from heating by the sun, from wind flow over mountains, or from the collision of air going in different directions with resultant vertical motions.

Moisture? There is always some in the air—sometimes enough to make thunderstorms when all the other ingredients are present, and sometimes not enough to make anything.

Build One

Once all the ingredients are present, how does nature construct a storm? A cumulus cloud is the basis for a thunderstorm. The action is upward in the cumulus. In unstable air, the vertical currents accelerate as the warm moist air of the cloud rises into the colder air above. The cloud feeds itself, attracting moisture from the surrounding atmosphere. In this cumulus stage, the updrafts extend from near the ground to a bit above the top of the cloud.

If there is enough lift and if the air is unstable enough, the cloud top goes on up through the freezing level. At some point in the development, the old saw about everything that goes up must come down takes over, and the moisture starts down—as rain, or as hail, if the moisture particles are held aloft long enough to freeze.

The precipitation usually starts within ten to fifteen minutes after the top of the cumulus builds through the freezing level. If there is not enough lifting action and instability for the cloud top to make it through the freezing level and to continue building rapidly, there won't be a thunderstorm. This is why, even in the summer, the freezing level is a useful bit of information. If you know the freezing level as you are moving along through a thicket of building cumulus, you will also know the point past which the tops must go to begin to qualify for admission into the thunderstorm club.

When the moisture starts down as precipitation, it brings air with it, forming a downdraft in what has just become a mature thunderstorm. The updrafts remain active around the outside of the storm at this stage.

As the downdraft approaches the surface it is deflected outward, and strong surface winds can result. The strongest wind will be in front of the storm, on the side toward which the storm is moving. The velocity of this wind is said to be the sum of the downdraft velocity and the forward speed of the storm over the ground. The interaction of the inflow and outflow is the producer of severe turbulence. Air going in opposite directions creates an area of crazy things betwixt and between.

The Climax

Early in the mature stage of a storm cell—right after the downdraft and precipitation make their move—the surrounding updrafts tend to increase and reach a climax. This can be the meanest moment in the life of a cell; it's all downhill from here. The updrafts begin to subside as the moisture falls out of a cloud and brings cool air down. Soon the updrafts are pretty well gone, and it is mostly downdraft. Things are relatively tame then. The life cycle of an individual storm cell is from 20 to 90 minutes, but if conditions are ripe, cells can form in lines or clusters; there can be gaggles of cells in various stages of development, maturity, and dissipation at any given time. What might look like one thunderstorm could really be several separate cells. The maturity of the group might run for several hours. Or, if the lifting, instability, and moisture supply are continuous, as with a squall line ahead of a cold front, the turbulent collection of clouds can exist until one of the factors is modified.

Drafts

Updrafts in a mature storm tend to increase in velocity through the lower two thirds of the storm, with maximum draft velocities found between 14,000 and 20,000 feet. They often reach 60 to 70 feet per second or more. Updraft strength is greater than that of downdrafts, but these also accelerate; the taller the storm, the stronger the downdraft. The 40-knot gust ahead of a storm converts to 67 feet per second, or 4,020 feet per minute, to give you some idea of strong downdraft strength. You would have to subtract some from that for the forward motion of the storm, but even 40 feet per second is quite strong. That's 2,400 feet per minute, which is well in excess of the rate of climb of most airplanes.

The air within a downdraft isn't so terribly turbulent. In fact, research has shown that the least turbulence in a storm might be found in the area of heaviest rain, in the downdraft. That is, of course, relative. It might still be plenty bumpy. What really hurts is moving from updraft to downdraft and through all the shears and eddies that develop when air rushing upward is next-door neighbor to air rushing downward. It is easy to visualize the tremendous turbulence that would develop in such a situation.

Experiment

It is also easy to estimate the effect of a thunderstorm on our airplane's ability to maintain altitude. Consider a garden-variety storm with maximum updrafts of 25 feet per second and downdrafts of 18 feet per second, for example. The updraft will be equivalent to 1,500 feet per minute and the downdraft equal to 1,080 feet per minute. Now, flying a light airplane at maneuvering speed, note the available rate of climb at full power and the available rate of descent when power is off. If the rate of climb is less than 1,080 feet per minute and the rate of descent is less than 1,500 feet per minute, then maintaining altitude is unlikely even with gross use of power. There are other factors that might affect rate of ascent and descent in a storm, but the example is useful for illustration. And remember, that is not too much of a thunderstorm.

Another useful mental exercise is to relate the turbulence from wind flow over rough terrain to that in a thunderstorm. Thirty knots is equal to 50 feet per second; a 30-knot wind over rough terrain can do some pretty enthusiastic things to an airplane flying downwind of the terrain. And consider that the force of those updrafts and downdrafts is mitigated by distance.

The point that must be understood is that it is extremely turbulent in and near any active thunderstorm cell, and the updrafts and downdrafts are likely to be more than an airplane's performance can handle, even if the pilot puts maximum effort into maintaining altitude. That's why the word on flying technique is always to maintain attitude and not to worry over altitude variations. Theoretically, the altitude might average out during passage through the storm.

Shear

As we consider the air rushing in around the sides to form the updraft and the downdraft in the center, we come to a logical reason why the worst turbulence is often found around instead of within storms. The downdraft must fan out as it nears the ground. The cold air of the downdraft pushes under the warm air around the storm, and as the storm continues gathering moisture from the surrounding airspace, air rushing in to feed the updraft is above the downdraft air. There is great turbulence where the two rub against each other; this can be found quite a distance away from the precipitation, in what is commonly called *wind shear*. The outer limit of severe shear should be at or above the point on the surface reached by the first gust from the storm, but turbulence related to air moving into the storm can be found farther away than that. Many storms give us a picture of the rolling and tumbling of air that takes place in the shear area between the updraft and downdraft. The illustration is in the roll cloud that forms a thousand or more feet above the ground, ahead of the storm cloud itself. In visualizing the turbulence caused by the interaction between the updrafts going in and the downdrafts coming out, also visualize how there can be a monumental amount of disturbance in the air between storm cells when conditions are ripe for thunderstorm development.

Lesson

Let's take what we have considered to this point and relate it to an air-carrier accident. It is very pertinent to general aviation flying because the airplane was only 4,000 feet above the ground as the accident started happening, and that is an altitude that we frequently use.

A line of thunderstorms lay between the point of departure and the destination, with the storms moving toward the point of departure. The pilot was aware of the line and the fact that it was an enthusiastic example of thunderstorm weather.

The flight requested a low altitude for penetration, and as the airplane neared the weather, the crew sought the controller's opinion on the situation. The controller told them that the line of weather appeared solid. The pilot also talked with another air-carrier flight in the area, which was in the process of penetrating the line from the other direction at a much higher altitude.

After considering the information gathered, and with the use of airborne radar and visual observations (it was dark, but there was a full moon in clear sky ahead of the line, as well as considerable lightning in the storms), the pilot requested a deviation from course. One can only assume that the deviation was to head for the most favorable point for penetration, based on the information at hand.

The airplane never reached the line of thunderstorms. According to information from traffic control radar, it broke up five or more miles from the nearest observable echo at the time of the accident. There was a roll cloud in the area, and the airplane apparently just reached the area of this cloud when it flew into catastrophic turbulence. Ground witnesses reported that some rain fell after the roll cloud passed, but no heavy rain was reported until 45 minutes later. Two funnel clouds were observed a half mile from the accident site approximately 8 minutes after the accident. (Reports of funnel clouds from the general public are often related more to the churning in and near a roll cloud than to an actual tornado. However, conditions in this instance were ideal for tornado formation.)

Two other air-carrier flights came through the squall line from the other direction at approximately the time of the accident. Crew statements and flight recorder readouts both indicated that the heaviest turbulence was encountered during a short period after passing through the precipitation. One of these flights flew through at about 2,000 feet above the ground; the other was more than 15,000 feet above the ground.

The airplane that was lost simply came to the wrong place at the wrong time. The storms were very tall with strong downdrafts, and there was continuous cell generation within the line of storms, because there was plenty of air rushing in to feed the updrafts. The airplane was flying at the proper turbulent-air-penetration speed as it approached the line of storms, but in flying into the shear area the aircraft experienced a momentary and substantial increase in airspeed. This could have been caused by a horizontal gust, or the increase in airspeed could have come as the airplane flew from an area where it had a very strong tailwind—it was flying toward the storm, and air at its level was being drawn into the storm—into an area with no tailwind. Airspeed will increase momentarily in that situation.

Whatever, the next ingredient was another gust. According to the accident report, this one probably was an angled gust and very strong. Visualize it as a stream of air, like a stream of water from a high-pressure hose, rushing upward at a 45-degree angle. The airplane flew into this with the airspeed still well above the turbulent air penetration speed—a situation caused by the gust encounter or abrupt tailwind decrease of a moment before—and the loads imposed on the structure as the airplane responded to this last gust were in excess of the limit load factor. The vertical fin and tail structure broke off almost simultaneously.

Again, this happened five or more miles from the closest weather return shown on the controller's scope. The airplane was at the proper penetration speed to begin with, and the low altitude penetration conformed with a long-held theory that lower is better around thunderstorms. The government publication *Aviation Weather* put it this way: "The softest altitude in a thunderstorm cloud is usually between 4,000 and 6,000 feet" above the ground. This has since been pretty well disproven in research flying; the turbulence exists throughout the height of the storm. With this example in mind, let's examine the considerations of speed and altitude.

How Fast?

In this accident, the speed was correct at the outset, but the movement of air ahead of the storm outfoxed the crew, caused an airspeed increase, and then took what might seem unfair advantage of the aircraft with another gust.

I think we have to recognize that such an airspeed increase is to be expected when approaching a thunderstorm, especially when flying toward the direction from which the storm is moving. Every factor in the construction of the storm works toward an increase in airspeed as the turbulent part of the weather is reached. The decreasing tailwind experienced as we fly from the area where air is rushing toward the storm to feed the updraft and into the shear between the updraft and downdraft is not to be dismissed lightly. For example, if the true airspeed is 200 knots and the groundspeed 240 knots because of a 40-knot tailwind, the groundspeed will tend to remain constant at 240 knots momentarily as the airplane enters the area of no tailwind. Quite a spike in airspeed will be experienced as a result.

Or, just considering the updraft itself, flying into air that is rushing upward will cause both an ascent and an increase in airspeed. Add this to the fact that the airplane is flying with a decreasing tailwind—the air is turning upward as it feeds the storm, and we are flying from an area where the flow was more parallel to the ground, affecting the airplane as a tailwind, and into an area where the tailwind will be lost and the updraft will be experienced—and you can see another reason why the airspeed increases. Also, flying into an updraft causes the nose to pitch down, another factor that would contribute to the increase in airspeed or at least cause the pilot to impose a little *g*-load in bringing the nose back to level.

There is a dual moral here. First, don't be in the position of trying to descend when near a thunderstorm cell. This can only compound the airspeed control problem that might be encountered. If you want to be at a lower altitude, get there well before reaching any area of questionable weather. Second, consider flying the airplane at a value somewhat below the turbulent air penetration speed if you suspect that the inflow/outflow effects of a storm might affect the airspeed. Flying at a speed below that recommended does bring added risk of stall if a strong vertical gust is encountered, but when we are talking about doing something that we really shouldn't do, such as flying near a storm, it becomes a matter of the lesser of risks.

The effect on airspeed reverses itself as you fly out of a thunderstorm, and the result can be a very bad sinking spell. When flying out of a storm at low altitude, the airplane is likely to experience an increasing tailwind component as the downdraft turns parallel to the ground and a rapidly increasing tailwind causes the airspeed to decrease. It can feel almost as if someone pulled the chair out from under you.

All this updraft-and-downdraft business and the interaction between the two should offer a pretty plain illustration of why it's next to impossible to maintain altitude in a mature storm, and why the airspeed will fluctuate and the turbulence will be rather wild if we attempt to pass near or through a storm.

Altitude

There have always been strong feelings about the best altitude to fly when working in thunderstorm areas. "The lower the better" is usually the consensus (except when you can top all clouds by a comfortable margin, but that is reserved for jets, and they can't always do it), but there are challenges to the theory. In thunderstorm-research flying, reports have been made suggesting there is equal turbulence at all levels.

Again considering the construction of the storm, the lowest possible altitude would tend to add risk of running into wind shear, but it would tend to minimize the risk of encountering a catastrophically strong vertical gust except in an extreme case such as experienced by the air carrier in the accident just related. When choosing between the devil and the deep blue sea, between wind shear and strong vertical gusts, wind shear seems the better one to accept in a light airplane. The light airplane's airspeed will be less affected by wind shear because the airplane adjusts more quickly to a "new" situation than does a heavy airplane with more mass momentum. Too, we can be willing to use power grossly in a light airplane, where the power response might not be as quick in a jet. The advantage is reversed when it comes to vertical-gust encounters, because an airplane's reaction to a vertical gust is more in proportion to wing loading than anything else, and larger airplanes have higher wing loading. The lowest possible altitude seems to me the best in a light airplane; higher is probably better in a jet. Again, it should be stressed that neither is really any good. The real best altitude is one in a location that is unaffected by the storm.

When flying at low altitude, the downdraft must be considered. It is true that a downdraft will not take an airplane to the ground, but it is equally true that a downdraft can put an airplane in a position where a collision with the ground is inevitable. The lower-is-better theory thus must be modified when the terrain in a storm area is anything other than flat. And even then, a strong enough storm could probably get you, because at some point that downdraft will result in a rapidly increasing tailwind for the airplane and there might not be enough altitude to handle that problem. But again, the light airplane handles wind shear better than the heavy airplane.

Several other things can be used to bolster the lower-is-better theory. One relates to the imbedded thunderstorms. These are often associated with warm fronts, where we find cold air near the surface and warm air aloft. (The height of the base of the warm air depends on the distance from the surface position of the front.) The meteorological fact of life is that the cold air is stable, with the instability and the thunderstorm bases aloft, on the slope of the warm front. Often a general aviation pilot will give a brave report of weathering a storm, and say "it wasn't so bad," in true ace fashion, when actually the pilot only flew below a storm that had a base at a high level. This is an entirely different situation from one in which the air is unstable from the ground up, and there is no question that low altitudes can produce good rides when the bases of the storms are high.

See

Another thing in favor of flying low is found in the possibility of staying in visual meteorological conditions so that you can eyeball the way ahead and avoid the areas of heavy precipitation by a good margin. If there is a general rainfall, some success can be found in always flying toward the areas that are lighter in appearance and avoiding the areas that are darker in appearance. Always do this, though, with the knowledge that the moment might come when all areas are dark in appearance.

Whatever, there is no doubt that the severity of a storm has at least as much to do with survival as does any operating procedure. Too, the mechanism that spawns the storm—a warm front, cold front, heating, or lifting along ridge line—has a lot to do with best operating altitudes, and it is an absolute certainty that severe storms offer only varying degrees of impossibility.

Another Old Wives' Tale

There's another thunderstorm parable that must be examined. It suggests that once in, the best way out is straight ahead. There is another air-carrier accident to use in studying this. Not to be picking on airliners, mind you, but the lessons are so much better when there are flight recorders and cockpit voice-recorder tapes to study.

This aircraft, a turboprop Lockheed Electra, was being operated at high altitude. Upon inspection of a line of storms 60 miles ahead to the northwest, the crew requested descent to a lower altitude and a deviation to the west. The airplane was cleared down to 15,000 feet, and later, to 14,000 feet, and then down to 5,000 feet, but it was lost before it reached 5,000 feet in a normal descent.

The line of storms was quite strong, and this crew headed toward an area that had been avoided by other aircraft and that did not appear a good penetration spot to the air traffic controller based on his radar picture. The cockpit voice-recorder tape suggests that the pilot felt they could go under the line of storms, presumably at 5,000 feet. The following excerpt from the National Transportation Safety Board report on the accident is worth some study:

At 1641:07, the captain made another announcement to the passengers, advising them that he was turning on the "Fasten Seat Belt" and "No Smoking" signs "just in the event it's a little choppy in the area." He stated that his radar was working and he was going to be able to "go well under and to the west of all the thundershowers, but they will be visible to you on the right. . . ." At 1641:42, the captain said (to the other crewmembers), "I guess I can go under." At 1644:16 the captain instructed the flight engineer to turn on the engine heat temporarily, "at least on number one, till we get about twelve degrees or a clear area." At approximately 1646:30, the captain instructed the first officer to ask the controller if he had any reports of hail, which the first officer did at 1646:32. The controller replied, "No, you're the closest one that's ever come to it yet.... I haven't been able to, anybody to, well I haven't tried really to get anybody to go through it, they've all deviated around to the east." Following this transmission, the captain advised the first officer, "No, don't talk to him too much. I'm hearing his conversation on this. He's trying to get us to admit [garbled words] big mistake coming through here." The first officer stated shortly after that, ". . . it looks worse to me over there." This statement was followed by the sound of the landing gear warning horn and the statement of the captain, "Let it ring." The captain then said, at 1647:20, "Let's make a one eighty," and three seconds later the first officer requested permission from the controller to make the turn. The turn was approved "right or left" at 1647:26.5. At 1647:29, a sound similar to hail or heavy rain was recorded, and at 1647:30.5, the first officer transmitted "three fifty-two." [That was the flight number.] One-half second later the captain said, "Let me know when we come back around there to reverse heading for rollout." There was no recorded reply to that instruction. At 1647:35.2, the first officer said "three forty," and immediately afterward the sound of the landing gear warning horn was heard, and the captain said "right." At 1647:41.3, the sound of a fire warning bell was heard and continued until the end of the recording. At 1647:41.9 a sound appeared that was described as being similar to breakup noise.

The Bumps

The flight recorder records *g* forces, and the readout was without remarkable excursions until only about 20 seconds before the captain ordered the 180-degree turn. At that time there was an increase of both frequency and amplitude of excursions, but there was no extraordinarily high *g* force until the aircraft broke up. Other flight-recorder data revealed that the airspeed increased rapidly from 206 knots, beginning at about the time the turn commenced, and reached 360 knots in about 8 seconds. Apparently the first officer's call of "three forty" was in relation to indicated airspeed.

The readout indicated that the airplane was initially rolled into a 24-degree bank, which was maintained for ten seconds. Then the bank increased to 66 degrees, and then to an even steeper bank as the airplane entered the dive in which it failed.

Another quote from the National Transportation Safety Board report is interesting: "After the penetration of the storm had been initiated, the decision to reverse course was not in keeping with recommended company procedures for operation in areas of turbulence. Normally, once in an area of turbulence, the crew is expected to maintain the attitude of the aircraft as nearly straight and level as possible, and maneuvering is kept to a minimum until the turbulent area is cleared."

There is nothing in the flight-recorder data to indicate an encounter with severe turbulence. Rather, the pilot lost control in the turn, and the breakup was probably related to the airspeed buildup after the loss of control.

Why did he lose control of the airplane? One item that I think must be strongly considered is related to the fact that noise draws the eye. In this case, there was enough noise from precipitation to be heard on the cockpit voice recorder. The streaming of water over the windshield also draws the eye, and if there was suspicion of hail, I guess the temptation would be to look to see if indeed it was there. That this might have diverted the pilot's attention away from the flight instruments is not offered as any explanation for the accident, but it would be a consideration in turning around in similar circumstances. I know from experience that it takes strong discipline to put 100 percent thought and effort into such a turn.

The corollary that you shouldn't turn at all once in a storm seems valid in this accident. The storm tends to be meanest in the direction in which it is going, and once you are into the heavy precipitation, the worst area of turbulence could be behind. This aircraft was in the heavy precipitation when it started to turn. If a turn was started soon after entering the precipitation—within 30 seconds—it would be reasonable to assume that it would take a minimum of 2 minutes to make the 180 and be back out of the weather—30 seconds in, a minute for the turn, and 30 seconds back out. In going straight ahead for this length of time, the aircraft would have flown more than 6 miles and would have been close to the back side of the weather.

Turning certainly increases the risk of loss of control, too. When the wings are level, the airplane is as far away from a roll upset (which is inevitably followed by a pitch upset) as possible. When it is banked, the airplane is just that many degrees closer to a roll upset.

The 180-degree turn is the perfect way to deal with thunderstorms only if the turn is started well before the effects of the storm are felt. Once in, the best way out might be straight ahead. For my nickel, exceptions might be found after entering an area of weather from the direction from which it is moving, from the back side of the line, for example, or after entering what has been described as a large area of imbedded activity.

The two accidents related almost seem to have a "you can and you can't, will and you won't, damned if you do, damned if you don't" ring to them. In the first case—the jet—it almost seems that only the act of not flying would have offered salvation. In the second, there are more alternatives, but it is still one of those "there but for the grace of God go I" situations. However, both were in severe weather, both weather situations were obvious to the eye and radar, and avoidance would have been simple in a light airplane. If we have and follow good rules, such events can be relegated to the category of the other pilot's problems.

If there is a common thread here that teaches a lesson, it is in relation to airspeed. Note that in both cases the airplane broke after the airspeed strayed from the proper value for turbulent-air penetration. As we poke around in weather, then, let's recognize airspeed control as a primary task if we are to avoid being devoured by a thunderstorm or any other form of turbulence. In most general aviation thunderstorm accidents it is possible to determine that the overload failure came not because of turbulence but because of pilot-induced loads. That generally means that the pilot lost control of the airplane, the airspeed increased, and the pilot pulled it apart in a recovery attempt. There are a few that involve airframe failure caused by an initial turbulence encounter, and in these the airspeed had to be too high because an airplane simply will not break if the airspeed is at or below the correct value. All of which is one way of saying that if the pilot doesn't understand the importance of keeping the speed on a proper value in turbulence, the airplane does. And once something breaks, reflecting the airplane's "understanding," there's no way to put it back together. Further, there's no question that airspeed will fluctuate in turbulence. But if the attitude of the aircraft is correct (that is, level), and if the power is reflective of the need of the moment, the airspeed should fluctuate within an acceptable range. As the aircraft moves through the drafts and the tumbling turbulence between updrafts and downdrafts, there will surely be pitch excursions, too, but if the pilot gently returns the aircraft to the proper attitude, the chances of passing through the storm are enhanced.

Radar/Stormscope

Both the airliners discussed had weather radar, and in both cases there was discussion with the controller about the depiction of the weather on traffic control radar. There was quite complete information, but neither radar nor any other device is magic. Above all, there is no device made that can be successfully used for the aerial penetration of severe weather. The guideline for radar use is to stay 5 miles away from the precipitation return of garden-variety storms and 20 miles away from the precipitation return when severe storms are forecast. The guidelines are based on experiences such as the two accidents related. When a pilot cuts it closer than those guidelines, the risk increases dramatically.

Even with a complete set of on-board weather avoidance gear, the controller's input can be useful. In flying a P210 with both weather radar and a Stormscope, I have found many instances where the addition of the controller's big picture was necessary to choose the best flight path.

A good example came late one afternoon at the end of a flight from Auburn, Alabama, to Trenton, New Jersey. The initial morning briefing (from "The Today Show") revealed that a lot of thunderstorm activity was expected up and down the east coast, along the route of flight. The northeast was flagged with the possibility of severe storms. It was thus no surprise when all the forecasts I got from the FSS called for the possibility of thunderstorms all along the way.

The trip was flown at Flight Level 190 (19,000 feet), where the visibility clear of clouds was quite good. Some deviations were made around small build-ups along the first three fourths of the route. As is so often the case, thunderstorms had been forecast over a wide area, but they were localized. In this case, the concentration was in our arrival area. Some very strong storms moved through about two hours before our ETA, spawning a rare New Jersey tornado. We could see the cloud mass from the storms ahead and to the right as we flew abeam Washington. There was another line of storms to the west, and there was definitely still some activity ahead. In this particular case, the Stormscope was giving the advance word. This device will detect electrical activity at a great distance, and it was showing the presence of such activity in the direction of Philadelphia, near the destination.

As we got closer, the radar started painting cells, and as we were trying to determine whether it would be better to zig or to zag to get into Trenton, the man with the big picture offered a suggestion. Based on the way the cells had been moving and based on the position of the two we were examining visually on radar and with the Stormscope, he suggested that we turn north, go between those two, and then turn back east to Trenton. That, he said, would give us the best shot. Left to my devices, I would have probably gone around the south side of the eastern storm. It would have been possible to get to Trenton that way, but it would have involved more flying. I took the controller's suggestion, and, using the radar and Stormscope to verify the best path between the two storms, flew on home without hitting a bump. Everything combined to give us a good ride.

When flying without airborne radar or a Stormscope, we have to rely primarily on eyeball information plus what we can learn from quizzing the air traffic controller about his radar depiction of weather. This can be frustrating or rewarding. Some controllers are helpful to the point of volunteering information and vectors. Others are reluctant, explain that their radar isn't designed to show weather, and give only the vaguest outline of the affected areas. And, while whatever information we get from the controller is better than nothing, anyone who uses it as something other than broad and general information had best be pretty sharp at flying instruments in turbulence.

Traffic radar is designed to show airplanes, not weather, and the radar systems incorporate circuitry that processes the radar return and displays only the weather deemed to be in excess of a certain precipitation rate, based on radar reflectivity. Back in the good old days, before computerized radar, some controllers could and would vector aircraft in areas of weather, taking them through the lightest areas, and this often worked well. Many IFR pilots have had some magnificent rides through fearful-looking skies with the traffic controller as tour guide.

The vectoring is less precise in weather areas with the computerized radar. Controllers, too, often seem reluctant to vector, because it is above and beyond the call of duty, and if a controller provides the service and the airplane doesn't make it, that is bad. There have been thunderstorm accidents where the controller was vectoring a pilot through the "lightest" area.

Good News

The good news is that the controllers have gotten, or are in the process of getting, better weather radar depictions as this book is being revised. That will mean better information for pilots, but it still will not be up to the controller to interpret the weather and provide the pilot with a smooth ride. The principles of meteorology simply don't allow that.

Procedure

I've found it helpful, regardless of what radar system the controller has, to use a series of questions to get information.

"Is there weather along my route of flight?"

"Affirmative."

"Well, would a deviation up along the north airway avoid the weather?"

"Negative."

"Okay, how about a deviation down around by the south airway?"

"That looks better."

In other words, even in the most extreme case, you can often find the best path with yes-or-no questions. Most controllers respond with better information, and most will give general information on areas of weather at the first pop of your question. But be prepared for the reluctant one.

Do be wary of the effect of time on radar information. As we noted, cells generate and dissipate rapidly, and an area of no return on radar 15 minutes ago might be filling in now. If conditions seem ripe, keep asking. And, again, remember that this information is best used for the broad avoidance of general areas of weather. The best way to avoid unpleasant rides when thunderstorms are out, regardless of the equipment installed, is to keep the airplane dry and well away from all rain.

Rainfall Levels

One of the reasons for keeping the airplane dry is that there is a fairly high likelihood of significant turbulence even in light precipitation returns. We need to define precipitation returns here because, with some equipment, controllers are able to give you precip returns in levels. Level One is light rain, Level Two is moderate rain, Level Three heavy rain. Four is very heavy, Five is intense, and Six is extreme. The fact that it is graded from one to six may lead some to believe it is okay up to, say, Level Three. That's not true. Anything greater than Level One might well be associated with a 20 to 30 percent chance of moderate turbulence and a 5 percent or greater chance of severe turbulence. Those are lousy odds.

Using airborne weather radar where green, yellow, and red are depicted as describing light, moderate, or heavy rain, the odds of unacceptable turbulence go beyond the acceptable in the yellow and become very high in the red. Perhaps a 10 percent chance of severe turbulence does not sound bad, but those are not much better odds than Russian roulette. Turbulence that is truly moderate means that you are straining against the belts, unsecured objects are dislodged, and changes in attitude and altitude occur, but the airplane can be controlled at all times. I have not encountered turbulence that strong very often and make every effort to stay away from it.

Attenuation

Earlier, I mentioned keeping the airplane dry. This is especially true with airborne radar because of a phenomenon called *attenuation*. A radar just puts out so much energy to be reflected back, to put that nice picture on the radar screen. Once all the energy is reflected or absorbed, the radar does not see any farther into the rain system, and the radar picture will look like the rain ends out there, five or ten or fifteen miles away. That is not likely to be what is happening. Instead, that's just as far into the rain that the radar can see. There can be heavy or intense rain beyond the distance at which the radar is attenuating and it won't show.

Whatever equipment help we have, the drill is to avoid thunderstorms. This includes avoiding the potential effects of wind shear on takeoff or landing.

One of the primary reasons we have to work so hard at avoidance is that thunderstorms huff and puff and ebb and flow—strong one minute, stronger the next. In many of the well-publicized airline accidents on approaches in thunderstorm areas, where a wind-shear encounter resulted in the larger airplane crashing, a smaller airplane had preceded the large one and completed the approach successfully. Some of this can be charged to the fact that light airplanes accelerate better than larger ones and can thus more easily fly out of a wind-shear encounter. Perhaps, but the storm becoming stronger might have also had a lot to do with the accidents. The way storms change also tells us that someone making it through an area ahead has absolutely no meaning to an airplane following along behind. What was okay a minute ago might well be impossible now.

Procedure

I was discussing all this with a training captain of an overseas airline, and he outlined a simple procedure they use to avoid approach problems when thunderstorm activity is suspected.

If there is a thunderstorm along the route and you are going to fly through it on the way to the airport, your airplane would first encounter an updraft. As far as this captain is concerned (and this is his line's recommendation), encountering the updraft means that the approach will be discontinued at that point. The updraft means that there will be a subsequent downdraft and increasing tailwind, which is the type shear that will put the airplane into the ground. They just don't want pilots flying ahead in the approach configuration into a condition that can only get worse. Wind-shear detection equipment is available for airline and corporate aircraft. For those of us who don't have it, the only solution is to refrain from flying where there might be strong enough wind shear to adversely affect the flight path of the airplane.

How Tough?

When we start poking around in weather, there's always some question about airframe strength. How strong are the airplanes? The answer is that they are strong enough if we make every effort to stay out of any clouds associated with thunderstorms, observe the recommended distances, and operate at the correct airspeed when in turbulence or when it is suspected. When airplanes are lost in thunderstorms, a loss of control precedes the usual airframe failure, though there have been cases where the airframe failed on the first encounter with turbulence, as in the air-carrier accident mentioned earlier. I like to think that, because I work very hard at avoiding the penetration of any cell, one I might accidentally graze should be of a milder variety and will be manageable if only I stick with the task of keeping the wings level and the airspeed at or slightly below the prescribed value.

Principles

There are some meteorological facts that we can keep in mind to help in planning storm avoidance. Storm cells tend to move with middle-level winds, which, in the U.S., are generally from the southwest when conditions are ripe for storms. An area of storms might move from the northwest, as in the case of a squall line ahead of a front, but the individual cells are likely moving from the southwest within the area of storms.

New cell generation in a cluster of storms tends to be on the side toward the low-level wind flow. The low-level wind is usually from the south or the southeast, so watch out for cell generation in this quadrant of a cluster and stay well clear. New cells also might develop on the side in which the area is moving, usually the east or northeast. These motions relate to frontal storms and those associated with active low-pressure storm systems. Air mass storms occasionally move toward the west.

Where a storm is moving in an unusual direction, visualize how this might affect the air around the storm; the previously mentioned principles apply. If there is to be hail, it is more likely to be in front of the storm, in the direction toward which it is moving. If there is a large high-level overhang of cloud off the top of the storm, don't fly under it, as there could be hail there.

Strong upper-level winds—jet streams—are a major contributor to the development of severe storm activity. To simplify completely, the thing to watch for is a low-pressure center or trough on the 500-millibar chart (approximately the 18,000-foot level), because when one of these is positioned to the west of your route of flight, cold air aloft is being drawn down around the south side of the low and then moved up over the warm air east of the low. When the jet stream takes such a trip, it creates ideal conditions for thunderstorm activity.

Because of circulation within the jet stream, the activity will be quite a distance to the east and southeast of the surface low-pressure center and associated cold front; it is when such conditions become strong that the classic and devastating tornado patterns develop in the springtime, or, for that matter, in any other season. So when the briefer says "thunderstorm," ask him to look at the 500-millibar chart and tell you if there's a low center or trough shown there. If there is a low aloft over central Texas, for example, and you are flying across Arkansas and Tennessee, beware. Any forecast of severe thunderstorm activity is likely to be accurate.

Emphasis

In leaving the topic of thunderstorms, I want to emphasize a few things. First and foremost is avoidance. Understanding the storm is an integral part of this, because if you understand how a thunderstorm is built and what it does to an airplane in flight, you'll be properly motivated for the avoidance role.

In checking weather before a flight, ascertain that you'll have a storm-free path for the beginning of the flight. The best information comes from weather radar and from convective sigmets. Next best is from teletype radar charts or the radar summary chart. The charted information is always dated; be sure you get the time the information was current and project it to the present time. Check the tops: the higher the tops, the meaner the storm. Check the movement of the storm. If it is moving at a good clip, it might be mean, although this is relative. A slow mover can also be violent. Relate the radar information to other available weather information. Study the weather map. A low-pressure trough can often spawn a collection of storms. Warm front or cold front? Storms associated with the latter are both more organized and more severe. Is there low-pressure to the west on the 500-millibar chart? Will there be a jetstream effect on the activity? What's the weather outside the thunderstorms? Is the activity scattered, broken, or solid? The last two can be bad news. Is the level of activity increasing? If it is increasing, surely things will get worse before they get better. Are severe storms forecast?

Once the decision to start out is made, the situation has to be continually evaluated. In a slow airplane it's okay to take it 20 miles at a time. Is it okay in the 20 miles just ahead? If not, in which direction would it be okay for the next 20 miles? Quiz the controller. If you can see, remember that human vision is the best storm-avoidance system available. Continually check weather along the way. If there is doubt, switch to an alternate plan of action. If you fly a lot, an investment in radar or a Stormscope adds to your available information.

A final thought is that thunderstorms are dynamic. They build and fade, and they move across the countryside. Often the most difficult thunderstorm situation imaginable will change its character in an hour or two. The pilot who loses the argument with a storm is the pilot who persists. Often the only solution is to land and relax while the storm does its thing in the airspace and moves off to harass the route of some other pilot.

9. Ice

The classic picture of an IFR pilot falling victim to ice begins with the aircraft struggling to maintain the minimum en route altitude as craggy peaks reach hungrily for the tender aluminum belly. The great festoons of ice continue to grow, and finally the airplane is overwhelmed. It's an impressive vision, but ice accidents don't always, or even often, happen that way. The IFR pilot who lets ice get the upper hand usually loses the battle later rather than sooner, while doing something that is relatively simple and that could easily have been done successfully.

For example, a surprising number of accidents occur after the pilot has extracted the airplane from the icing condition and is maneuvering the iced aircraft for landing. At that point the stall-speed-increasing properties of ice hold sway, and the event ends as a stall-spin accident.

Ice, like the thunderstorm, is well respected by general aviation pilots, and that is probably why it is not a direct and overwhelming factor in a lot of accidents. Too, ice seems somewhat easier to manage than thunderstorms, because detection of it is easy; ice allows us to trespass, sniff around at the situation, and leave. It also comes in a better variety than thunderstorms. Ice is light, moderate, and heavy. Thunderstorms are bad, worse, and impossible. The thing that we learn quickly about ice is that it need only be treated promptly to be managed.

Given a proper respect for ice, a pilot will always react to any ice accumulation with an action that will move the airplane out of the icing condition. This might mean climbing, descending, or retreating. The key is in accepting the formation of ice as a mandate. The pilot who watches it accumulate and hopes that it will go away is the pilot who is likely to gather enough of the frosty stuff to have a real problem.

Ice is illogical, anyway. If the temperature is below freezing, you'd just naturally think all the liquid in the atmosphere would be frozen. But a phenomenon known as *supercooling* defeats the logic. Even though the temperature is below freezing, the supercooled water droplet remains liquid until it is disturbed. Then it freezes. If we charge through a collection of supercooled water droplets in our airplane, disturbing their reverie with complete abandon, they will take umbrage at our splattering them and freeze in retaliation. The temperature and the cloud formations have a lot to do with the nature of the resulting ice.

Rime Ice

In stratus clouds the droplets are small, and the small droplets will freeze and become ice crystals if the temperature drops to a value well below freezing. Thus we come up with one of the rules of thumb for evacuating an icing situation: climb to colder air. The ice that does form in stratus clouds, usually rough in texture, is called *rime ice*, because it is a collection of very small water droplets that freeze quickly, that is to say, without splattering all over the place. Stratus clouds don't have great vertical depth, so any icing condition that is found in pure stratus clouds can often be handled by climbing to on top or to a colder level where the supercooled water droplets have become ice crystals. The important thing is to do it. Even a very light ice accumulation is something to flee.

Next, you might logically ask how one determines the nature of the cloud in which he or she is flying. There's no "welcome to stratus" sign on the clouds, but it is relatively easy to tell one cloud from another. There is no vertical development in stratus, so the air should be smooth. Also, the water droplets are small, and this fact is quite easy to note by just glancing at the moisture flowing on the windshield. The rivulets are fine. If ice does accumulate, it takes the form of a rough and rather milky substance right at the leading edge of the wing. The ice on the windshield looks almost like a fine frost.

Stratocumulus

When considering cloud types and ice, it is all downhill after stratus. The stratocumulus cloud likely has many of the properties of stratus in the lower portion of the cloud, but as you climb higher, the cumulus part holds sway. There is vertical development and greater depth, and larger supercooled water droplets are encountered.

Ice formation in anything related to a cumulus cloud is immediately serious because the accumulation rate is likely to be more rapid than that in stratus. The lifting that makes the cloud a cumulus results in bigger and juicier droplets that maintain their supercooled status to outside air temperatures that would have long since frozen the supercooled droplets in stratus clouds.

If we start off in the bottom of a stratocumulus with the idea of climbing to get above icing, the accumulation might well start off in the classic stratus rime icing pattern. Higher in the cloud, though, the droplets will be bigger. The accumulation might then start taking the form of clear ice, which comes when we burst really big supercooled water droplets. Instead of freezing in a tiny and almost ball-like shape at the leading edge, the droplet splatters, and the clear ice forms both right at the leading edge and back a ways, as the water flows some before freezing. The closer the temperature is to freezing, the farther the water will run back before turning to ice.

Two things introduce us to the problems of the stratocumulus. One, the air is generally a bit bumpy. Two, the droplets are bigger. Just look out at a wing for proof of that. The kicker in a stratocumulus layer comes as we get close to the top of it. There we'll likely find maximum supercooled water droplet size and quantity, the maximum rate of ice accumulation, and some turbulence. If the plan for ice was to climb on top, and if there is a suspicion that the clouds are stratocumulus, watch out. The tops might well be about 10,000 feet, even in low country, and if the airplane isn't turbocharged, you're going to reach the level of maximum ice accumulation with a partially frozen airplane and an engine that is capable of producing only about 75 percent power or less.

Behind the Front

Some pretty classic ice accumulations can be found in stratocumulus that form behind slower-moving cold fronts, or cold fronts that stop and that cover a wide area. We talked about the pitfalls of climbing in such a situation; if you happen to be flying up over such a cloud deck, beware an altitude assignment on descent that will put you in the upper part of the cloud formation for an extended period of time. The clouds look innocent enough from above. The tops of a stratocumulus layer look almost flat. But there can be plenty of ice in there. It is likely to be cold on the ground, too, so you might have to land with any ice that accumulates during the descent. The message is to work toward an unrestricted descent, at least through the top few thousand feet of the stratocumulus.

Cumulus

Moving from stratocumulus into cumulus is like jumping from the frying pan into the fire. While pure cumulus clouds are not likely to be continuous—you'll be in and out of them—the ice buildup can be rapid when you are in cloud as the airplane encounters supercooled water droplets of maximum size. Some notable collections of wintertime cumulus are found over mountainous terrain—caused by the lifting effect of circulation over the ridges—and this results in a confrontation with ice at the least desirable place. If you are flying on top to avoid icing and are approaching mountains, you can bet your sweet tooth that the tops will likely become higher over the mountains, too.

Another place where lifting makes a lot of ice is on the lee side of the Great Lakes. A flow of colder air over the lakes results in instability—the lake being warmer than the air flowing over it—and if there is moisture available, there will be building clouds. These produce the classic lake-effect snows, and they can result in some of the fanciest icing in the clouds that you have ever seen. Lake-effect icing can be present at quite low temperatures—lower than -15°C—and the depth of the icing can be nothing short of amazing. I have been at 16,000 feet wishing for Flight Level 180, collecting ice in cloud tops, with ice reported below practically all the way to the ground. Fly over the lake and to the other side and the tops drop off dramatically.

Rules of thumb are not always good, but I have found, in the winter, that the tops of the lake-effect cumulus-type clouds can and do extend up to 16,000 to 18,000 feet, and they blow off hundreds of miles downwind. The westerly flows are the usual culprits, meaning that the highest clouds will be east or southeast of the lakes. Other flows, though, can result in lake-effect icing. The pilot's job is to know which side of the lake is the lee side and expect big trouble there if the air aloft is below freezing.

Cumulobumpus

It's quite easy to tell when flying in a cumulus. The bumps tell the tale plainly, and you can look at the wing and note the rapid clear ice buildup as the airplane passes through the cumulus. I'm not talking about real turbulence here, just bumps, even light jiggles. The cumulus of winter are not as enthusiastic as the ones of summer, and the only winter ones that contain turbulence that would be a significant factor—except for the ice—would be in thunder snow showers or over ridges when there is a relatively strong wind flow perpendicular to the ridges.

When operating in an area of cumulus development, it is tempting to try to rationalize some hope into the situation as the airplane passes from areas of icing through areas with no icing and then back into the areas of icing. But the fact that the buildup is not continuous should not be used as an excuse to carry on. The sporadic buildup in areas of cumulus can easily exceed the buildup found during continuous flight in stratus clouds.

Unless the airplane has exceptional altitude capability, the odds on climbing out of a cumulus icing situation are quite against you. An unturbocharged airplane would have little chance in such a situation. The way out is almost always to warmer air below, to a position beneath the clouds or back to the air from which you came.

One of the principles of meteorology does work in our favor. Cumulus clouds are found when the air is unstable; when the air is unstable it cools more rapidly with altitude. In reverse, that means it warms more rapidly as you descend, so the chances of finding warm air beneath are better than in a stratus or stratocumulus icing encounter, for example. There's no guarantee, though, especially in rough terrain, where there might well be no warm air above ridge level when cumulus clouds are producing large amounts of ice.

Clouds tend to mix it up and become difficult to identify in many situations, but the rule of thumb about icing in cloud being worse when there is turbulence is a good one. For example, when flying in the quadrant to the northeast of a low-pressure system, especially a developing low-pressure system, there is generally both instability and moisture. You might not see a textbook picture of a cumulus cloud when flying in such a situation, but you sure can experience the ice and feel the bumps.

. . . And in Precipitation

The weather people always forecast icing in clouds and in precipitation when conditions offer any potential, and there is one particular form of precipitation to beware. Freezing rain is the cause of frequently mentioned fantasic ice accumulations in a short period of time. Freezing rain occurs when rain falls from warm air above into cold air below. This can happen north of a warm front or when cold air at the surface is moved by the circulation around a high pressure area to a position beneath warm air aloft.

The procedure when encountering freezing rain is often said to be a climb to the warm air above. When flying IFR this might work okay but then the drill becomes to fly to where there is no freezing rain to land. If you make an approach in freezing rain, conditions will continually worsen during the approach. While there will still be warm air above, the airplane might accumulate so much ice on the approach that it won't climb well enough to get back to the warm air. Seeing is another consideration. Unless the airplane has a heated windshield or heated element on the windshield, there won't likely be any view ahead. A typical defroster won't even begin to melt the ice of freezing rain. Any approach and landing in freezing rain simply falls in the high-risk category and is something to avoid.

Other than freezing rain, there is not really any significant ice in precipitation. Snow will make a white line down the leading edge of the wing, but it doesn't really accumulate as ice. The wetter the snow, the greater the accumulation. Dry snow just passes by. Any snow can accumulate inside the cowling and has been known to clog ducts and do other mischief. Dry snow can also cause precipitation static, which can ace radios and play particular havoc with loran receivers. If the static wicks are good and if all the control surfaces are properly bonded, though, this is minimized.

With wet snow, it has to be considered that this often comes from cumulus clouds, and if you are flying in the cloud as well as in the snow, there might be a generous amount if ice. Clouds, really, are the key to icing in a snow situation. If there is a serious ice problem with snow it's because the airplane is in cloud. And there are times when, with snow, there are no clouds as such. To the west of a low, for example, where the flow is northerly and all the moisture has made the long trip around the top of the low, what appears to be cloud might really be obscurement of the sky by snow. The moisture, having mixed with colder air in the trip around the north side of the low, is all frozen. On the other hand, if temperatures aloft are freezing and the wind aloft is from a southerly or easterly direction, the clouds are probably plentiful, as well as laden with supercooled water droplets.

The Worst

If I had to pick the worst possible icing situation, I'd go back to the beginning and pick that airway in mountainous terrain, with the airplane accumulating ice while flying at the minimum en route altitude, which also happens to be at or about the airplane's service ceiling. That situation is the worst because it is without options. Second worst would be where there is a lot of ice between the airplane and the ground—freezing rain and lake-effect icing would be two examples—and not enough fuel to fly to where the problem doesn't exist.

We simply must have options when ice starts forming on an airplane. When you have none, you are good as whipped. From the optionless stereotypes, move on to the more likely ice encounter and see how the cards might be played. Fly into an icing condition in cloud during climb, soon after takeoff. This one is pretty simple. If it doesn't go away in a couple of thousand feet of climb, return and land. A return to Mother Earth can be the most attractive option of all. En route, fly into an icing condition at a moderate cruising level—say, 6,000 feet. The options here are wide, even without turbocharging: go higher or lower, retreat, or continue without change. The last is the poorest choice. If the situation went from one with no ice to one with ice, the chances of its getting worse before it gets better are quite good. Some basic change in the situation created the ice, and it's just not likely to go away quickly. Another change is required and it is up to the pilot-in-command.

Higher might be the best option if the air remains smooth. If a definite tops report could be obtained, and if that level is easily within the capability of the airplane, climbing would be by far the best deal. A lower altitude would depend on the surface temperatures and the minimum en route altitude. If the country is flat, and MEAs down to a substantially lower altitude are available, that might be a pretty good deal if the temperature at 6,000 is just below freezing. Another consideration on lower altitudes is the availability of places to land. If there are adequate airports with approaches (and minimums) beneath, the lower altitude is always a good deal. A retreat to the ice-free air from whence you came can also be an excellent solution.

Know Thy Situation

Some basic knowledge of the weather situation can be applied to this situation, too. For example, if you are flying toward colder air, level at 6,000, and ice starts forming, any descent to a lower altitude might provide only temporary relief. The temperature at 4,000 might soon drop below freezing. And the temperature at 2,000 might do the same as more miles slip by. Watching the surface temperatures is quite important if the decision is to descend, but don't kid yourself with surface temperatures that are close to freezing.

The temperature can drop as rapidly as 5 degrees per 1,000 feet, though the temperature in cloud drops less rapidly than that. At any rate, a surface temperature of 34° or 35°F is nothing to consider as much of an option. Even with a surface temperature as high as 40°, the minimum IFR altitudes might all be icy, even over flat terrain. You really need to correlate surface temperatures with what is being experienced at the cruising level to get some picture of available relief at lower altitudes. If you are flying at 6,000 feet over flat terrain and it's freezing, and if the surface temperature nearby is 39°F, you'll probably be able to do some good by descending. But remember that it might not last if you are flying toward colder instead of warmer air.

For further illustration, assume that our response to an ice accumulation was to climb instead of descend. The climb might well be a long one, but let's say that we reached either an on-top situation or a temperature too cold (likely -15°C and even lower in cumulus clouds) for icing at 12,000 feet. Now things are better—no more ice is forming—but still not ideal. The airplane has some accumulation and little more climb is available (unless the airplane is turbocharged). There will thus be one less option if ice starts to build again. The location of the airplane in relation to weather systems is always important, especially if on top and near the ceiling of the airplane. If flying toward a weather system, toward higher terrain, or toward the lee of the Great Lakes, things will definitely get worse.

E-Flat

Here it might be noted that ice accumulations can make an airplane emit a strange collection of noises. Some airplanes practically shriek when iced. Fixed-gear Cessnas certainly do this, and I've always thought it must be some result of ice formation on the nose gear—at least that's where the sound seems to be coming from. Also note that the ice affects airspeed, and the range of the airplane will be cut. Ice on a maximum-range flight is good reason to review the fuel reserves. Just a little might slow the airplane by 10 knots.

Those factors acknowledged, move now into further icing at 12,000 feet. More is accumulating; what shall we do about it? With the options reduced, a pilot in this situation has to face a lot of basic facts. If the airplane is not capable of climb, then much more ice accumulation will probably make it incapable of staying at 12,000 feet. What is below? If there is warm air below, fine. If there is a between-layers situation below, fine. Go for either, but go with an out. Maybe that lower altitude isn't as warm or cloud-free now as indicated on a pilot report a few hours old, or maybe the forecast is wrong. Don't count on anything unless there is a brand-new pilot report to back it up.

Whatever is done here, the thought should really be of getting the airplane safely on the ground. When leaving 12,000 feet for alleged warm or cloud-free air below, I'd try to add the option of an airport with an instrument approach and comfortably above-minimum weather conditions available nearby to use as a haven in case the prediction of good things turns out to be a fiction.

What if there is no airport, and no hopeful situation below? Well, you can spend a millisecond cursing the fates or use the judgment you exercised in bringing the airplane this far and go on to the best possible option. I would fly the airplane at the highest altitude it would maintain until within striking distance of an airport that I felt reasonably confident of hitting on the first instrument approach. Then, and only then, would I start intentionally descending. Altitude in this situation is the only thing in your favor. It is stored energy and can be translated into distance.

Don't give it up prematurely. An airport for such an arrival should be chosen with care. Ideally, it would have an ILS and reported weather well above ILS minimums. I would arrange for a straight-in approach—no circling—and would try for about a ten-mile turn on final. I think that I'd leave the gear up on a retractable until I had the airport made; I'd use flaps according to the pilot's operating handbook recommendation for icing conditions (usually no flaps, sometime partial flaps); and I'd keep the airspeed 20 to 25 knots above the normal approach speed until runway is beneath the airplane. That is, of course, assuming quite a collection of ice. And you would have quite a collection after flying some miles in a gradual descent from 12,000 feet in icing conditions all the way down.

Hopefully you will never do things badly enough to have to fly an iced airplane on an approach. The worst one I have done was in a Cessna Caravan; the ice was so bad that the boots had to be cycled every minute, and even then, the maximum allowable power had to be exceeded to keep the airplane on the glideslope. Any speed below 140 knots resulted in an increase in the descent rate—all this in an airplane approved for flight in icing conditions. The power was not reduced until the airplane was about 15 feet high and the flaps-up landing was at extremely high speed. The ceiling was 500 feet, and at 800 feet the flight director failed, to make it more exciting. Fortunately, this happened in a simulator, where the only bruises after a crash are on the old ego, but it was still an interesting experience.

High Country

There are some areas where 12,000 feet isn't a lot of altitude. One of the higher minimum en route altitudes in the country is between Pueblo and Gunnison, in Colorado. The chart says that 16,000 feet is the minimum; fly it at that and you'd say that 20,000 feet or even more would be a lot more comfortable. There is a lot of vertical real estate, and perhaps the best way to avoid ice problems along such airways is to refrain from flying in clouds along them unless in a turbocharged airplane with deicing equipment. Even that is no cure-all, because the turbocharged airplane is, in the high country, in much the same shape as the unturbocharged airplane out in the flat country. It'll operate perhaps 10,000 feet above the minimum en route altitude, so a turbocharged pilot approaches ice in the mountains with the same vertical limitations that the nonturbocharged pilot finds between Chicago and St. Louis. One big difference: between Chicago and St. Louis, you might settle into a farmer's field with an iced airplane. There aren't many such fields in the Rockies.

Hardware

Deicing equipment is good stuff to have if you fly a lot of wintertime IFR, but there is certainly no magic to it. Just as radar won't allow penetration of thunderstorms, deicing equipment won't solve every ice problem. In heavy icing situations, enough can accumulate on surfaces that aren't deiced to cause a considerable problem. There are accidents on record involving deiced airplanes that accumulated so much ice they just couldn't continue flying. I've even gotten enough ice accumulation on heated props to cause quite a bit of vibration. (The ice formed right next to the prop hubs in extremely cold temperatures close to the top of a stratocumulus deck.)

What deicing does is expand the time available to choose one of the options available for fleeing the icing situation. A pilot would be purely foolish to remain at an icing altitude and depend on the deicing to keep things cleaned off. It just doesn't work that way.

There's long been an argument about which is best to deice—props or flying surfaces. Naturally, it is better to deice both, but for many, there's no way to deice the surfaces. Boots or weeping wing systems that emit a deicing solution along the leading edge of the wing are presently the only way, and these systems are not approved for most single-engine airplanes. Perhaps the unavailability and expense of surface deice systems plus the availability of a simple deterrent to prop ice is what has led so many of us to say that keeping the prop clear is the most important item. Self-deception, perhaps, but keeping the prop clear is better than nothing, and it does avoid vibration caused by a little more ice on one blade than the other.

There are some ice-deterrent preparations available in spray cans, and these have served me well on propellers lacking heated elements or alcohol systems. I kept my prop filed silky-smooth and squirted some of that stuff on the propeller blades before each flight that had the slightest chance of passing through any icing condition. And I never had any problem with propeller ice. (The knocking sound you hear is four knuckles on the piece of wood that I always keep handy.) Many pilots also spray the antennas, and I've seen some spray the leading edges. I've done the latter but have noted no advantage to it. The stuff might keep ice off, but only for a minute or two. The reason that it works well on the prop is related to centrifugal force and propeller-blade flexing and vibration coupled with a slight lingering slickness of the preparation. If the airplane is flown in rain, the slick stuff would no longer be slick. Using this should not embolden anyone to go out and tackle ice. It is strictly a "what if" precaution.

With a Full Deck

In fourteen years of operating a P210 for over 6,000 hours with full deice, I have learned that the equipment is used many times more in dealing with forecasts while flight planning than in actual flying. I have used the boots in anger only maybe a dozen or so times, and found that ice on unprotected surfaces can have quite an effect on airspeed if allowed to build to a substantial amount. As a result, I have come to think of the deicing equipment only as something to use while fleeing ice. There's no way I'd slog along in ice, using boots on a rather continuous basis to clean the airplane.

There's an item of technique to using boots. If they are cycled with just a little ice, the stuff might not blow off when the boots inflate. The result can be a rough leading edge, with new ice building on top of old ice. The book says not to cycle the boots until from ¼- to ½-inch of ice has accumulated. I use a combination of how it looks and a 15- to 20-knot loss in indicated airspeed to determine when to cycle the boots. If Icex, a slick preparation, is not applied to the boots on a regular basis, they do a pretty poor job of shucking ice.

Having approved deicing equipment might take care of the legality of the matter. There is no Part 91 (operating rules) prohibition about flying in ice; the operating limitations of the airplane govern. Flight into icing is generally prohibited. Even the FAA has trouble defining *icing*, though, and the fact of the matter is that only those who have an accident or declare an emergency in a situation where icing was forecast are likely to be cited for a violation.

Some time back, the FAA tried to define *icing* but their definition would have virtually grounded the general aviation fleet on all but clear days in the wintertime. They retreated from their ridiculous position.

Go or No?

There are not many hard-and-fast rules to use in making the preflight start/don't start decision as it relates to icing conditions. The forecasts of icing and freezing levels in airmets and sigmets have to be studied. Because the forecasters paint with such a broad brush, especially in airmets that cover moderate icing, there will almost always be some forecast of icing. That can't be ignored—the system has warned of the possibility and it then becomes the pilot's job to make certain that the air to be used will not include ice that could be hazardous to the flight.

Pilot reports can help, too, but there are some considerations here. First, the pilot report needs to be new. Older ones are just not any good. If it is a report of tops, that has to be combined with the big picture. Remember, if flying toward a weather system, mountains, or the Great Lakes, the tops will likely be higher.

The type aircraft from which the pilot report comes is important, too. There is a temperature rise on the surface of the airplane as speed increases, so a faster airplane might encounter no ice where a slower one finds plenty of it. At light airplane speeds, the temperature differences are not that great, but when you get to jets, the temperature rise becomes significant.

Perhaps the primary thing is in examining options. Surface temperatures are important. So are temperatures aloft, though these (more often than not) will be forecasts, so you are working with opinion and not fact. As with thunderstorms, the important thing is to ensure that it is okay to start out and that there are options from the beginning.

In a freezing-rain situation there may be no such options. With cloud bases of 1,000 feet, surface temperatures 37°F, 5 degrees above freezing, and icing forecast in the clouds, you might have a look with the option of returning, but any actual report of ice in the clouds would suggest waiting.

The weather map is important to preflight icing deliberations, too. Is there something out there that will create lifting and cumulus clouds? Warm front, cold front, or terrain effects? How about a low pressure to the west or south? Are you close to the Great Lakes? Some of the classic icing situations in the central and eastern U.S. occur as a low-pressure area moves to the south in the wintertime, bringing moist air up to mix with cold air from the north.

Another ice item is related to air traffic control. We might flight plan for an altitude that appears it will be ice-free only to find out that because of traffic or procedural reasons, the desired altitude cannot be approved. That might leave the airplane flying along in ice. If this happens, request a different altitude, and if the controller doesn't approve it, ask if a vector or a different route would enable him to approve the new altitude. Failing this, the other alternative would be to land at the nearest suitable airport as soon as ice is encountered.

Pilots used to be much more candid with controllers about ice, but then the FAA went out on an aggressive enforcement campaign, trying to catch pilots flying in ice without approved equipment. I was leaving Kansas City one day and climbing through a cloud layer, when there was a forecast for icing, and the controller asked me if there was any ice in the clouds. There wasn't, but I felt like he was asking me for a reason. Later, on an icy day, most pilots were requesting altitude changes because of "turbulence." The air was smooth but icy at some altitudes. Still, if ice is about to become a hazard and you feel you need priority to ensure the safety of the flight, tell the controller about the problem. Better do that and face the music because you got priority handling than face the possibility of the music coming from the angels singing.

Ice is neither mysterious nor complicated, and when a pilot actively wonders about what is the most dangerous thing about ice, there is but one answer. *Procrastination* is the prime hazard. Eliminate the procrastination and you might not always get where you wanted to be, but you'll have a lot better chance of always landing at an airport.

There is another important thing to understand about ice. Some airplanes fly better with it than others, but none go on indefinitely. And in most airplanes the ice doesn't seem to affect the airplane much up to a point. Past that point, it suddenly starts to matter a great deal, and the airplane might seem okay one minute and badly in trouble the next. That is another reason that procrastination is so hazardous. There is enough margin in most airplanes, in most icing situations, to allow an escape as long as it begins as soon as the ice starts forming on the airplane.

Too, good knowledge of the weather picture can prevent surprises. Just knowing whether it is warmer, colder, or about the same in the area toward which you are flying can tell you a lot about what to expect. Watch the temperature trend on your outside air temperature gauge. If the airplane is moving along in cloud and the temperature has slowly dropped until it is at the freezing point, don't be surprised at the ice that forms. And don't forget that turning around and returning to the warm air behind you will make it go away.

10. Doing It in the Dark

First, acknowledge two things about flying instruments at night. One, it is something that most of us do not do with regularity. Two, the accident rate in IFR flying is very much higher at night than in the daytime—I don't think any of us realized how *much* higher until the AOPA Air Safety Foundation developed an accident database from which you could easily extract the numbers. The accident rate might be as much as ten times higher in the dark than in the daytime.

Next, add one more fact: the involvement of actual mechanical engine failure in single-engine airplanes during night IFR flying is so insignificant that it becomes quite a minor factor. Certainly it can happen and has happened, and anyone who isn't comfortable in a single should buy a twin or just not fly IFR at night or not fly at night even in clear weather. It just doesn't happen very often. In those first night-IFR experiences, almost every pilot must occasionally have that "What am I doing here?" feeling. I still do, at times, and I suppose it comes from a realization that night IFR requires stronger discipline than any other form of flying. The work that we must do is more difficult. The airplane doesn't matter so much. I have the feeling in twins just as strongly as in singles. There's just something different about night IFR because a lot more visual accommodations must be made.

Start with the end of a flight and compare a daytime instrument approach with a nighttime instrument approach. By day, if there is an 800-foot ceiling, the approach might well be a piece of cake. We'll be in visual flight conditions at almost a normal traffic pattern altitude, and the final landing approach, whether it be straight-in or circling, becomes a normal VFR operation. Even somewhat lower approaches in the daytime offer visual flying toward the last, with relatively reliable clues. It's not until we get down to the really low ones—ceiling 300 feet or below and visibility 1 mile or below—that the daytime approach starts offering visual bear traps.

By Night

It's entirely different at night. There are no reliable visual clues on a night instrument approach. This holds true even if the ceiling is at or above normal pattern altitude. This was once illustrated in a study by a manufacturer of air-carrier aircraft. They had experienced pilots "fly" a night-visual-approach simulator (no instruments) that offered the opportunity to fly to and land on a runway, heads up all the way—strictly visual. It was found to be very difficult to avoid landing short, in the rough, especially with certain combinations of ground lighting.

The situations in which it was most difficult to judge height accurately were: a long, straight-in approach to an airport located on the near side of the city; a runway length-width relationship that was unfamiliar to the pilot; an airport situated at a lower elevation and on a different slope from the surrounding terrain; approaches from a navigational facility located some distance from the airport; substandard runway lighting and no other landing aids available; a sprawling city with an irregular matrix of lights spread over various hillsides in the back of the airport; industrial smoke or other obscurities that made lights look dimmer or farther away.

As we make an approach to a strange airport at night, there's no way to know that one or more of these visually misleading factors won't be present, so it is best to assume that a trap will be there. Add another one to the list, too. Precipitation often gives an illusion of greater-than-actual height. Whenever it's raining or snowing, be especially wary of what you think you see.

ILS

If an airport has a full instrument landing system, the glideslope provides vertical guidance to the runway, and should be followed until the runway is beneath the wheels. In the daytime it's important not to change anything when becoming visual on an ILS approach—just maintain the rate of descent and power setting that has been tracking the glideslope and don't reduce power until time to flare. At night this is even more important. Pilots who are prone to go below the glideslope when changing to visual flight in the daytime are even more prone to do so at night.

Approach lights can be a trap at night because they become visible sooner than they do in the daytime and they make an offer that is not really there. The approach lights seem to penetrate cloud and say, "Come on, we'll lead you down the runway." It is true that they will lead you on in a left-right sense, but they offer absolutely no up-and-down guidance. Only the runway itself can offer a valid cue for visual approach slope judgment. You have to see the aiming point to aim, and if the approach lights are accepted as offering anything in the vertical sense, they become the aiming point. Drive in your car to the approach zone some day and look at the poles on which they mount those approach lights. Very uncomfortable aiming points. And unless you take approach lights as an item of incidental information, you run a good chance of tangling with those lights and poles. One light system that does help lead you to a proper point in the up-down sense is the *visual approach slope indicator*. The VASI or other approach slope system is invaluable on a night approach.

Nonprecision

Moving from the full ILS back to a nonprecision approach (one without electronic vertical guidance) to a runway without a VASI, we find ourselves in the aeronautical dark ages (no pun intended). In recalling the things that can create erroneous visual impressions, we know that there is no way to count on making an accurate approach visually, and we know that there is nothing on the instrument panel that will directly calculate a proper approach slope for us. The pilot's difficult task begins at the time the airplane leaves the safety of minimum descent altitude, and it becomes one of very careful interpretation and interpolation.

A long final to an airport in the distance can be quite demanding. I recall making one such approach to a runway that was much wider than I was used to. A feeling of uncertainty crept into the proceedings when I was a couple of miles out on final (or was it three miles or four?). According to the altimeter I was only 800 feet above the airport. I thought the runway was pretty far away, yet the urge was to descend. The visual suggestion was one of being too high. I just could not quite resolve the problem, so I gave up on my straight-in approach. I remained at the MDA listed on the chart for a circling approach, flew up over the airport, made a normal pattern, and landed. By so doing, I was at a known position when I started my descent. When I was over the airport, I knew right where it was. That was a lot better than the previous situation of flying over an inky abyss with runway lights an unknown distance away.

Judging the Slope

There is a valid technique for judging the proper approach slope, and I will repeat it here. A 15:1 approach slope will clear all obstructions on a VFR or IFR runway. So decide that 15:1 will be the minimum acceptable slope for your approach. That's 15 feet forward for each foot down. At 90 knots groundspeed, we are moving forward at a rate of about 9,060 feet per minute. Divide by 15 and you'll find that 600 feet per minute would be a minimum allowable rate of descent when the groundspeed is 90 knots.

The point on the ground toward which the airplane is tracking remains in a constant spot in the windshield. This is somewhat easier to see at night than in the daytime because of the runway lights against a generally dark background. If you are making good a descent toward a point one light or two past the approach end of the runway, if the groundspeed is 90 knots and the rate of descent is 600 or more feet per minute, then you know that your approach slope is 15:1 or steeper. If the airplane were tracking toward the runway at 90 knots with a rate of descent of only 300 feet per minute, the slope would be dangerously shallow.

So there is information on the panel you can use. It isn't as good as a glideslope, to be sure, but it's better than nothing. The altimeter, airspeed, and vertical speed all give solid messages; combined with visual observations, they can help keep the airplane out of the trees. And while these instruments are important when maneuvering visually in the daytime, their messages are absolutely essential at night, when it is at least somewhat IFR all the way to touchdown every time. Think in terms of steep approaches with minimum acceptable rates of descent to track to the end of the runway. If the slope is too shallow, fly level or even climb until closer and then resume a descent.

Circle to Land

In the mention of a flight up over the airport for a circle instead of sticking with a straight-in one dark and lonely night, I contradicted a long-held feeling that a circling approach to minimums at night in turbulence and precipitation is the most difficult maneuver that can be attempted in an airplane. What I was doing in the switch to a circle that night was moving away from something without points of reference—the long straight-in—to something with points of reference. On that flight it might have felt more comfortable, but that didn't make it easy.

The circle at night is difficult because the discipline on altitude control is absolute, visual factors might try to make you fly lower than you should, and there is no way to see where you are going.

The approach plate does tell us how to stay out of trouble while flying a circling approach. Say the MDA is 458 feet above the ground and the visibility minimum is one mile. Follow the published final approach course while flying at the MDA until within one mile of the airport. Then start the circle, remaining within one mile of the airport. I would not leave the MDA until turning onto final, for at 90 knots the required rate of descent to lose 458 feet in a mile is a bit less than 700 feet per minute—just about right, although you would be a bit closer than a mile when the turn onto final was completed. That rate of descent is still quite easy to handle in a light airplane, it gives a satisfyingly steep approach, and it leaves me at the safe haven of MDA until I can draw a bead on the aiming point.

There are a lot of reasons why it is best not to leave the circling approach MDA until turning final. There are also good reasons not to make a night approach to an airport that does not have a visual approach slope indication system. The rules say not to leave MDA unless in a position from which a normal landing can be made and the runway, approach lights, or other markings identifiable with the end of the runway are clearly visible to the pilot. What the rule does not say is that you shouldn't leave MDA unless you expect these things to remain true. At night, there's no way to see cruddy scud between you and the runway until you turn final and take aim on the runway. There is no way to assess the flight path ahead and make a determination that it will indeed be possible to fly visually on to the runway unless you are looking down your approach slope to that runway. Only after turning final are you sighting through the air between you and the place you want to be. So only after turning final should you leave a known safe altitude.

In high-performance airplanes, the descent rates on final required after flying a circling approach in this manner might not be too desirable. In such a case, it might be best to stick with a higher-than-published MDA and make a wider circle, still to leave MDA only after turning final. If that isn't possible, surely there's a nearby airport with an ILS. Even an ILS has not proven to be magic. Most of the night IFR accidents occur on approaches or missed approaches, and a lot of them occur on full ILS approaches. Perhaps we do better than expected on non-precision approaches, including circles, because the degree of difficulty is so obvious. The night ILS, though, is just like a day ILS. That might be true in theory, but a lot of pilots hit before the airport on an ILS after being lured away from the electronic guidance by the twinkle of lights or by the approach lights.

Go Up, Young Person

The following is true day or night, but it seems to be a more difficult point of discipline at night, so it is emphasized here. If, after leaving MDA or DH, the view of the runway is lost or even becomes the least fuzzy, take this as a mandate to go up. It is never a signal to descend, and pilots who descend and try to maintain visual contact with the runway after flying into scud are those most likely to fly into the ground on day or night IFR approaches—especially night approaches.

Discipline is more difficult at night, because where we have only a gray mass scooting beneath us in the daytime, lights beckon at night.

Lights tend to penetrate cloud, they tend to suggest that you come on down, they tend to suggest that the visibility is better than it really is. The night approach isn't easy, and its difficulty combines with visual illusions to make it a critical area for risk management. Take no chances. Follow the book to the letter and the altitudes to the foot.

Preparation

Backing up, preparing for the approach, and studying the paperwork is more difficult at night because cockpit lighting is never ideal. Too, as you add a touch of age, your night vision is the first thing that suffers. You can walk out of the aviation medical examiner's office fresh from a physical and still notice some difficulty in adjusting to the visual demands of night IFR. Many pilots have a stronger correction in the glasses they reserve for night flying, and some bifocal wearers switch to trifocals in the dark. One word of caution: if you get special glasses for night flying, don't wear them for the first time when the chips are down. Take them flying on a nice night to make sure they allow a clear picture of everything.

Oxygen helps night vision, and I find it quite refreshing to spend a few minutes on oxygen before leaving altitude for terminal area maneuvering at night. A small flashlight is essential for chart reading, too, because few map lights direct a bright enough stream of light at the chart.

The things we do to prepare for an approach in the daytime need special emphasis at night. If you aren't a frequent night flyer, getting behind is both easier and more serious. The arrival needs to be planned carefully, and any sign that the flight isn't following the script is a clear call for a reassessment of the activity.

I'll never forget hearing a pilot come to grips with reality one bumpy night. He missed a VOR approach and was working his way around for a second approach when he told the controller that he'd just like to change plan and go to another airport—one with an ILS. The pilot recognized that he was not organized, that he was pushing a non-precision approach, and that he'd feel better with more electronic guidance. Wise man.

I also recall a night approach I flew that involved special pressures. I was in a twin, they held me up above 10,000 feet until I was practically at the destination, and the descent was made in an abbreviated holding pattern. "Just do 360s while you descend." By the time I leveled at the glideslope-interception altitude and started inbound on the ILS, I was pinching myself and doubling up on the challenge and response (all by myself) to make certain that the required disciplines were intact for the approach to minimums. I would have much preferred a "normal" arrival, but you have to adjust to actual situations, and in this case I found that a lot of extra effort was necessary to make the adjustment.

Missed Approach

Another night approach made me go out and practice some at night. This one was at the end of a long day and a long flight nonstop from Wichita, Kansas, to Maryland in my P210. As I descended I listened to the AWOS for what was then my home base, Carroll County airport. The ceiling was given as 500 feet. The minimum descent altitude is higher than that, and where I might or might not have made the approach to see if the AWOS was correct in the daytime, there's no way I'd start a night approach with the reported weather below minimums. I have read far too many accident reports where pilots did that; it has proven to be one of the deadliest of sins.

Anyway, nearby Frederick, Maryland, has an ILS. At the time they had no AWOS, but Carroll County was the lowest reported weather in the area, so I felt confident that the ILS to Frederick would work well. Cleared for it, down, down, 100 feet above DH, nothing, down, 50 feet, nothing, DH, nothing, missed approach.

Up to that point I felt as though I was working very hard and that night approaches are a lot of times more demanding than day approaches. The workload on the missed approach, though, is even higher. Power up, gear up, flaps up, trim, fly. Looking back on the event, I am convinced that the missed approach at night involves the highest workload of anything we do in retractables or light twins.

Having missed the approach, I had no desire to try another. I knew the weather was below minimums at Frederick, so I opted to go to Baltimore. To do that, I had to get the proper approach plate out and study the approach. I felt a little like there was a conspiracy that evening, too, because they were using a back course approach that uses a number of DME fixes as step-down points—just what you need on a dark night. The ceiling there was 1,100 feet and the visibility a few miles. I was a happy fellow when the runway appeared in the murk.

The activities of that evening illustrated something else. In a fairly significant number of night instrument approach accidents, the pilot loses control of the airplane and crashes. This happens both while the pilot is maneuvering to land and during missed approaches, and it's easy to see how it happens. The pilot's attention is diverted from the instruments when the chart must be selected or consulted and, where in the daytime your peripheral vision might pick up clues on the panel, at night you tend to see only that which is in your direct line of vision. Throw in a little confusion, and the seeds are there for a loss of control.

Along the Way

En route, the thunderstorm is worthy of a special night thought because there are a number of thunderstorm problems involving IFR night flights each year. It is hard to pinpoint a reason why night would offer more problems than day in relation to storms. Some feel that being able to see lightning should actually make the night avoidance task easier, but apparently this is true only when avoidance means staying a gross distance away from any lightning discharges. Perhaps the ability to see lightning leads pilots to use it as a visual aid for penetration, and the clues from lightning are far from adequate to use in avoiding cells at close range.

Also, it is often noted that strobe lights and flashing or rotating beacons should be doused when flying in cloud at night. I think that most of us have turned them on just to sample the effect or have left them on for a moment after flying into cloud. The results can be spectacular. I doubt that they really cause spatial disorientation; rather, the illumination of the cloud's innards is so bright that it probably draws the eye and makes you neglect the instrument scan. Same result.

Takeoff

Moving back to the departure, there are some special considerations for night IFR takeoffs. When we launch in the daytime, the ceiling can be "seen," if there is a ceiling. On a day with, say, a 600-foot ceiling, I might fly visually up to the point just before cloud penetration. Then I change over to instruments. That's perhaps not the best way, but when you can see, it is hard to resist looking, right up to the last minute.

At night, there's no way to see a ceiling clearly, and it is not wise to depend on the reported value to decide when you are going to have to change to instruments. At night, I turn the panel lights up full bright, make the takeoff without landing lights unless there is some compelling reason to use them, and then switch to instruments at liftoff. This way, I'm ready for the clouds at whatever level they choose to envelope the airplane.

The sensations of a night takeoff and initial climb can be more bothersome than a daytime IFR departure, and a dedication to the gauges helps relieve the discomfort. In many situations, regardless of the weather, the flight instruments give the only valid visual clues on a night departure, especially if launching from a well-lighted airport and flying out over a dark or sparsely lighted area. A definite transition to gauges can make the first 1,000 feet of climb a much more precise exercise in such conditions. If you must, after reaching that altitude, look outside if it appears the airplane is in visual meteorological conditions. Look for other traffic and think you are flying visually. But scan back to the gauges, because only they give the straight poop.

Preflight

There are some special preflight actions that can help make night departures more routine. The business of arranging the first part of the flight—presetting everything that can be preset and knowing the path and altitude that will be prescribed for the first part of the flight—is important. Where you can glance at a chart-on-lap by day to refresh your memory, at night you have to arrange for lighting and then *squint* at the chart-on-lap. There's a big difference.

Have the flashlight ready on the takeoff roll, too. I learned the value of this one very dark and rainy night when departing from a 3,000-foot-long runway with minimum runway lighting and virtually no ground lighting around the airport. The airplane was a light twin, we were at gross weight, and as the aircraft reached liftoff speed pretty far down the runway, the panel lights flickered a couple of times. I mentioned to the lad riding shotgun that he should have the flashlight ready. We were just off, gear coming up, when the panel lights went out entirely. It was a bad moment. The airplane was just beginning to climb, and my scan had been arranged to hold a heading and a pitch attitude to insure a positive rate of climb and to verify a proper airspeed. Then there was nothing but darkness, the drone of a couple of Continentals, and the pitter-patter of rain on the windshield.

Fortunately, my flying companion for the evening was fast on the draw with that light. I asked him to shine it on the artificial horizon. Everything was still okay, and I left the engines at full bore and climbed at the best rate-of-climb speed to a good altitude. I had a flashlight in my pocket, too, and I wasn't particularly concerned about running out of battery power, but the view of the panel was somewhat restricted. And I felt rather dumb when one of the passengers, who had watched the whole procedure, wondered aloud if it would help us to turn on the dome light. He pressed the button. It did a fine job of lighting the instrument panel, and we flew on home. But we'd have been in a difficult situation at the moment of lighting failure had we not had the flashlight ready.

On the theory that confession is good for the soul, I offer another flashlight story. This one was on a before-daybreak flight after the flight just described. I had a flashlight ready in my lap. It was one that turns on with a push button on the side. I had gotten a clearance with a void time over the phone and was to contact the center when airborne. Now, are you ready for this? When it was time to call the center, I picked up the flashlight, held it like the mike, pressed the button and illuminated my face. It was red.

Weather

There's a weather-related item to watch at night, too. Generally, ceilings and visibilities will drop at night in an area of inclement weather. And the reporting of weather at night seems to me much less accurate than the reporting of weather in the daytime. It is not unusual to find yourself flying to the final approach fix at night, 1,500 feet above the ground, in cloud, with a reported ceiling of 5,000 feet or better. The observers are looking at instruments and a lot of black sky at night. In the daytime they can see clouds and are less likely to miss the fact that lower clouds are banked to the west of the airport, for example.

One final item on night IFR. I noted in the beginning that mechanical engine failure is statistically insignificant in nighttime IFR accidents. One thing needs to be added on this point. One of the reasons that engine failure is statistically insignificant is because the overall record is so bad. If pilots didn't crash so many airplanes on approaches, engine failure would become a more significant part of the picture.

There is an engine-failure question that must be noted, too. It is not related to things breaking, but rather to fuel. There are cases of fuel exhaustion on night IFR flights, and occasionally a pilot will position a fuel selector incorrectly and wind up with a dandy case of fuel starvation while trying to juggle all the balls of an instrument arrival. Either event can be quite unhandy.

On fuel quantity, it's wise to be super-conservative at night. If you land with an hour's fuel on board by day, land with two hours' fuel on board at night. Weather conditions are more likely to go below landing minimums at night than in the daytime, and if the weather area is of any size, the trip to an alternate could be a long one.

On fuel selection, use a flashlight to illuminate the fuel selector(s) if lighting is not provided. Also, make the final selection for landing before leaving the cruising level and entering the terminal area. As well as we often think we know an airplane, it is still possible to turn something in the wrong direction. But if you shine a light on it and select "Right," for example, then you'll know that it is indeed on "Right."

There's nothing wrong with night IFR, nothing at all. It's all a matter of recognizing the extra demands—there are a lot of them—and catering to those demands. And when compared with night VFR in marginal weather, the night IFR is one of the best deals going.

Interlude—A Vignette: Everybody's Gotta Be Somewhere

You've probably heard the old story about what the fellow said when he was discovered hiding in the closet. Everyone does have to be somewhere, and in instrument flying, our location in space is the thing by which we live. A pilot who is always aware of position and altitude as well as aircraft attitude and speed is a pilot doing his IFR work properly.

It's often amusing to respond to a passenger's question about location with "Beats me" as we move along in cloud. It had better be a joke, though. When flying IFR, you must know exactly where you are and what you are doing at all times. Instead of "Beats me," a better answer might be: "We are 52 miles northeast of Little Rock, flying at 7,000 feet on an airway that has a minimum en route altitude of 2,500 feet. Our groundspeed is 150 knots, and we'll be over Gilmore at 45 past the hour."

Altitude is a critical part of our position space. When pilots crash on an approach or while maneuvering in a terminal area, it is usually because they are flying too low. There are bad altitudes, and there are worse altitudes in thunderstorms. Altitude is an important consideration when dealing with ice. Selection of the best altitude for winds might make the difference between getting there with good reserves and sweating fuel to the last drop. Flying at too high an altitude without oxygen or pressurization can fuzz the mind for a critical approach. Flying at the wrong altitude can create a collision hazard. First, is the altitude a safe one? Second, is the altitude the best possible safe altitude for efficiency and comfort?

When we fly VFR, we draw the line of the chart. Avoiding terrain and obstructions becomes a matter of noting elevations on the chart and visually verifying that the selected altitude is a safe one. When we fly IFR, the lines are drawn on the chart for us, and there is always a minimum allowable altitude for each line. These minimums are not to be taken lightly. There is good air at and above the numbers; below are trees, rocks, and TV towers.

Acknowledge, too, that there is often temptation on an approach to fly at a lower altitude than is safe or legal. The devil on your shoulder might say: "There's always a ceiling, so it's okay to descend below MDA to an altitude beneath the ceiling." The devil is correct. There is always a ceiling. But it might be halfway up a tree, or it might be zero. Just before you fly into the top half of the tree, the devil that made you do it will hop off and go find another sucker's shoulder to ride on. Altitude and position are the sum of what we do. Knowing both is imperative. "This is my position and altitude, and this is a safe altitude for this position." Ask the question continuously. It's critically important by day and even more important at night.

11. Middle-Altitude IFR

Turbocharging has become so popular that a high percentage of the high-performance singles and light twins are so equipped. This effectively doubles the vertical operating envelope of the airplanes and introduces a lot of new factors to flying. And one thing is certain: flying in the middle altitudes, from 10,000 to 25,000 feet, is best done IFR. Sure, it's legal to fly VFR at 17,500 and below, but it's not a good idea except on a sparkling clear day.

A pilot doesn't have to fly high many times to realize that it's a long way down. A lot of weather can get between the airplane and the runway. Even when cruising along up high on what seems a pretty good day, it can be quite difficult to judge whether or not it'll be VFR ahead at the selected flight level, or whether or not a VFR descent will be possible.

Another reason IFR is wise above 10,000 is related to the speed limit regulations. The really high-performance airplanes have to slow to 250 knots before descending below 10,000 feet; above that level there is no speed limit. Closure rates are thus greater and collision avoidance is more difficult. The overtaking situation can be critical. With a single or light twin, the "be seen" part of the equation is relatively small, and we can't do much for the "see" part if a jet is overtaking us. The speed at which a jet overtakes a single or light twin might be as much as 200 to 300 knots, depending on the airplanes involved. Simply put, seeing and being seen become a lot more difficult above 10,000 feet. It is true that all airplanes above 10,000 have transponders and that controllers should give you as traffic to any air carrier aircraft when you are flying above 10,000 feet. Many jets have on-board collision avoidance gear as well. There is always the opportunity for a lapse, though, and this becomes much smaller if you always fly IFR above 10,000 feet, where the closure rates can be much higher.

The Machines

The serious IFR pilot will go much farther than the usual cursory check-out when starting out with a turbocharged airplane. The machines are complex. Operation of them is demanding in the mechanical sense, in the flying sense, and in the physiological sense. No type rating is required, but we should approach the turbocharged airplane on much the same basis as an airplane for which a type rating is required (a jet, for example), both in initial training and proficiency flying. Cessna built the P210 (Pressurized Centurion) for several years before they recognized the need for a special training course for the airplane. When formulating the course, one of their training people made the remark that the P210, in appearance the simplest airplane for which they offer training, is in truth the most complex to operate. Some manufacturers offer training for other turbocharged light twins and singles—usually if the airplane is pressurized, and there are excellent training courses for simpler airplanes. Regardless of whether or not training is offered, it's best not to settle for less than a complete understanding of a turbocharged airplane and its systems along with a flight training program that includes the complete operating envelope of the airplane and middle-altitude IFR flying.

Malibu

The Piper Malibu had a training course from the very beginning, but the airplane had trouble in the hands of pilots anyway. The original training course for the airplane put very little emphasis on IFR operation and the use of the autopilot (this was later changed), and there appears to be a connection between these items and a series of accidents. The certification of the airplane and the autopilot came under FAA scrutiny, and the National Transportation Safety Board did an exhaustive study of the accidents.

Anyone who flies high in any airplane, or aspires to, can certainly learn from the NTSB study. It is especially pertinent to this chapter, because the NTSB made specific recommendations for training for many pilots operating in the middle altitudes, and these might become law during the lifespan of this book.

Five Malibus were involved in fatal accidents in the United States in less than two years. All were IFR accidents and in each case the airplane broke up in flight.

A summary of the first accident reveals that the pilot was flying at 16,000 feet when he asked about weather ahead. The controller advised that there was weather about 70 miles directly ahead. The pilot requested a deviation to the left and was cleared to 17,000 feet. A bit later the pilot advised that he was going to make a turn to get out of some of the weather; the turn was approved. Then the pilot said that "he was having a little point control problem and did not want to get into bad weather." It was speculated that the "point control" was probably a reference to dots on the Stormscope installed in the airplane.

Next, the controller cleared the airplane down to 13,000 feet because the pilot was nearing his destination. The pilot requested an even lower altitude and the controller gave the pilot a vector for the descent. Shortly afterward, the pilot said, "Present heading is three five zero and we're getting in a big cell and we've got to get out of here." The controller advised, "Deviation left of course out of weather is approved as needed, maintain one two thousand." Sixteen seconds later the pilot advised that he couldn't hold it and the airplane crashed shortly thereafter. Control of the aircraft was obviously lost. The radar plot showed that the airplane entered a steeply banked turn to the right from the north, and its speed increased from 170 knots to 200 knots (indicated airspeeds, developed using the radar track) and the altitude decreased to 11,100 in 17 seconds. From its original northerly ground track, the airplane traveled 1.5 miles to the east before it broke up. Weather radar data showed that the airplane had entered an area of very strong weather echoes containing thunderstorms with heavy rain-showers. Witnesses reported thunder and lightning but no rain where the airplane crashed. This pilot had 17 hours in the Malibu and 3.9 hours of instrument time in the airplane. The airplane had a WX-10A Stormscope installed, but no mention was made of radar, so there obviously was none.

When we are flying at the higher levels, thunderstorms, in some conditions, can actually be more a factor than they are at low altitudes. The weather near this crash site was reported as VFR, but the pilot was apparently dealing with congested cumulus that were likely building. As has been noted previously, a Stormscope is not suitable for penetrating areas of thunderstorms (nor, in my opinion, is radar, in most cases) and this airplane actually had a placard declaring that the Stormscope shouldn't be used for thunderstorm area penetration.

This accident had more to do with a pilot vs. thunderstorms than anything else, though the pilot's relatively low time and instrument time in the type could have put him at a flying disadvantage. There is also the possibility that he was trying to use the autopilot and did not fully understand its limitations.

The second Malibu accident is not really pertinent to high altitude flying because its filed altitude was 9,000 feet. In this case, the airplane leveled at 9,000 feet, then climbed to 9,400 feet, where the airplane entered a very rapid descent. The transponder return disappeared when the airplane reached 5,400 feet. The airframe had failed in flight.

This pilot had some difficulty with instrument flying and left the Piper factory school with word that 10 hours more of instrument instruction were needed before he could fly in instrument meteorological conditions. The pilot then got 9.4 hours of dual in the Malibu with a local instructor, who said he then possessed adequate skills to fly instruments.

Weather data indicated that clouds were present with tops above 18,000 feet as well as the probable presence of light to moderate icing between 8,000 and 10,000 feet. Documentation of cockpit switches indicated that all anti-ice switches were off, including the pitot heat.

It will be useful to summarize the other three files before relating all this to middle-altitude flying.

Forecast Thunderstorms

The next pilot was flying toward a front with rainshowers and thunder-storms forecast in connection with the front. The activity was on the radar summary, and there was an absence of activity in one area. The pilot asked for deviations and progressively higher altitudes, telling the controller that he was "going to try to get over it. . . ." The pilot checked in with a new controller and reported that he was climbing to Flight Level 220, to which he had been cleared. The controller acknowledged the transmission, but after that, the pilot failed to respond to transmissions from the controller. The reason for the lack of response was that the pilot had switched to a Flight Service Station frequency, where he had a discussion about weather. Because the destination weather was not good, the pilot indicated to the FSS Specialist that he would be changing destinations. Then, still on the FSS frequency, the pilot transmitted, "I'm having a bit of trouble, I'm trying to level out at Flight Level 200 (tone)." Then the pilot transmitted, "I've lost my ah . . . Mayday, Mayday, Mayday."

Witnesses saw the aircraft descend out of an overcast sky with the nose 15-20 degrees down and the wings level and the landing gear extended. The base of the overcast was estimated at 2,000 feet. Shortly after the airplane flew out of the overcast, the wings broke off with what a witness described as an explosion.

Weather radar data showed that the airplane was about five miles from a moderate (Level 2) convective echo when the trouble occurred. Cloud tops were about 33,000 feet and light to moderate icing was possible above the freezing level, 13,000 feet.

The flightpath study showed an erratic vertical track. After being cleared to FL220, the airplane ascended from FL200 to FL227. Then it descended to FL204 and reached a descent rate of 3,200 fpm. The airspeed (as interpolated from groundspeed readouts) increased from 110 to 198 knots. The descent stopped at FL204 and the airplane then transitioned into a climb to FL231, during which the airplane reached a climb angle of about 25 degrees and the airspeed decreased to well within the range of stall. After that the airplane descended, the speed apparently increased dramatically, and the airframe probably failed when the pilot sighted the ground and tried to pull out of the dive.

The pitot heat switch was in the "Off" position. The pilot had 54 hours of instrument time in the Malibu.

In Climb

The next pilot was climbing to a cruising level of 15,000 feet. There was a chance of thunderstorms in the area, but there was no discussion of these in the communications. The freezing level in the area was just below 13,000 feet. In fact, communications and everything else were normal as the airplane passed thorugh 13,300 feet. Then, near 13,900 feet, the airspeed had decreased to less than 80 knots and the airplane made a shallow turn to the left followed by a steeper turn to the right. The airplane then entered a rapid descent with some maneuvering as the airspeed rapidly increased. Studies suggested that the aircraft broke apart in a rapid descent between 9,000 and 6,000 feet. The pitot heat switch was off.

Another Climb

The next pilot was climbing to a cruising level of FL220 in an area of inclement weather when, at 17,300 feet, the airplane started to descend erratically. The pilot transmitted, ". . .we're having a problem." The controller asked him to repeat and this time the pilot said, ". . .we're having a . . . ."

When it reached 17,300 feet in the climb, this airplane entered a descent followed by an abrupt, steeply banked turn to the right. About 20 seconds elapsed from the start of the descent to the completion of a heading change from north to east. The airplane flew east for about a minute while further altitude excursions occurred. The airplane's altitude decreased to 15,400 feet and it accelerated to more than 230 knots on the easterly heading. Then it ascended to 17,200 feet in about 20 seconds, losing much of the airspeed. Further excursions followed before the airplane entered a final descent with a substantial right bank angle. The airframe failed in flight.

This pilot had flown 2.7 hours instrument time in the past six months. The weather analysis indicates that the freezing level was near 13,000 feet and that the airplane was in clouds at 17,000 feet. Cumulus clouds were forming within 10 miles north of where the first deviation from normal flight occurred, and correlation of radar data showed the airplane to have been in or near a moderate convective echo at the time of the first deviation.

P210

It is useful here to add the accident history of the Cessna P210. It and the Malibu spend a far higher percentage of their flying time at high altitude than do unpressurized turbocharged airplanes, and I think it is from them that we learn the most about high altitude flight.

Even though the P210 is in the fleet in larger numbers than the Malibu, the airplane had only four accidents in a five-year period that relate to this subject. (It had a lot of other accidents that don't relate, especially approach accidents.)

One P210 accident, early in the airplane's history, involved a failed vacuum pump and subsequent airframe failure. The P210s were later fitted with standby vacuum or standby electrically operated instrumentation, mandated by an airworthiness directive.

In the next P210 accident, the pilot penetrated an area of Level 5 (intense) thunderstorms at FL190 and an airframe failure followed. There would likely have been severe ice as well as severe turbulence in the area.

A P210 was lost from 14,000 feet, flying in an area where both ice and thunderstorms would have been a consideration. The pilot had reported ice at 14,000 and had been cleared to 12,000 feet when it was lost.

The fourth P210 was at 16,000 feet with no ice forecast above 14,000 and apparently no significant weather in the area. It was daytime. The pilot was relatively inexperienced, with 417 hours, 29 on actual instruments, and 30 in type. The airplane dropped off the radar scope and, because the airplane crashed into the ocean, not enough wreckage was recovered to make any determination of what might have happened.

Not the Airplane

It was determined in all the Malibu investigations that there was nothing wrong with the airplane or the autopilot. When comparing the P210 with the Malibu, one item stands out. The total flying experience, as well as the experience in type, is much greater in the P210 accidents than in the Malibu accidents. Would experience prompt pilots to be better about such a simple procedure as turning on the pitot heat? Perhaps, though that is certainly something that could be taught.

One thing that does come to mind relates to experience. Pilots who fly frequently in the middle altitudes quickly become aware that icing in those levels occurs in the summer as well as in the other seasons. The best procedure to follow on pitot heat is to use it whenever flying in visible moisture. Some modify this with a temperature requirement and turn it on when the moisture is there and the temperature is below +10°C. The main thing is to have a procedure that results in the heat being on when it is needed.

The loss of control after a loss of airspeed indication is something that could certainly be avoided if the pilot recognized the problem. Doing this is not easy, and there is one case on record of an airline jet being lost because the pitot heat was not turned on, airspeed indication was lost, and the crew lost control of the aircraft and crashed—apparently never realizing what had caused the problem.

What's So Different?

Where the NTSB related only one of the accidents to a thunderstorm, three of the other Malibus lost were in close proximity to activity or were flying in an area where activity was forecast. The aircraft could have encountered turbulence—perhaps not thunderstorm turbulence, but enough to get things going. Add some ice to that, along with what the NTSB thought might be unfamiliarity with the flight control system in the airplane, and you have the level of confusion that can lead a pilot down the path. Certainly it was not shown that anything was wrong with the airplanes or flight control systems. It just comes back to that old and often noted situation where the pilot was not up to the task at hand.

Wind at Altitude

Beside knowing everything there is to know about the airplanes and giving any convective activity a wide berth, we need to understand some other things about conditions that will be encountered in the middle levels.

Wind is a big operational consideration in middle-altitude IFR. When the jet stream is active, winds in the 18,000- to 25,000-foot levels can run in the 100-knot range. Earlier, we discussed how critical the winds aloft can be for flight planning in an airplane that cruises 120 knots. Well, a 100-knot wind is as critical to a 190-knot cruise turbocharged single as a 65-knot wind is to a Skyhawk.

The first thing we learn about winds aloft is that the forecasts are as approximate for the higher levels as they are for the lower levels. They should be taken as an indication of the general flow, and then with a grain of salt. For example, on a trip in my P210, I planned a flight with a forecast calling for a tailwind beginning at 45 knots, increasing to 55 knots after about 200 miles of flight, and remaining at that level for the final 850 miles. Actually, the wind started off at 55 knots and remained at that level for about 500 miles. It then increased to 85 knots for about 200 miles and finally dropped back to 45 knots for the last 350 miles. Those might seem like relatively small variations, but they do have a pronounced effect on flight planning. I was using a maximum range cruise setting on this flight, with a true airspeed of 165 knots at 21,000 feet, so the wind velocity was a high percentage of true airspeed. The fuel reserves were predicated on the 45-knot tailwind. When it picked up to 85 knots, the temptation was strong to base the ETA on the new and spectacular groundspeed and to increase cruise power to do even better. That would have been a mistake.

The high velocity winds aloft can be a big factor when crosswind. For example, cruising at 180 knots true with an 85-knot wind exactly 90 degrees to the airway being flown results in a loss of over 20 knots as you track the airway. Blow off course a bit and make a 20-degree correction to get back on the airway and you'll shed about 30 additional knots as you work (slowly) back to the airway. Or, if the wind forecast was correct on the velocity but 20 degrees more toward the nose on direction, the groundspeed would be 30 knots below that anticipated when planning. So it's not only the wind that's right on the nose that hurts.

This is offered mainly to underscore the importance of advance as well as en route fuel planning. More than one turbocharged airplane has crashed out of fuel because the pilot wasn't precise and realistic when attempting a maximum range trip.

The Bumpy Clues

There's often a clear sign that the wind is changing at altitude. Turbulence tells the tale. It is surprising how often the air isn't smooth in the middle levels, and when it is jiggly it's usually because of wind shear or a change in wind direction and/or velocity as you move along. This change in wind is what causes the clear-air turbulence that bothers jets flying at higher altitudes and sometimes bothers airplanes flying in the middle levels.

I do think that light airplanes do much better in clear air turbulence than heavier ones. I know that I've heard jets reporting moderate chop at levels and in areas where I was flying and experiencing nothing particularly uncomfortable.

The National Weather Service uses a change of 40 knots in velocity in 150 miles as a guideline in forecasting severe clear air turbulence, and I've experienced such changes in velocity with a ride that wasn't too bad. On the flight described earlier, the wind increased by 30 and then dropped back 40 in the course of less than 300 miles, and while the ride wasn't exactly smooth, it wasn't bad. The NWS forecasts moderate clear air turbulence based on a wind change of 18 knots in 150 miles. When flying in the middle levels, a bumpy ride in clear air means that the wind is changing. Be ready to recalculate fuel reserves.

Vertical shear, a change in velocity, usually an increase with height, can also create turbulence. Light turbulence can be caused by a change of 3 to 5 knots per 1,000 feet, 6 to 9 knots can cause moderate turbulence, and 10 knots or more can result in severe turbulence. Climbing into an increasing headwind can be seen as a momentary increase in climb rate; the reverse is true for climbing into an increasing tailwind. These factors can be very useful in evaluating the winds aloft during a climb.

The forecaster usually shows an increase in wind velocity with altitude. To counter this, turbocharged airplanes will offer an increase in true airspeed of 1½ to 2 knots per 1,000 feet, on the same fuel flow, as the cruising level is increased. But which increases faster, the cruising speed or the wind? How do we choose the best altitude?

The first thing most of us do is fly at a comfortable level. For flying across the Appalachians, 6,000 feet might be the minimum en route altitude with the lowest wind velocity, but in a strong westerly flow it is a very uncomfortable altitude. With a turbocharged airplane, you'd probably look at a minimum of 12,000 to clear the turbulence and the snowshowers, possibly higher. But would this do grievous harm to the groundspeed? Probably not.

It has been my experience that once you get above 3,000 or 4,000 feet or into the smooth air above low-level turbulence, the wind aloft increases less rapidly with altitude than either the true airspeed or the wind forecast. With turbocharging, the better groundspeeds are usually found higher rather than lower. Many a time I've responded to a low groundspeed at, say, 16,000 feet by descending to the minimum en route altitude—only to find a bad ride and the same or a lower groundspeed there. I'm a slow learner, but I've finally concluded from experience that a forecast of 25 knots at 6,000, 40 knots at 9,000, 48 knots at 12,000, and 60 knots at 18,000 is not always accurate. Velocities are usually more uniform over that altitude range.

The big exception to higher being better is when there is jetstream activity aloft. In this case, the flow will be strong at all levels but will become very strong as you go higher. Turbulence in clear air in the climb, or an increase or decrease in rate of climb as the airplane climbs, is a sign that wind velocities are probably increasing with altitude much more rapidly than the true airspeed will increase with altitude. The groundspeed readout on the DME, Loran, or GPS will also tell the tale, but the turbulence and rate of climb can be very useful in pinpointing the altitude where the change occurred. Do calculate true airspeeds in climb, so that you'll know what the wind is doing to you as you read the groundspeed.

Another thing to consider: it's been my experience that the engineers do a rather inexact job of determining cruising speeds of some turbocharged airplanes. True airspeeds of some increase more rapidly with altitude than is suggested in the pilot's operating handbook. Some are faster at high altitudes than the book shows, while some barely cling to the book figures, and weight below gross gives some of the airplanes a big jump in cruising speed while helping others less. The key is in getting to know the fuel flows and true airspeeds of a particular airplane before tackling those extra long trips.

Ups and Downs

One of the first things I noticed when starting to fly a turbocharged airplane at high altitude on a regular basis was that the total average fuel burn was a bit higher than I expected for each trip, and the average groundspeed was a bit lower. This is a direct result of spending a smaller percentage of the time at cruise, in the steady state, in a turbocharged airplane as opposed to a normally aspirated one.

In operating in the high teens and low twenties, for example, 30 minutes might be spent climbing. In virtually all turbocharged airplanes, extra fuel is used to cool the engine during climb. When you add the start, taxi, and takeoff fuel to the climb fuel, you will likely find that the first 30 minutes uses as much or almost as much fuel as will be used in an hour of cruising with the power set on a nominal value. And on the other end, there will be 30 minutes of descent, with the fuel flow probably very close to what it was at cruise. Sometimes when we are cruising at 3,000-4,000 feet, we feel almost as if we have arrived when starting to descend for landing. This isn't so in a high-flying airplane. The pilot who leaves a high altitude with the fuel gauges flirting with empty and calculations based on being down to the last few gallons on landing might well use it all before getting the airplane down.

A P210 (the 1978 through 1981 models) has 89 gallons (534 pounds) of usable fuel. If you think of using a mid-range cruise setting that burns 15 gallons, or 90 pounds, of fuel per hour, the endurance figure that pops to mind is somewhere close to six hours. Not so. On a high altitude flight, you have to subtract about half an hour from the number you get by dividing total fuel by flow at cruise: on a 90-pound-per-hour flight a P210 would be at dry tanks in about 5½ hours. Take an hour off that for reserve and it allows 4 plus 30 to the destination and to the alternate. The pilot's operating handbook provides the information to use in calculating fuel required to climb, and some good sessions with the book provide a basis on which to plan flights.

The 210s, Ps, and others have also been the subject of an abnormal number of fuel exhaustion accidents as well as an airworthiness directive on the subject. The airplanes are not easy to fill to the rated 89 gallons, and if the wings are not level in a left-right sense when the airplane is fueled, there is no way to get the rated amount of fuel in the tanks.

Stealing Candy

I hope you don't think I'm trying to spoil all the fun, but it's also necessary to say that when flying high with a tailwind, the descents are always a disappointment. There's no way you can fly along at Flight Level 210 (21,000 feet), look at the groundspeed and the estimated time of arrival on an electronic device, and expect to arrive at that time. All the evil forces in the world conspire against speed on descents. Where the groundspeed will show a big spike when you first start down, that's more than offset later by lower true airspeeds at lower altitudes, often by lighter winds down low, and by maneuvering for landing.

For example, on one trip I was whistling along at 227 knots groundspeed at FL 210, 187 nautical miles from my destination. It took me 58 minutes to cover that last 187 miles. If I had been in a questionable fuel state and had read my calculator through rose-colored glasses, I might have gotten to the last cookie in the jar. I've found that if you want to use groundspeed at high altitude cruise in calculating the ETA, you have to add at least 10 minutes to the computed ETA.

One other thought on fuel: some turbocharged airplanes have the word *turbocharged* or *turbo* painted on the cowling or on the nacelles. This might give the pilot's ego as much boost as the little device gives the engine, but it can be confusing to people who put fuel in airplanes. More than one lineman has seen the word *turbo* and filled the tanks of a turbocharged, piston-engine airplane with jet fuel. The words have been removed from virtually all turbocharged airplanes, but one line person explained away jet fuel in a turbocharged airplane because it had polished spinners and he thought that meant it was turbine powered. Unfortunately, with a mixture of jet fuel and avgas, one will start and often run enough to become airborne before the engine or engines cease running. The cure is to drain the sumps and *smell the fuel* after every refueling. If the sump fuel drains directly on the ground, put your fingers in it and then sniff them. Jet fuel is basically kerosene, which, to put it politely, stinks. Rub it between your fingers. It's also more oily and slick than avgas.

Back to Basics

Another basic that bedevils the pilot who moves from Victor up into

Jet airways is the heading. (The change to jet airways is at 18,000 feet, where altitudes become Flight Levels and the altimeter is always set on 29.92.) Flying a precise heading isn't as important here as on an approach, but it can do a lot to minimize the miles flown. Pilots have an initial problem because of greater distances between navaids in the high altitude airways system, and because the relatively slow speeds of the turbocharged airplanes mean that any heading change will take a long time to show on the navigation needles.

On an airway that I fly frequently, the distance between two Vortacs is 311 miles. When flying a VOR, one degree off course is one mile off course when the airplane is 60 miles from the station. So, at 150 miles, about half way between the two stations, a degree is 2.5 miles; when 2 degrees off course, the airplane would be 5 miles away from the centerline of the airway. A full-scale deflection on a VOR is 10 degrees; 2 doesn't look like a lot and is probably the minimum that prompts a pilot to think about a correction.

When far from a station, any correction takes effect in very slow motion. The result is that a pilot used to flying VOR at lower altitudes, where the stations have to be closer together, gets impatient and takes 10 degrees more, or 20 degrees more, because that apparent slight deviation from course wasn't quickly fixed by the initial correction. It's common for a pilot who isn't heading-conscious to wander around, varying thirty degrees either side of the correct heading. The air traffic controller often calls and asks, "Hey, 40RC, where are you going?" Tracking an airway is just like flying an ILS—as long as the wind remains constant, one heading will do it. Find that heading and fly it and remember that everything happens in slow motion when the distance to the station is great.

If the airplane has a Loran or GPS that gives the ground track being made good, that can be used for the quick solution to the heading that should be flown. The device will also show the bearing to where you are going; the difference between that number and the track is the heading correction that will be necessary to track toward the point.

Powerplant Management

There's a lot to powerplant management when flying a turbocharged airplane, and this can add to IFR workload—especially if the pilot doesn't really understand what's going on under the cowling.

Engine temperatures can be a critical item. Temperatures will increase as you climb even though the outside air temperature decreases. The higher you go, the harder the turbocharger works to maintain the intake air at the same density as at sea level. Compressing the air generates heat. A pilot accustomed to a normally aspirated airplane thinks in terms of lower power at higher altitudes, thus less critical temperatures and mixture leaning considerations. The exact opposite is true with a turbocharged engine. The higher you go, the more critical the temperatures and the greater the possibility of harming the engine when leaning.

To minimize workload when IFR, leave the precise leaning until there's extra time to spend with it. I leave the fuel flow on a P210 10 pounds per hour above the prescribed cruise climb setting on an IFR departure, just as an extra margin. And when leveling at cruise, I don't lean until the engine has cooled a bit from the climb. These two things probably add only a gallon or two to the fuel consumption on each flight, but I think there is a good return in reliability.

Turbocharging systems vary, and the pilot's operating handbook usually gives a good description of how the system works in a particular airplane. A pilot who flies away without a complete understanding can not only become confused about what is going on, he can do serious damage to the engine.

Weather Outlook

A pilot flying in the middle altitudes comes to have a different outlook on weather. This new outlook should be examined, because we tend to neglect some things that aren't as apparent as when flying IFR at lower altitudes.

One feels a certain detachment from the ground when flying high, but this must not be allowed to lessen attention to what is going on below. The surface observations along the route ahead, at the destination and at the alternate, need to be checked as frequently by the pilot flying at Flight Level 210 as by the pilot flying at 5,000 feet.

The descent area weather is of special importance. When flying low, we are usually flying in the conditions in which the descent will be conducted. That's not so when flying high. You can be on top of a lot of weather, the descent will encompass about 30 minutes, and icing in the clouds or turbulent cumulus can make that a very interesting half hour. Flying in the mid-twenties, you can be on top of clouds from which a lot of rain is falling, or on top of thundershowers.

It's often said that getting a turbocharger means you'll almost always be on top. Not so. I'll always remember a speech in which Senator Barry Goldwater reminisced about his progression from very basic airplanes through high performance jets. With each step up, he felt sure that all en route flying would be on top. But he soon found that the tops of all clouds are generally found 1,000 feet above the service ceiling of the airplane being flown. I certainly found that to be true when moving from a Cardinal RG that was normally operated below 10,000 feet to a P210, normally operated in the high teens and low twenties. The percentage of flying hours actually in cloud was the same for both airplanes. And there were some interesting new twists. Icing, for example, is often a summertime problem at higher altitudes. The freezing level in a warm front is often between 15,000 and 20,000 feet in the summer, and you can get quite a dose of ice there. It's not a serious problem because there are scads of warm air altitudes beneath, but it's there. In the wintertime, ice is almost never a problem in the normal cruising altitudes because it's too cold. The clouds tend to be composed of ice crystals. But ice is something to deal with in the climb or descent.

Physiological Factors

The law sets 12,500 feet as a basic altitude above which oxygen must be used; 10,000 feet is a better altitude at which to don the mask—especially if there's instrument flying to be done. That's a simple rule by which to live. Another altitude should be considered. Just double the 10,000 and consider 20,000 feet as an altitude at which things change again. Above this altitude a problem with the oxygen system or the depressurization of a pressurized airplane offers a big problem and a limited time for solution—the solution being a fast descent. At or below 20,000, you call the controller, give him a few seconds to assimilate the message, and then get on with the descent.

A person has some minutes of useful consciousness at or below 20,000 feet. But the time of useful consciousness decreases very rapidly at altitudes above 20,000. If, for example, you were cruising at 25,000 and had a pressurization or oxygen system failure, you'd have to start an emergency descent immediately, and staying conscious would be touch and go for the first few minutes of the descent.

It's important to monitor oxygen flow. The higher you fly, the more important it becomes. Nothing obvious happens if the oxygen stops moving through the tubes and to the masks, so you have to watch the flow indicator. You might not be able to perceive a failure by the way you feel. The progression through hypoxia just doesn't register on some people. It's possible to think things are okay up to the point where you lose useful consciousness. In a pressurized airplane, any failure is rather obvious. A sudden depressurization is a noisy and uncomfortable event. A gradual depressurization would be perceived at least through ear discomfort. And pressurized airplanes have warning systems that alert the pilot when the cabin altitude goes above a safe level.

Training in the oxygen chamber is available at some Air Force and Navy installations. Your nearest FAA Flight Standards District Office should have details. Every pilot intending to fly over 10,000 feet should seek this training.

Let's Fly

To get some feel for IFR middle-level flying, follow along on a day's worth in a P210. This was a long trip—from Tucson, Arizona, to Trenton, New Jersey—but it illustrates the benefits of middle-altitude capability as well as some of the challenges found in this type of flying.

From Tucson to Wichita is 763 nautical miles as the trip was filed, and it appeared from the wind forecasts that it might be a fast flight. The wind out of Tucson would be a bit of a crosswind from the northwest, but it was forecast to shift to southwesterly. The velocity was pegged at 50 knots at 18,000 feet; we'd be flying at Flight Level 190. Based on the wind forecasts, I filed for 3 hours and 55 minutes. I calculated that we'd burn 15 gallons an hour at cruise and would have groundspeeds of over 200 knots for better than half the flight. Wichita's forecast called for 2,000 overcast with unlimited visibility with occasional 1,000 overcast, two miles, light rain, or snow and fog. There was the chance of a thunderstorm, and the surface wind was to be out of the north at about 15. There were three low-pressure systems on the map, one of which was west of Wichita. Another was south, and the third was to the northeast. None was strong.

The weather was fine out of Tucson, but the wind aloft was a distinct disappointment. They had missed by a few degrees, and from takeoff to a point 254 nautical miles along the way, we had averaged only 141 knots groundspeed. The climb was part of that, but level and tracking the airway, the airplane's DME was showing only 155. In other words, we had a headwind component.

It was improving, working up to 175, but this was in the area where I was counting on a strong southwesterly flow and direct tailwind. Based on preflight deliberations, I would have anticipated a groundspeed of 230 at this point in the flight. It was 55 knots lower than that.

This dictated a recalculation of the fuel plan. The quick, easy, and often proper solution is a fuel stop, but if one can be avoided, it's money in the bank. I figure it costs 15 gallons of fuel and an hour of time when a stop is added.

I calculated that if I reduced to a maximum-range setting and if the wind shifted enough to keep the groundspeed on 175, we would consume 71 gallons of fuel in getting to Wichita, leaving 18. The forecasts over the area were still good, but the actual weather was becoming suspect. Wichita was 400 broken, 2,300 overcast, and two miles with rainshowers. We were headed for a small airport in the Wichita area; the major airport with an ILS had been my alternate. Now I had to start thinking about something else in case there was a weather problem in the Wichita area. Oklahoma City, which would be off to the right about 45 minutes before we reached Wichita, was my real alternate. If anything untoward happened to the Wichita weather, I'd divert to Oke City, which had better weather.

Calculated to the last drop, it was a legal alternate with the 45 minutes reserve. My plan wasn't to stretch it to that, though. I'd make a decision to divert before reaching Wichita, to add to the fuel reserve.

The flight was above clouds, in smooth air, as we flew across Oklahoma. But there were higher clouds to the northeast, and we were in them as we began our descent into Wichita. Then came the day's first mention of thunderstorms: they were scattered in the Wichita area, according to the controller. So the descent was into an area of convective activity. While such things seem distant when you are droning along in clear air, en route, they become quite real on the radarscope.

The descent was relatively routine, though, with only a couple of zigs and a zag to get around one thundershower that was clearly shown on airborne as well as traffic control radar. The fuel bill was for 71 gallons, the amount projected during inflight planning. But the time en route was 57 minutes greater than that calculated in preflight planning—proof of the fact that the planning you do *after* takeoff is important.

From the Fire

That flight had been from good weather into an area of inclement weather. Our next hop started out in the area of bad weather. I thought we'd have a little help from the wind, that the radar would help us get around the showers in the area, and that at Flight Level 210 we would be on top.

There was some turbulence in the climb, caused by building cumulus, but the one thundershower shown on radar required only a slight deviation. At FL 210 we were barely on top. The controller was reporting a large area of precipitation, but it wasn't possible to separate the precip from the ground clutter when the airplane's radar antenna was tilted down to examine the clouds ahead and below.

The hop from Wichita to Trenton is one that I've made nonstop many times. All it requires is a 45-knot tailwind component at either FL 190 or FL 210, and that's not an unusual situation in the fall, winter, or spring. Since this trip was flown, too, I have added 30 gallons to the fuel supply of my P210 in the form of a baggage compartment tank. This makes nonstops out of one stops, and I figure the tank paid for itself pretty quickly in stops it eliminated.

Back to Wichita to Trenton. This flight was in the springtime, and while the wind forecast was for better than 45, I didn't even plan a nonstop. For one thing, the wind forecast earlier put me off. For another, the weather along the east coast was bad, and when that's the case, I like to get there with a lot of fuel. It is usually possible to conjure up a legal alternate, but the east coast has been known to fold completely, meaning that you have to retreat westward or to the northwest, into the wind that helped you get there, and this is best done only with plenty of fuel.

The flight to the fuel stop—Columbus, Ohio—was on top of all clouds and in smooth air. There was precious little tailwind, and I was glad that I hadn't entertained the thought of a nonstop. I was using relatively high power, was truing about 190 knots, and the best groundspeed was 210. The weather at Columbus was 600 overcast and two miles.

En route conditions looked okay for the flight from Columbus on home. More of the same, really. When you've been flying along at a relatively high altitude, looking at miles and miles of flat-topped clouds far below, you get a feeling for the general weather situation. The forecaster was promising a better tailwind for this leg, which I'd gratefully accept though I didn't depend on it. The weather at Trenton was forecast to be comfortably above IFR minimums.

Takeoff from Columbus was at sunset, and it was soon dark. To me, the first hours of darkness are critical where you have a widespread area of low clouds, rain, and drizzle. Weather tends to fold then, so I kept close tabs on current conditions as the airplane moved serenely through the night sky. Trenton was reporting 400 broken, 600 overcast, and 2 in light rain and fog. That could turn into something much lower, but Harrisburg's 1,600 overcast and 10 was heartening.

Some airplanes at lower altitudes were heard working on altitude changes because of icing as we flew over the mountains, but that was not a problem at 17,000. The groundspeed was up to 220, and everything looked good. I was amusing myself with the old game of "what if," and it's amazing how much of the time you are within gliding distance of a good airport when flying in the middle altitudes.

A little realism was added to the game, when, with a flash, half the panel lights went out. That caused a quick check of both the primary and the standby flashlights. A few minutes later, the DME dropped off the line. No real bother so late in a flight, but it caused the other pilot in the airplane to wonder what would go next. A careful survey of all the instruments and indications revealed nothing to tie together the light and DME glitches.

We were descending by this time, and the descent from altitude is a busier time the higher you fly because it takes longer. Planning is required, to comply with any altitude-crossing restrictions on descent, such as "cleared to descend to 9,000, cross Harrisburg at or below 14,000" and there is other work. The destination ATIS needs a little attention, and there should be a couple of checklist points on the descent. I use 10,000 as a key to prompt a recheck that the altimeter was reset leaving 18,000, that the fuel is on a tank with more than enough for the arrival, approach, and missed approach, that all the lights are on, that ice protection is selected as necessary, and that the approach chart is at hand and is understood.

What next? As the descent continued, we moved into airspace controlled by Philadelphia Approach Control, and after the initial contact with them, we could no longer converse. There was apparently some onboard problem. The avionics in the airplane had a sidetone feature—you could hear yourself transmit—but there was nothing there when either transmitter was used. There was no click in the audio when the microphone was keyed or unkeyed. We could hear the controller.

My "what if" bag was on the back seat. First I got another microphone and replaced the one we had been using. That didn't help. I delved more deeply into the bag and extricated my handheld transceiver and gave approach a call on that. They answered, relieved that communications had been established. I used that little radio the rest of the way, to complete what had been a routine use of a turbocharged airplane.

While the avionics problem came late in the flight, it can be used as an illustration of how such things take on greater importance the higher you fly. If, for example, we had lost transmitting capability while at 17,000 feet, headed toward the congested airspace of the northeastern states, it would have caused quite a ripple. And the higher you fly, the less likely you'll be able to get down VFR in case of radio failure.

This raises the question of redundant equipment. In twenty-four years of IFR at low altitudes, I had never been moved to incorporate much redundant equipment into my airplane. After fourteen years of turbocharged flying and encounters with vacuum and electrical problems, I had dual gyro instrumentation—both electric and vacuum heading indicators and artificial horizons—and have a standby vacuum system. My handheld transceiver has become two handhelds, and there's an external antenna that I can use with them. I also have an emergency bus that ties one nav/comm directly to the battery. Given these additions to equipment, no one system failure leaves me without answers.

As long as you recognize the need for proficiency and equipment a cut above basic, there's a lot of flexibility and reliability to be found in a turbocharged airplane. The extra demand on both the planning and flying is nothing more than what you would expect in return for all the good things offered.

12. IFR Emergencies and Glitches

My dictionary defines *emergency* as "a sudden, urgent, usually unforeseen occurrence or occasion requiring immediate action." If they would just take *unforeseen* out, it would be an excellent word to use for aviation in general and IFR flying in particular. As it is, the word *emergency* doesn't quite fit, because *unforeseen* has no place in flying. A person must learn to expect anything and everything when operating an airplane, and must have a plan to use in handling any problem. "OhmyGodwhatdoIdonow?" just doesn't work in airplanes.

The part of the definition about immediate action is applicable, but consider that "immediate" doesn't mean that things should be done before you have taken the time to verify that the chosen action is indeed a correct one.

Start with a simple thing, an event that doesn't threaten the actual safety of the flight but does demand attention. Right after you punch into the overcast, the baggage door of the airplane comes open and starts distributing the contents, dirty underwear and all, over the terrain below. In such a case it might be tempting to immediately duck back down, get VFR, return, and land. That's no good, though. Once the airplane is in cloud, the only thing to do is to follow IFR procedures. In this case, the solution would be to request clearance for an approach back to the airport of departure or to a nearby airport. Do it routinely. Do not cut corners. A lot of airplanes have been destroyed after a door inadvertently came open, but in general aviation it is usually precipitious action on the part of the pilot and not the actual opening of the door that causes the accident.

There are numerous other things that can come open or come loose on an airplane, and the event is always best handled by a routine IFR return and landing. The inconvenience of this is why the IFR preflight should be extra thorough. Landing to close a door when flying VFR is no big deal. It becomes quite a production on an IFR flight.

Can't Hear

Moving on, there's a relatively simple thing right after takeoff that often plagues pilots. Somehow, if there is to be communications difficulty, it seems to come more often as we depart. Perhaps the number-two radio is not used until we try to talk with the departure controller, and the radio isn't up to snuff or the squelch is incorrectly set. Or perhaps the audio switches are positioned incorrectly, or the frequency is simply not the correct one. Whatever, the result is an unanswered call to departure control.

Loss of radio contact shouldn't be considered an emergency, or even an event of air-shaking importance, because there are procedures to study and follow. A pilot should always have a plan in mind for continuation in the event of loss of two-way communications. It is a cinch you can't park the airplane on a cloud, and generally the controller is going to expect you to behave as flight-planned unless there might be a good reason not to do so.

For example, were the trip a very long one, the lost communications procedures would serve but would probably also foul up the air traffic control system over a great distance. In such a case, the controller at the airport of departure might hope you can land somewhere else VFR or make an approach back into the airport of departure.

Loss of communication is far less critical in a radar environment, too, because they are watching and will protect a lot of airspace for an IFR airplane with which they can't communicate. If they see the aircraft maneuvering for a return-and-land, they would clear the airspace.

The chances of no communication being possible, especially if you have a handheld, are pretty remote, and if it ever happens, knowledge of the lost communications procedures coupled with some logic and common sense will likely save the day.

Nav Loss

Consider other avionics failures. A rule requires a report on the loss of navigational gear. Don't fail to make such a report or to ask for any special favors that might seem in order because of the failure. For example, if, after losing one VOR, you are told to hold at an intersection identified only by two VOR radials, ask for relief. Holding at such a point with one VOR is certainly possible, but the attempt is better avoided. There was once a tragic collision between airliners that was related to an intersection and an airplane with only one VOR receiver, and that lesson shouldn't be lost on us.

Even though the rules don't specifically require it, any other failure—such as a vacuum pump or alternator—should be reported to the controller. The people on the ground should know about anything that might have an effect on the pilot's performance in the system.

Low Fuel

If you get your hand in the cookie jar on fuel and it looks as if it might be close, air traffic control should be told that the flight is arriving with minimum fuel. That'll help smooth the way. But watch out for cutting corners on any such approach. An extra mile or two on final to get it all lined up consumes a lot less fuel than a missed approach, and a missed approach is a likely follow-up to an over-expedited arrival. If the fuel might likely be less than "minimum" and priority handling will be necessary to land with any fuel, then the word is *emergency.*

While making any approach in a retractable, consider what you might do if the landing gear extension system should malfunction. The landing gear shouldn't normally be extended until at the final-approach fix inbound. Dragging an extended landing gear farther than necessary is a pure waste of fuel, and wasting fuel is bad, regardless of how much is in the tanks. Waiting until this late in the approach does mean that the gear probably can't be extended with the emergency system while you are continuing the approach. If the pilot already has one problem, such as low fuel, a malfunction of the gear-extension system means that the dominoes have begun to tumble. Low on fuel, I for one might well follow the path of least resistance and just continue and land wheels up. That would beat running the risk of encountering still another problem, such as fuel exhaustion, while flying around trying to get the wheels down.

Watch for Flags

The approach is a good time to give some more serious thought to navigational-system failures. The instruments have flags on them to indicate failures, but the flags are often hard to see. Too, we tend to look past flags. Many a pilot has thought that he or she was doing a perfect job of flying a needle, when in reality the needle was remaining centered because it was dead. I always set both nav receivers to the ILS frequency when on that type of approach; if ever the needles did not agree, I'd pull up and investigate. Many airplanes do not have dual glideslope receivers, so there we must watch for the flag and monitor altitude for logic. The glideslope altitude over the markers is published on the approach charts for a double-check. On a VOR approach, I set both nav receivers as appropriate for the approach whenever possible, for a consensus. On any approach, I monitor the ident of the facility continuously. Admittedly, this is a throw-back to the old days when the tower or other controlling facility would communicate with us over the navigational frequencies, but if letting down to within a few hundred feet of the ground based on information from a station, it's nice to know the thing is still beeping away. When GPS and Loran become common for approaches, I guess this will go away and we'll rely only on flags.

Air and Lights

Either of two system failures—vacuum or electrical—can pose serious problems, especially in single-engine airplanes, but either is manageable with a modicum of attentiveness and planning. Either failure does suggest a landing at the nearest suitable airport, which means that while you have to compensate, you don't have to do it for long. I've noted in Chapter 2, on partial-panel flying, what happens when the vacuum system fails. If the alternator fails, the critical thing is to catch the failure when it occurs. A low-voltage warning light is excellent for this, because it will come on very shortly after an alternator fails. Planning to maximize the energy stored in the battery can then start at the very beginning. If you don't catch a failed alternator for an hour, chances are you'll catch it when things start to fade. At that point, you are left with few options.

How long a battery lasts depends on a lot of things, including temperature, the condition of the battery, and current drain. There's nothing we can do about temperature. The only way we can influence battery condition is to service it regularly and buy a new one at specified intervals—every year, or two years at the most—instead of when the old one just falls over dead. Current drain is our controllable ace in the hole, and if it is minimized from the moment of alternator failure, there should be enough in the battery to last through an approach and landing.

It is safe to say that a good battery should handle one nav/com radio for at least an hour after an alternator failure. It should actually last much longer than that, but there is seldom a time when there's not a place to land within an hour. An alternator failure is a mandate to land as soon as possible, so there's nothing wrong with a 1-hour limit. I'd try to be down in 30 minutes. Turn off as much electrical stuff as possible and operate with one nav-com. If the controller insists, you might use the transponder, but it should be easy to work a deal to have the transponder operating only when and if absolutely necessary for the controller to handle the flight in an expeditious manner. In turning things off, be very methodical. If, for example, you missed the pitot heat, you'd have left on the item of highest electrical drain.

If you are really curious about how long your battery will last, the investment required is one battery charge. Turn on what you'd need to fly and make an approach, minimum, and then sit there, on the ramp, without the engine running, and see how long it takes the battery to become ineffective.

I'm a belt-and-suspenders man and have purchased a little hardware to make the failure of any system a bit less bothersome. I fitted my P210 with electric gyros—directional gyro and artificial horizon—

to back up the vacuum pump and instruments, and the vacuum pump itself is backed up with a standby. I carry two handhelds and about seven flashlights, which folks kid me greatly about. I have used a handheld only on that stormy night as I was plunging through clouds in the Philadelphia terminal area. I got my trusty little radio out of the briefcase and was soon back in contact with the controller. That made carrying it seem worthwhile forever.

It goes without saying that a complete engine failure is an honest IFR emergency. This is true whether the airplane is a single or a twin.

Engine Loss

In a single, there's not a lot of decision-making when the power fails completely. There are many things to do, though. First and foremost is to get the engine going again if possible. The chances are good that it stopped because of something the pilot did, and unless this happened to be using all the fuel, the next step is to right the wrong.

In case of fuel-system mismanagement, it takes time to get an engine going again. This is why tank-switching should be done at a non-critical time in flight. That last switch before an approach should be back at the time the descent was started from cruising level, for example. There, a mistake can be handled easily. Switch tanks incorrectly just before crossing the outer marker inbound, though, and the mistake will be difficult to handle.

In the unlikely event an engine failure is not pilot-induced, there are still many things that might bring life back to the power plant. If applicable, the carburetor heat control should have been pulled at the first sign of power loss. Move the magneto switch from "Both" to "Left" to "Right." If it runs, or runs better, on "Left" or "Right," leave the switch in that position. Turn on the auxiliary fuel pump if there is one. Enrich the mixture. Check the primer as locked, if applicable. Switch tanks even if there is gas in the one selected. Change anything that has a relationship to the engine. True mechanical breakages are rare. Engine failures are more likely related to fuel or ignition, and these things have handles and switches to set and reset. Try everything.

All the while, be active with the radio but do not change to 121.5 the instant something happens, and don't squawk 7700. If IFR, you are likely in contact with a controller, and if there is radar coverage in the area, you would be in radar contact. Just stay on the assigned frequency, tell the controller about the unhappy event, and let him get on with clearing any aircraft that might be IFR at a lower altitude. If he wants a change in frequency or transponder code, he'll say so.

The controller might also be able to give information on a nearby airport. There have been successful power-off IFR approaches (I know—my father made one once), and you'd hate to miss the chance to pull that off if there was an airport around. If you have a Loran or GPS with a "nearest airport" feature, you can probably get this information more quickly than the controller can give it to you.

If there is no airport within gliding range, spend the time devising the best gliding plan for the terrain. If there are ridges, glide parallel to them. If there is an Interstate highway, glide in that direction. The controller can help you with information on what is available. If you are over a lake, glide toward the shore. Too, it is good to be aware of the surface wind so that your impromptu arrival can be into the wind.

Unless it's zero-zero, you are going to break out of the clouds before reaching the ground. From there on in, it is the same as landing VFR. If there is any doubt at all about how much ceiling there will be, the airplane should be configured for the softest possible touchdown early in the proceedings. This varies from airplane to airplane, and it is a good idea to know the gear/flaps/speed arrangement that results in the lowest possible combination of forward speed and sink rate while still allowing good aircraft control. Try it out in the practice area some day. Note, too, that this would be a time when shoulder harnesses would appear to be the most valuable equipment in the airplane. Given anything other than the most impossible circumstance, shoulder harnesses will help make such a landing nothing more than a bruising inconvenience.

If you don't care to think about this, or if you don't feel comfortable flying in clouds with just one engine, there is a whole fleet of twins out there for sale. None, however, offer any automatic "safe" feature.

Twin

A power failure when IFR in a twin actually involves as much as or more than a power failure in a single. The event simply evolves in a different manner. There are more decisions to make, and a bad decision in a twin can be a lot more costly than a bad decision in a single.

To begin, the drill in a twin is much the same as in a single. Communicate the problem while trying to get the engine running again. If it won't run, feather the prop. Then take stock of the airplane's capability.

If you're flying in an area where the minimum en route altitude is higher than the airplane's single engine service ceiling, the outcome of an engine failure might be much the same as in a single. The task is thus the same. Arrange things in the most advantageous manner, considering the terrain. The operating engine can be used to minimize the descent rate, but watch the airspeed. If you get a bit slow in a conventional twin with one engine operating and the other one shut down, the loss of control that could follow is likely much more serious than any forced landing you have ever imagined.

A more likely event in a twin finds the airplane capable of making it to an airport after one engine fails. All the pilot must do is take advantage of the airplane's capability. This, however, can be a difficult task. The *i*s must be dotted and the *t*s must be crossed with a precision that is unknown to many general aviation pilots. That's why the twin has relatively more engine-failure-related fatal accidents than the single. We'll explore proficiency in Chapter 15 and confine the discussion here to the decisions.

Once it is decided that the airplane is maintaining altitude, the next step is to choose the airport for an arrival. Snap judgment might well suggest the closest airport, but this isn't always the best place to go. Weather, field length, and terrain are all important considerations.

For example, rather than flying a VOR approach to minimums at an airport with a 3,500-foot runway that just happens to be 10 miles away, I'd rather fly 100 miles on one engine to a big airport with an ILS and a bigger runway. Why? Because once you reach a certain point in the engine-out approach with a twin, the airplane demands absolutely perfect flying technique. There is a point on the approach at which you become committed to the landing. I would rather try perfection with a precision approach and a long runway.

Another item: I would hesitate to fly an approach in poor weather at an airport without weather reporting facilities. The chance of a missed approach would be too great. It would seem a bad idea to give up the relative safety of altitude unless there was a good idea that the approach could be flown to completion. An engine failure is like a systems failure—the airplane should be flown to the nearest suitable airport and landed. The pilot's job is to balance all the factors in deciding on the nearest suitable airport.

All the while I was flying a twin somewhere to fly that engine-out approach, I would be much more at ease if I had gone to the trouble of maintaining proficiency in instrument approaches to minimums with one engine out. Once the approach begins, the decisions must be based on closing doors behind the twin with an engine out. Specifically, when the decision is made to descend below 500 feet above the ground, or to extend full flaps, I would accept that as a decision to land the airplane. Some might choose a lower altitude for this decision, based on conditions and the performance capability of the airplane. Once past certain things, though, the average light twin's available engine-out performance is too marginal to consider anything other than a landing.

This is one of those places where a pilot has to make decisions and be comfortable with those decisions. There might be cases where a go-around or missed approach would work, but at least a pilot should be aware that the best deal of all comes from flying the first approach perfectly and landing out of that approach.

Weather Emergencies

There are what might be considered emergencies in relation to weather. If, for example, a pilot bumbles into a thunderstorm, he or she may consider that an emergency. It isn't one in the true sense of the word, because there is no applicable immediate action other than remembering principles and doing the best possible job of keeping the airplane upright. The storm will pass, and unless the airplane sustains structural damage, the flight after the storm will return to a routine operation as the pilot's knees slowly cease knocking.

Ice can be considered a weather emergency, and has already been covered.

The other weather emergency that we might someday face has to do with blown forecasts. What do we do if the destination goes to zero-

zero, the alternate goes to zero-zero, and nothing else within fuel range has landing minimums? I think it goes without saying that a pilot who backs into such a corner has probably made some unwise weather decisions based on wishful thinking, but once there, you still have every right to try to extricate yourself without damage. One of the more difficult things to overcome might be the helpless, or hopeless, feeling that would have to exist after flying into a condition where this has to be contemplated.

It is extremely hazardous to even think about an emergency landing in below-minimum conditions unless the airport has a full ILS system. With the ILS, things look up, and a sharp aviator can put an airplane on an ILS runway in foggy weather if the airplane is flown with absolute precision. The ILS is precise enough, and if the runway is long and wide, it makes a good target.

In making an ILS approach in below-minimum conditions, I'd configure the airplane for landing when passing the outer marker. I'd put the gear down if in a retractable and set the flaps at the takeoff or approach position. If no takeoff or approach flap position is specified, I'd go for a partial flap setting that reduces stalling speed but still leaves the airplane in a more or less level flight attitude on the approach. For an approach speed, I'd select a value 40 to 50 percent above the stalling speed. Then I'd fly the ILS in the normal manner until reaching decision height. At DH, I would leave the descent as it had been while tracking the glideslope. Power and aircraft attitude would remain exactly unchanged. I'd then disregard the glideslope needle and concentrate on the localizer. If the localizer needle is kept in the center, the aircraft will fly to the center of the runway. The glideslope will usually lead the airplane lower than 200 feet with precision, but you really don't need it.

If the airplane has been tracking toward the runway in a vertical sense, and if it is on the glideslope at the decision height, a continuation of the status quo will lead to the runway. The glideslope leads the airplane to a point 1,000 feet down the runway, so there is some margin. There's less margin in the left-right sense. That is why the localizer needs all the attention. It's seldom so zero-zero that you won't see any runway and won't be able to flare. But if it were that bad, I might make a very slight nose-up adjustment in attitude at about 50 feet. That's all.

Then I'd work like the very devil on keeping the localizer needle centered and wait for the wheels to contact the runway.

GCA

Better yet, if I were to be backed into a corner with nothing but zero-zero around for an approach, I'd go to a military base and ask for a precision *ground-controlled approach.* I had a friend who once did this in a light twin. He was deluged with paperwork after his landing, but he strongly felt that it was worth every bit of it. With only a few gallons of fuel on board, had he not gotten to the proper place and made the approach the first time, he'd have been up a tree. Or *in* a tree.

One thing to consider here is the accident history of airplanes attempting very low approaches. In some cases, the airplane crashes before it gets to the airport. With information on the instrument panel about the location of both the runway centerline and a proper glidepath to follow to the airport, this is certainly uncalled for.

What If?

One of the most profitable ways to spend time while droning along en route is playing the old "what if" game. What if the cabin fills with smoke? What if the low voltage light comes on? What if the engine (or an engine) stops producing power? (On the latter, it's interesting to see how quickly you can calculate the potential gliding distance and the availability of airports within gliding range.) There are a multitude of situations to think through to a successful conclusion. And if you've thought it through enough times, you'll be able to fly with a steady hand and a cool head should a bad thing ever actually occur. It takes a lot of self-discipline to remain calm, collected, and well organized when things start going to the devil in a handbasket, but this is what succeeds if the motivation is there. And having thought through the problem a lot of times in advance makes the actual event at least one word removed from a true emergency. That word is "unforeseen."

13. The System

I like to think of "the system" as the direct government involvement with flying. Some consider it to be just the traffic control business, but there is enough interrelationship for us to consider the total. And, from the beginning, do acknowledge that the system is not something that works automatically or that protects us. The system is something that pilots must make work for themselves. What we get out of it is in direct proportion to what we put into it.

In examining the government's relationship with the IFR pilot, look first at the rules on qualifying to become one. We don't have to fly actual instruments in cloud to get the rating. Instrument instructors may have never flown in cloud, and I'd be willing to bet that there are FAA inspectors who have never conducted actual IFR operations in a light airplane and who would not willingly do so. A pilot who goes through and gets an instrument rating in such sterile conditions, from people without actual experience, had best know that his or her rating is only an indication of success at jumping through a government-prescribed hoop. Ability and knowledge have to expand far beyond that, in hand and mind, any time a rating is acquired under those conditions. The pilot need only recognize this to be okay. Ideally, it would be recognized early in the training process, and the pilot could switch to a school or an instructor that teaches instrument flying instead of test-pass. But if a pilot winds up with a "dry" instrument rating (meaning that he hasn't actually been in a cloud), there is nothing to keep that pilot from hiring another instructor for getting the rating wet.

The government's reluctance to prescribe the actual experience in training is as it should be. The rules are minimums. We have to be wise enough to know what the word *minimum* means. Look it up in your dictonary if you need a refresher.

The minimum relationship is also there as we move to the rules governing proficiency. Note that the only requirement is for so many hours of instrument flying in the recent past plus a prescribed number of approaches. We desperately need a better proficiency program than the one required by law, and this will be discussed in Chapter 16. Look next at the rules governing hardware—the airplane and equipment. Again, the word is *minimum*, and very few general aviation pilots fly IFR with anything approaching the minimum in equipment. Some of the requirements—altimeter and transponder checks, for example—seem of more nuisance value than anything else, but the government must play its game.

Altitudes

When we come to altitudes, we must really come to terms with the meaning of the word "minimums." Some feel that government-prescribed altitude minimums are a decree of how we should fly. That is not the case. Instead, think of minimums as numbers defining the lowest possible altitude at which we can fly without hurting. The margin for error in minimum altitudes is slim, especially on approach, and we cannot fly with the thought of being plus or minus a hundred or so feet. It had best be all plus.

Ice and Storms

The rules don't help much when it comes to bad things like thunderstorms and ice. There is no rule against flying into a thunderstorm, and there is no specific operating rule about flying IFR into icing conditions in a light airplane that is not for hire. (Flight in icing is prohibited in aircaft limitations.) The lack of regulation here is good, because any law prohibiting flight in relation to dynamic weather situations is impractical at best. When the FAA does try to write a rule on ice, the rule becomes ambiguous.

For example, the air-taxi operating regulations prohibit flight into known or forecast icing conditions (unless the airplane is equipped with deicing equipment) and then hedge by saying that if current reports and briefing information indicate the ice won't be there, it is okay to fly on. The buck is clearly passed to the pilot. That's where it belongs, and that's the only place it can be handled. The pilot must only realize that no outside source, no mystical "they," no system, and no regulation offers any protection against the elements.

To this point we've talked about regulations. There is no shortage of those, and while we can find some guidance in them, common sense and a strong feeling of responsibility will often carry the day better than any rule.

For example, a new flight instructor asked me what I would do if I had a communications failure and then encountered potentially debilitating icing conditions at the altitude I would be expected to fly according to prescribed lost-communications procedures. No rule covers that. I'd squawk 7700, the emergency code, on the transponder, and go about the business of extricating the airplane from the icing condition in the quickest and most effective way I could devise. In fairness to others, I would try to imagine where other IFR traffic might be operating and would do everything possible to avoid any possible conflict. I sure wouldn't look to any rulebook for guidance.

The People

When we set out to fly an actual IFR flight, the point of first system contact might be the flight service station, unless you get your weather information with a computer. The FSS is an important part of the general aviation pilot's IFR system because it is where we start working with people. It can also be the prime point of information. Again, remember that the system is not automatic. Even with government people involved, we have to make it work for us to get maximum benefit.

Some pilots tend to put themselves at the mercy of the FSS briefer, as if to leave the go/no-go decision in his or her hands. This is bad, because if a pilot doesn't have the intelligence to obtain information, interpret it, and make a sound decision on a flight, then the pilot's training is inadequate and his or her fanny is in danger. Don't forget that an IFR pilot should, for self protection, strive to know more about the effects of weather on the airplane than any briefer at a flight service station might know. Meteorological knowledge becomes increasingly important as the FAA phases out the concept of one-to-one weather briefings from flight service stations and leaves the pilot to automated means of extracting weather information from government or private sources. A pilot will have to be able to evaluate the general situation in order to know what specific information to seek. As always, an overview—the big picture—will be important. Fortunately, this is available on TV.

Air Traffic Control

So far as human relationships go, the IFR pilot spends far more time in the company of the air traffic controller than with any other person we deal with in flying. In a lifetime, an active pilot might spend more time in conversation with air traffic controllers than with his or her own kids. Certainly we spend more time with the controllers than with an instructor, inspector, or flight service station specialist. The proper relationship with the air traffic controller should not be master/slave (in either direction). And the old question asked of a controller by an airline captain must be qualified. The captain asked: "Am I up here because you're down there, or are you down there because I'm up here?" In truth, it works both ways. If we didn't fly IFR, they wouldn't have a job, but if they weren't doing their job, an IFR flight wouldn't work very well.

The part about making the system work for you is very pertinent when dealing with air traffic control. The controller makes it work for himself—the job, pay, and working conditions are quite good—and the controller will make the overall traffic control system work for everyone on general terms. But the individual pilot must find the proper piece of airspace in which to fly, file a flight plan outlining the use of that airspace, operate the airplane per the clearance, and request any changes deemed advisable or necessary once en route.

It is very important not to feel like a slave to the system in time of need. For example, if you need to fly at a lower altitude—the published minimum en route altitude shown on the chart, for example—the controller might balk. If there is controller reluctance to this, it might be caused by the fact that radio or radar coverage isn't good at low altitudes, and controllers do not like to lose contact with airplanes. But there is a way to do it, and if you need that low altitude and make the request clearly, it should be honored. The controller is paid to do any extra work that might result from your being out of contact for a while.

Difference of Opinion

Often a controller will not approve a routine pilot request. Sometimes this is because there is conflicting traffic; often it is for procedural reasons. In case of the latter, all airplanes are sent along certain paths at certain altitudes regardless of inconvenience, even if there is no traffic in the airspace the pilot would prefer to use. As illogical as it seems to us, there is some justification for this. It brings a predictability to the flow of traffic and makes the controller's job easier. But if it still bothers you as a pilot, don't hesitate to speak up. Do so on the phone, to the chief of the facility involved. Do not argue about such things on the radio.

Other Side

Pilots are certainly not perfect; in fact, controllers do their work in a more uniform and skillful manner than do general aviation pilots. If we are to pick at their system, we need to work to understand their problems and to correct our own areas of need. One way to start is by trying to understand the basics of the air traffic control task.

An IFR pilot who has not visited both an air route traffic control center and a terminal radar control room is lacking the important overview of the system that is necessary to keep from being a misfit. Just watching the handling of a flight helps to shed light on many areas of misunderstanding. For example, you can't really get a feel for the controller's problem at a big and busy airport until you watch the line of blips on final, three miles apart, all fed to that line from various fixes in the terminal area. Watch that for long enough and a general aviation airplane will show up, at which point the controller is likely to ask the question, "What will be your speed on final?" Speed is an important thing to the controller, and we should understand that the more nearly we conform to the flow of traffic, the better.

One rainy day at Washington National, I heard a Bonanza pilot illustrate how *not* to do it by answering: "Eighty knots." He didn't understand the problem. The big jets are going to be flying at least 120 knots when inside the marker, and fitting an 80-knotter into the string is difficult. The controller had no choice but to make extra room. The Bonanza pilot could just as well have flown his final at 120 knots, smoothing both the flow and the general aviation pilot's image.

In watching controllers do their work, a pilot may find the two-dimensional nature of the air traffic control system to be the most impressive thing. The airplanes all appear on one flat radar screen. The controller has to look at and interpret the altitude readout to know that the airplanes are properly separated. That is why the altitude reporting transponder is so important to the air traffic control system.

As we fly along VFR, we might not see a lot of traffic because we have random vertical as well as horizontal separation. But the scope can indeed appear crowded and hectic to the controller at the same time. The way the controller sees it is okay for his purposes, because the task is to keep airplanes separated as they move to and from airports, and in the crucial beginning and end, flying is two-dimensional. All airplanes start and stop on the ground.

The Relationship

There have been and always will be differences of opinion between pilots and controllers. The depth of this disagreement was illustrated in the 1981 controller's strike. The strikers literally found themselves without support in their argument with the government. Few pilots were on their side. I was flying, or trying to fly, the day the strike started and was in the lobby at a general aviation airport when President Reagan announced that he would fire the strikers if they didn't return to work. A large number of pilots were watching the TV in the lobby, and a loud cheer rang out for Reagan's determination.

Part of the pilot-controller schism was a result of the times. A strike by any other group of public employees would have aroused the same sentiments. A widening gap between pilots and controllers before the strike contributed strongly, though. An ever-smaller number of controllers are pilots, and a pilot working as a controller just puts more feeling into the work and has a better understanding of the problems on the other end. When a person calls in and requests an altitude change because of turbulence or ice, a controller-pilot might well have been in a similar situation himself. He knows the discomfort. Likewise, one who has flown in the canyons of cumulus knows how helpful it is to have word of any weather return from the traffic control scope.

The controller who doesn't fly is more likely to look at the job as a task that isn't even related to aviation. The atmosphere in a radar room just doesn't have an aeronautical flavor. It's more like a TV station, and the individual controller's workplace and scope might be said to resemble a slow-motion video game. Having said all that, I'd add that the non-pilot controllers, on balance, do an excellent job—just not with the same feeling or understanding.

Other than visiting a center or tracon, we can do something else to further pilot/controller understanding. AOPA has long promoted a "fly-a-controller" program, and it is a constructive effort. I went through it a while back and found that, just as the picture became clearer to me when I visited their place, the picture became clearer to them when they flew in my airplane. I took two out on a round-robin IFR, including a climb to 19,000 feet. I knew that controllers have trouble grasping the somewhat weak climb capability of airplanes like mine, and I wanted them to see how it looked from inside the cockpit.

The Mighty Computer

Fitting into the computerized scheme of things in our air traffic control system program is important. If an airport has published standard instrument departures and/or arrivals, the flight plan had best be based on the use of these. If there are preferred routes published for the trip, the flight plan should be based on the published routes. This makes us feel subservient to the computer, but you can take some long delays while they fool with a flight plan that doesn't fit into the programmed way to go. If the program is ridiculous, as some are, take it up later with the powers that be at the traffic control facility involved. If you do want to fly direct routes with Loran or GPS or other area navigation gear, file the direct legs but start the direct part once clear of any terminal area and fly direct to a point before entering the destination terminal. For example, leaving the Washington area, I usually get a direct clearance to anywhere after reaching the Kessel vortac, which is west and well clear of the terminal area.

Using general aviation airports for IFR operations is at times complicated by the fact that there is no direct communication with air traffic control when you are on the ground awaiting departure. Where there is a will, there is a way, though, and if there is no radio contact, the telephone becomes one means of communication. Even that can have its perplexing moments.

I remember arriving by car at a small field early one Sunday morning before the office opened. I had an IFR on file, and the weather was below VFR minimums, so it wouldn't be possible to depart and then get a clearance when in radio contact. There was no place to call at the airport, for sure, but then I remembered a roadside phone booth a few miles back. I drove there, called the approach control facility covering the airspace, and got a clearance with a void time. It worked fine, and I was soon off.

Do be wary on IFR departures from VFR airports. If an airport with an approved approach has any necessity for special departure procedures to avoid terrain or obstructions, this will be noted on the chart. Leaving a VFR airport under IFR conditions, you must study the situation yourself and make certain the climb path and gradient will provide proper clearances. The system offers no protection in such a case.

The air traffic control system was designed for the air carriers, but the by-product that has become our part of the system is still quite good and workable. But again, we must make it work for ourselves. The local airport won't have an instrument approach unless someone requests that one be approved. Your IFR flight plan doesn't go on file until you make the call. The decision on weather is yours. Once you're en route, the altitude changes and deviations in flight path necessary for comfort and safety are of your choosing. The friends (or enemies) we make as we fit into the flow of traffic are products of individual actions. And our relationship with the people of "the system" is made good or bad on an individual basis. Be assertive, but smile when you speak, and things should go more smoothly.

14. The Machines

The first airplane that I used for instrument flying was a Piper Pacer. It was a basic airplane that taught me a lot of lessons about the machine versus the IFR environment. My Pacer IFR flying was done in the mid-fifties, and while the airplane was well equipped for its time, it was a little short by more modern standards. As a primary bit of avionic gear, I had a Narco Omnigator, which provided VOR and localizer plus VHF communications and a marker-beacon receiver. An ADF was fitted, and in three years I went through as many different radios in a space on the right side of the panel.

First there was a low-frequency receiver and VHF transmitter. But low-frequency ranges were on the way out, and I replaced it with another Narco, a Superhomer, that gave me a backup VOR but with accuracy that was not really adequate for IFR flying. That gave way to a crystal-controlled 60-channel transceiver, an improvement on my ability to communicate. The Pacer also had a wing-leveler autopilot that used the rudder instead of the ailerons, as more modern units do. Except in the rare instances when a radio would malfunction, I never felt short. I could navigate and talk—enough for the time—and the wing-leveler would handle that chore when I needed to look at a map. It was before the advent of Loran, GPS, DME, and transponders, so those items were not even missed. And to my knowledge there was not a glideslope receiver available for smaller general aviation aircraft, so I had no real basis for wanting in that area. In retrospect, it was the lack of a glideslope that put the most severe limitation on the IFR use of the Pacer.

Minimum descent altitudes (they were just plain minimums then) for VOR or for localizer approaches were usually 400 to 500 feet above the ground, with required visibility values from a low of half a mile on some localizer approaches to up to a norm of a mile for most non-precision approaches.

The weather seems to know about those minimums, and the majority of instrument approaches were either in conditions comfortably above the 500-and-1 specified for many nonprecision approaches, or between that value and the 200-and-½ we most often see listed as the acceptable decision height and visibility values for a full ILS approach.

Pitting an airplane of the Pacer's performance and range—100 knots, 5 to 6 hours of fuel—against a basic 500-and-1 weather requirement often created sticky situations. This was especially true when there was a headwind to contend with. The thing that I learned quickly was that endurance is extremely important in an IFR airplane, especially in a slow IFR airplane, and that a glideslope receiver is a very desirable item because of the lower minimums it affords.

Endurance

Endurance is of critical importance in a relatively slow airplane because it takes a lot of it to create range, especially with a headwind. The weather in which you fly is influenced by the progress you make in moving through the features on the map. If the southeast is socked in, as it often is in January, the closest haven might be way on the other side of the Appalachian Mountains. If you were milling about the Atlanta area in a 120-knot airplane with fuel for an hour and a half, you would be running on fumes by the time you reached Nashville— even without a headwind.

For an example of how endurance with a headwind becomes more critical the slower an airplane cruises, let's look at three airplanes with five hours' endurance. With no wind, a 120-knot-cruise airplane starts with 600 nm absolute range; a 140 knotter will go 700, and a 160 knotter, 800. Now, point those airplanes into a 40-knot headwind. The 120-knot airplane will go 400, the 140 can manage 500, and the 160-knot airplane will still cover 600 nm. So, a headwind of a given value slices a greater percentage off the range of the slower airplane. The 120-knot airplane is down to two-thirds of its original range; the 160-knot airplane hangs in there with three-fourths of its original range.

The effect is more pronounced when the IFR reserve and alternate requirement is considered. Given 45 minutes for the law and 80 nm to fly to the alternate, the 120-knot airplane with five hours' fuel has only 3 plus 55 to match against en route distance. With a 40-knot headwind, the available range for flight planning is only around 300 nm with the absolute minimum reserve requirements and no fuel set aside for contingencies. The real range is more like 250 nm. The departure point, destination, and the alternate can all be under the influence of the same weather system on hops that short. Add the higher weather minimums required in a no-glideslope airplane to the range restrictions, and you can see why the ability to fly lower approaches and choose alternates with a worse forecast is worth a lot in a slower airplane. To say nothing of having plenty of fuel. I'd add that the basic four-place airplanes are still excellent IFR machines, especially with long range tanks. The Skyhawk, for example, with its largest tanks, is a seven-hour airplane.

There's another factor on fuel, too. As our fleet of airplanes ages, there are more and more modifications available to give them a little extra something. One mod I added to my P210 was a 29.4-gallon fuselage tank. This makes a dramatic difference in that the total of this fuel can be added to the en route portion of the flight because the alternate and reserve is already taken care of. Where with a solid hour in reserve it used to be a four-hours-and-down airplane at high cruise power, it is now good for five hours and forty-five minutes. Add thirty minutes for moderate cruise power. In either case, if an hour had to be taken off for a trip to the closest legal alternate, that extra 30 gallons would increase the range of the airplane by a lot.

West Virginia

Endurance combined with greater speed can make a more dramatic difference than is immediately apparent in some hypothetical IFR trips. A good example relates to West Virginia—not a large state but one of the most difficult eastern states to get across westbound in the wintertime.

While the West Virginia mountains are not really big ones like the Rockies, they affect the flying air from 50 to 100 miles to the lee side when the westerlies are strong. Long before you reach Martinsburg, West Virginia, which is east of most of the mountains, strong updrafts and downdrafts can be encountered. Cloud tops become higher. A flight that was doing perfectly well at 8,000 feet becomes uncomfortable. Then 10,000 becomes uncomfortable, and 12,000 is no bargain. The area below the clouds is quite turbulent, even if there is plenty of clearance between the clouds and the mountains. From the point where you start working with the updrafts and downdrafts and with higher cloud tops to where it all starts to taper off is about 200 nautical miles. This means that with the usual headwind, a slower airplane might test its maximum IFR range just getting through the effect of westerlies over the mountains in a relatively small state.

Often the choice is between landing and refueling just before starting across, or facing the possibility of a stop in the mountains. I'll always remember testing the endurance of my Pacer one winter day in going from Martinsburg, West Virginia, all the way to Charleston, West Virginia. Nonstop!

Up and Over
Climbing and ceiling go hand-in-hand with speed because some of the extra power used to make the airplane go faster can just as well be applied to climbing. The basic four-place airplanes climb between 600 and 700 feet per minute and hit the ceiling at 13,000 feet. The 140-knot airplanes climb half again as well, and most have ceilings of around 15,000 feet. The 160-knot airplanes are usually quite a bit heavier and don't show a lot of climb and ceiling performance advantage when flown at gross weight. But with the same payload as a smaller airplane, they climb a lot better. Turbocharged airplanes are quite a different matter, as we saw in Chapter 11.

An airplane's altitude ability can be a factor in winter flying. It's often the only tool to use in dealing with ice, and an airplane that is unable to get to at least 15,000 feet can be at quite a disadvantage. An example comes to mind. The flight was across West Virginia in a Cardinal RG; luckily, it was eastbound. I had my oxygen bottles along. In fact, oxygen can be necessary equipment for wintertime IFR in a non-pressurized airplane because it can be a go/no-go item. You can't fly as high as 15,000 or 17,000 feet without it, and the flight in question would not have been possible at lower altitudes.

It took some coaxing to get the Cardinal RG to 17,000 feet, but it finally made it. I was able to avoid most clouds (and thus the ice) in the climb. The tops started at about 11,000 feet and then sloped upward as I moved toward the mountains. The highest general tops were 15,000, with some buildups to 17,000 feet. The trip was smooth and serene with a few deviations around buildups. A lower trip would have been turbulent. Had I been blessed with a turbocharged airplane this day, I'd have whipped on up to Flight Level 210 (21,000 feet) and enjoyed an even better trip.

There's one other factor to consider in your IFR airplane. Useful load is important, because if you don't have enough of it for your average mission, fuel will have to be left out, thus cutting endurance and range. The old saw about buying two more seats than you'll ever use usually handles this pretty well, though a lot of airplanes have payload/range capability that allows all seats to be filled. Just don't fail to consider this carefully—in advance.

Which?

We have considered speed, endurance, climb, and ceiling as performance parameters with a definite effect on instrument flying. It is interesting to try to put the four in order. Which one means the most? It's tempting to go for speed, but that's not worth a whole lot without reasonable endurance. And I think it takes a great speed advantage to overcome a great endurance advantage.

Take, for example, that Skyhawk with seven hours' fuel. It'll chug along at 120 knots. Would a 140-knot airplane with four hours of fuel be more useful? I think not. You'd have to stop too often. Of course a lot of this depends on average trip length. If you move around within a couple of hundred miles of home base, neither speed nor endurance variations between popular light airplanes will have a lot of effect on your missions. Start running around half the country, though, and the speed/endurance equation demands careful analysis.

Rate of climb does a lot of things for an airplane in instrument flying. I remember a comment that was made while I was leaving Dallas one warm winter day in my Skyhawk. A colleague was flying the airplane, which was loaded to maximum weight. As we struggled upward at 500 or fewer feet per minute, he remarked that a larger engine would surely be nice in the airplane, if for no other reason than to improve the anemic climb rate. "Why," he said, "if you encountered the least ice and the tops were as low as 5,000 or 6,000 feet, you might never make it on top when climbing like this."

There are two ways to buy climb capability. One is with raw horsepower, the other is with turbocharging. When gross-weight climb figures are examined, the best sea-level climb we generally see for single-engine airplanes is in the neighborhood of 1,000 feet per minute, plus or minus some. Add turbocharging to a single, and it won't climb any better at sea level but it will maintain rate of climb as it goes up. Couple this with a high service ceiling and increasing true airspeeds aloft, and it is obvious that the turbocharger can offer answers to IFR questions. The combination of an aerodynamically clean airframe and an efficient and reliable turbocharging system is hard to beat.

Buying a twin is another way to get more rate of climb. If a twin will climb at all on one engine, that means that the power of the other engine can be devoted to extra rate of climb when you are operating with both engines. The results are comparatively spectacular. Most light twins go up half again as well as the best singles, or even better. The rub comes at the gas pump, and with fuel efficiency and cost a big thing, carrying a lot of extra horsepower around for the sole purpose of being able to climb better might not be an enduring proposition.

Most IFR users find an airplane that climbs somewhere near 1,000 feet per minute to be adequate. Climb rates below that involve compromise and might cause an occasional cancellation due to low rate of climb or correspondingly low service ceiling. Poor climb can also perplex air traffic controllers, who are used to watching high performance airplanes climb.

When comparing high initial rate of climb, as with an untur-bocharged twin, and high service ceiling, as with a turbocharged single, the practical IFR aviator would probably opt for the turbocharged single. The value there would have to be balanced against the missions flown. In the west, an airplane simply is not an IFR airplane unless it is turbocharged. In the east, wintertime trips can often beg for tur-bocharging to avoid ice or to take advantage of strong westerlies aloft on eastbound trips. In the summertime, turbocharging can keep the climb rate peppy up to comfortable IFR altitudes, and can often make possible a flight on top of haze and murk. Without it you are down where you can't see the cumulus and cumulonimbus imbedded in the smaze until the last minute; with it you can be at Flight Level 200, sur-veying the scene without restriction to visibility.

Handling Qualities

How an airplane flies is very important to the IFR aviator, and prefer-ence here is usually based more on the pilot than on any envisioned mission. If the pilot is a tiger about staying proficient, the aerodynami-cally slickest airplane is the best deal, because it is the most efficient. If a pilot feels that he or she won't be doing a lot of IFR flying and the missions are generally short, then an airplane that is slower might be more forgiving of error and the better deal. An airplane in the class of the Piper Warrior, for example, is very good for a pilot who wants a nice stable platform that doesn't rush things. Remember: the faster you fly, the faster you have to think. An IFR flight between here and there involves about the same number of tasks in a Learjet and a Warrior, but there is less time for the work in a Learjet.

Before going on with the subject of handling qualities, it is impor-tant to consider that while an instrument rating gives the legal okay to fly IFR in a lot of different airplanes, this doesn't mean that it is advis-able for a pilot to fly IFR in all airplanes for which he is rated. If you get a rating and are proficient in a Beech Sundowner, for example, best not tangle with a Bonanza or a Baron in IFR operations without some IFR dual flying in those airplanes.

In considering the fine points—control forces, trim changes, roll and pitch stability—it is best to fly an airplane and see if it fits your hand and bottom. Some pilots like light control forces, some like heavy control forces, and there are arguments for both sides. It has been said that there is a correlation between light elevator forces and in-flight airframe failures. This is logical. Virtually all in-flight failures come after the pilot has lost control of the airplane. This means high airspeed and a gangbusters rate of descent. The pilot perceives a problem and attempts a recovery. The lighter the elevator forces, the less effort the pilot has to expend to break the airframe in a recovery attempt when the airspeed is far in excess of the limit. There's one hitch to the theory. The Bonanza, with light elevator forces, and the Cessna 210, with heavy elevator forces, apparently have an involvement in airframe failures that is about equal. The key is in the pilot's remaining in control of the airplane.

Pilots tend to think of airplanes that are light on the controls as being more responsive. This can be a factor in instrument flying. The slightest inadvertent movement of the controls changes the status quo, and if changes in heading could be magnified to hundredths of a degree, you'd probably find a pilot flying an airplane that is light on the controls darting about from one heading to another, while a pilot flying a less responsive airplane would show a much more stable heading. I know that in flying different types of airplanes for evaluation, I can usually do a better job of flying a strange airplane that is heavy on the controls. And I must admit that for transportation flying and IFR work, my personal preference is for one that is heavy on the controls. Once you learn the amount of force necessary to achieve the desired results, the airplane can be very accurately nudged around.

Rudder

We usually think of the ailerons and elevators as the controls most used, with the rudder being more of a trimming device used to keep the ball in the center. On many airplanes, though, the rudder can be a good primary flight control. In fact, some of the very first wing-leveler autopilots used the rudder, not the ailerons, to keep things on an even keel. The value of using rudder varies from airplane to airplane, but on most it can be effectively used to keep the wings level. If, for example, you want to look at a chart in relatively smooth air, it can be effective to take your hands off the wheel and use slight rudder pressures to influence any divergence from a wings-level attitude noticed in cross-checking from chart to artificial horizon.

The use of trim in relation to trim changes is important. First and foremost is the fact that you can't fly the airplane with trim. Its purpose is to relieve control pressures that have been applied to maintain a desired attitude. Trying to fly an airplane with trim alone results in a rather continuous swooping and dipping. What an airplane needs is to be held as desired until everything stabilizes. Then pressures should be gently trimmed away.

On my P210, the trim change that most often bothers people is a strong one that comes when extending full flaps. It takes a very strong push forward on the wheel to keep the airplane on the glideslope as the flaps extend—more push than many pilots are accustomed to—and I have watched a lot of people divert their attention to trim instead of shoving as necessary, stabilizing the airplane in the new configuration and then trimming.

Ride Quality

An airplane's response to turbulence is quite important in instrument flying because this combines with handling qualities to put the pilot's ability to the test in turbulence. Roll stability in turbulence is by far the most important, because a roll upset almost always precedes a pitch upset in a light airplane. Directional stability is also important, as is proven by the amount of money spent for yaw damper systems on more exotic airplanes. Whether any correlation could ever be drawn between yaw stability and loss of control, I know not. I can only say that I have never seen an airplane prone to yaw in turbulence develop an unusual desire to do anything other than just yaw.

Dutch roll, the roll/directional couple, is tough to deal with in turbulence. The airplane rolls and yaws from side to side (the wing tip makes circles on the horizon); fortunately, no current production airplanes have an extremely strong dutch-roll tendency.

The size of the tail surfaces on an airplane often tells a tale of how it will ride in turbulence as well as how it will fly. Bigger is usually better; so is a tail that is farther aft of the wing. In examining numbers, wing loading is the one most directly related to riding qualities. The higher the wing loading, the better the ride. Other things do indeed affect bounce qualities, but wing loading is the primary number to look at.

Another number to consider is span loading. We never thought much about this in general aviation until the Malibu came out. It has a lot of span for the same weight as some like airplanes and its ride in certain types of turbulence is busier.

Certainly, in picking an IFR mount, it is good to fly the airplane in turbulence and sample its ride and handling qualities.

Maneuvering Speed

Maneuvering speed is worthy of note, because this is the speed at which you'll be flying when the going gets rough. If maneuvering speed is quite a bit below the normal indicated airspeed at cruise, it will mean slowing down just that much in turbulence. Some see a low maneuvering speed as an all-bad thing, but it can have its advantages. You might have to slow down in turbulence, but a low maneuvering speed also means a low stalling speed, which in turn is a better deal should it ever become necessary to land the airplane on some surface other than a runway. The lower maneuvering speed often also means lighter wing loading, though, and thus more response to turbulence and a bumpier ride.

Perhaps the best of all worlds is having an airplane with a high flaps-up stalling speed, a corresponding high maneuvering speed, and an effective flap system that lowers the stalling speed as much as possible for landing.

Because maneuvering speed is generally used as the turbulent air penetration speed, we need to look a little more deeply into the subject.

While the airplane's strength in relation to gusts is based on top-of-the-green airspeed (that's why airspeed in the yellow is for smooth air only, as well as for pilots braver than I am), this is not the value most often given for turbulent air penetration. The best speed is one where the airplane will stall just as the limit-load factor is reached. As it relates to maneuvering loads, this is maneuvering speed and it is based on a simple mathematical formula. Multiply the square root of the limit load factor (3.8 g for Normal Category) by the stalling speed for the clean configuration and weight, and you have the maneuvering speed.

It can be estimated for maximum weight by doubling the number at the bottom of the green arc.

Because the technical definition of maneuvering speed relates to full or abrupt control movements, it might be modified slightly by strength considerations in the aft section of the wing, the horizontal tail, or of control surface or system considerations. Gusts, on the other hand, start their work at the leading edge of the surfaces. The end result—g-loading—is the same, but the onset is different. Also, turbulence is likely to be a series of increases and decreases in g-loading where maneuvering loads may be smoother in application.

Actually, the best speed in turbulence from a structural standpoint might be somewhat higher than maneuvering speed when only turbulence is considered. That doesn't really work, though, because the pilot is likely to be working the controls pretty hard in turbulence, so a speed that gives the best deal against abrupt control use might be the best. While maneuvering speed might be conservative, it has withstood the test of time.

Another advantage to the conservative nature of maneuvering speed is found in the nature of the gusts that we plow through, whether they are from mechanical or convective turbulence. There are both horizontal and vertical motions out there and this can affect airspeed, which will increase if the gust value is increasing from ahead. The airspeed jumps around a lot in bumps and there's little chance we will keep it pegged precisely. Some margin is thus required, and maneuvering speed gives this.

In discussing this, the related question has to do with the strength of airplanes. They are really quite strong. Airplane manufacturers design extra strength into airplanes to exceed the FAA's requirements. In testing, the manufacturer is required to go to one-and-a-half times the limit load factor without a failure. A Normal Category 3.8-g airplane must test to 5.7-g without breaking, although things are allowed to bend. Most go beyond the requirement to see what happens, and at times this is done to develop information to use in defending a lawsuit. I was once told that this was done with the wings of a Cessna 210 and that they broke when the static load in ground testing reached the equivalent of over 7-g. That is a static load, though, and flights loads can be a lot different, especially if the airplane is operated outside the allowable speed envelope, which it usually is after a loss of control.

Examining accident reports reveals that most but certainly not all airplanes that are lost around thunderstorms are lost because of a loss of control. The turbulence may cause the loss of control but, in itself, turbulence does not usually break the airframe.

When an airplane goes outside the speed envelope, one of the bad things that can happen is *flutter*. This is the development of an unstable oscillation in part of the airplane. A horizontal tail or wing has some elasticity, and at very high speeds or conditons of loading, the aerodynamic forces can interact with the airframe in a manner that can excite the structure and cause flutter. Excessive play in a control system could contribute, and once flutter starts, the airframe probably fails in a very short time. There have been cases of pilots encountering flutter and coming back to tell about it, but these are rare.

Again, flutter occurs only at speeds well above the limits, and those speeds are reached only when the pilot loses control of the airplane. Aerodynamically clean airplanes accelerate more rapidly when control is lost; the result is that most airframe failures occur in retractables.

Getting Down

Another important speed-related item is an airplane's descent capacity. The most demanding IFR descent situation is where the desire is to lose altitude as rapidly as possible in an area of turbulence that necessitates flying at maneuvering speed. Keeping the engine(s) warm during such a descent is also a consideration, and many airplanes offer more questions than answers in such a situation. If there is no way to descend at a rate of 1,000 feet per minute at maneuvering speed with the engine developing enough power to stay warm, there will be awkward moments or times of rapid engine cooling. The latter can have a very detrimental effect on engine life. Note also that in almost all airplanes, the use of approach flaps would not be allowed in this descent situation, because the use of flaps lowers the limit-load factor of the airplane. That is not a good thing to do in turbulence.

When flying a retractable, the landing gear often serves well as a speed brake in a descent. Do note the relationship between the maximum allowable landing-gear speeds and maneuvering speed, though. The ideal situation is with the gear speed at or above maneuvering speed.

Being able to control speed in turbulence is important, and one related factor is worth noting again and again: generally, the turbulent air speed should be reduced when the airplane is flown at light weights. I know this is contrary to what some think is logical, and it always raises arguments. But it is based on sound principles and fact. For one thing, the span-wise distribution of weight changes with fuel burnoff, resulting in a greater concentration of weight in the center and less relieving weight in the wings. This increases bending loads. Too, the wing loading is lower at lighter weights, so the airplane will experience greater accelerations in any given gust, putting greater stresses on the total airframe.

Some misinterpret all this as suggesting that the airplane is stronger when flown at heavier weights. That is not necessarily true. Basically, the whole airplane is a known and established quantity at its maximum weight. If the total machine's ability to withstand a vertical gust of a given strength is to be maintained at weights lighter than gross, the speed must be reduced to help manage the product of that gust.

Fuel Injection

A powerplant feature worth pondering is fuel injection. This often offers the disadvantage of hard starting when hot or poor idling in hot weather, but all the minus points are related to that limited time, and fuel injection is very nice when flying IFR. There is no carburetor heat to fool with, and most systems either have an automatic alternate air source or an air supply that is not subject to impact ice or to clogging in heavy snow. Too, fuel-injection engines have better mixture distribution and can be leaned more precisely. All around, it is a better deal for an IFR airplane, though I have flown many an IFR mile in a carburetted Skylane. A carburetor air temperature gauge is very helpful here because it, instead of engine spluttering, tells you when to get some heat on.

The Panel

Moving from the basics of the machine to the inside, we find an almost unlimited selection of things to do with and for an airplane. The first step is to establish a basic IFR requirement and elaborate from that point as finances allow. A basic avionics package might consist of two contemporary nav-com radios or two separate com and two separate nav radios, plus glideslope, ADF, transponder, encoding altimeter, audio selector, and a marker-beacon receiver.

Before expanding that package, I'd next add some special IFR items that are not always included in aircraft. Static wicks are a necessity to help get rid of precipitation static, and even the wicks on some turbo-prop aircraft are nothing short of pitiful. Static wicks and the proper bonding of the control surfaces are essential items if Loran is to be used, because it is more affected than anything else on an aircraft.

A better navigational radio antenna than the standard cat's whiskers is also strongly advisable. Besides improving reception and accuracy, one of the good antennas will minimize the effects of precipitation static on the nav radios.

Next, consider the warning systems in the airplane, especially if it is single engine. Is there a low-voltage light that would quickly alert you to an alternator failure? If not, add one. Relying on the eye to catch a needle showing a discharge as the only available indication of alternator failure is pure foolishness. What about vacuum? Vacuum-failure warning systems are not as widely available as low-voltage lights, but unless the vacuum gauge is on the flight panel and is methodically included in the scan, some obvious indication of vacuum failure should be included on the panel. A better system is a standby vacuum source, required unless you are willing to bet everything on your ability at partial-panel flying.

The static wicks, antennas, and warning lights are minimum items, but they are things that are often left off. Too bad, because each contributes to serenity (or safety) of flight way out of proportion to cost.

A more personal item to add is a microphone switch on the control wheel. A lot of pilots resist the use of headsets, but use of these can cut the workload enough to make a difficult arrival easier. Just not having to pick up the microphone is an improvement and, if you also add an intercom, the communication with the person in the right seat is easier. I flew for years without headsets, and my hearing suffered, along with the ease of flying. Some argue that you can't hear what is going on with the airplane while wearing headsets, but I don't find that to be true. Fly with them for a bit and you know what normal sounds like, and anything abnormal is actually easier to hear.

Once past the basics, the choices are harder to make. In equipping a single, my next move past basic avionics would be redundant systems. I have already described what I have in my airplane, and for any airplane I would want a handheld and some backup for the attitude indication system—either an electric artificial horizon or standby vacuum.

Autopilot

A lot of pilots feel that an autopilot is a primary piece of IFR gear, and it can indeed be one of the friendliest things in an airplane. There are, however, considerations to autopilot use. The basis for an autopilot might well be in the pilot's outlook on its go/no-go status. In a single or light twin, if a pilot would not conduct normal IFR operations with the autopilot inoperative, then the pilot is probably depending too much on that autopilot. And if a pilot ever lets an autopilot fly an approach that the pilot would not attempt, said pilot is engaging in a terrible game of transistorized Russian roulette.

That aside, an autopilot is wonderful. Engage it, slide the seat back a notch, and carefully monitor the instruments as the mechanical wizard does its thing. Most autopilots fly more smoothly than humans, and you can actually improve your own technique by watching the machine's deft handling of the airplane. It works in a manner that puts a recalcitrant needle back in the center with a minimum of fuss. In the terminal area, let a good autopilot intercept the ILS and note how it nails the needles. Keep a hand lightly on the wheel and feel how smoothly it flies. Never, though, try to override an autopilot. Only one pilot can fly the airplane at a time, and overriding most autopilots in pitch will cause them to trim against you—all the way to an uncontrollable state, if you persist.

Should you ever let the autopilot fly the approach in actual IFR conditions? Absolutely. Why? Because it gives you the best possible deal. The autopilot will fly the approach with precision, and you are there to monitor its performance. If anything goes wrong, you can jump in and save its bacon. If you are flying the approach personally and goof up, the turned-off autopilot can't help you. But for each low approach you let the autopilot fly, hand-fly three or four under the hood on a proficiency flight and don't settle for any less perfection than that demonstrated by the autopilot.

When monitoring autopilot's performance, watch it closely. An autopilot is likely to malfunction every 500 to 1,000 hours. If you were flying with a real pilot you knew would likely have a heart attack while flying in the next 500 to 1,000 hours, you'd watch him like a hawk. Do the same for the machinery.

Be certain that you understand the effect of various failures on the autopilot. From which instruments does the autopilot derive information? What does the autopilot do when an instrument fails from loss of power source or any other reason? Also, what are the parameters that, when exceeded, cause the autopilot to shut down? All this information is in the flight manual supplement that covers the autopilot.

One area of primary and almost necessary use for an autopilot is when operating IFR in marginal VFR weather conditions. Given, for example, virtually clear skies but limited visibility in summertime haze, the autopilot can be given the primary task of maintaining heading and altitude while the pilot keeps up an active scan for traffic. When flying in such conditions, there is just no way to do a precise job of hand-flying the airplane while also doing the IFR chores and a thorough job of looking for traffic.

Flight Director

The flight director is an autopilot adjunct that uses the information given to the autopilot to command the human pilot to move the controls as necessary to make the airplane fly as per the program. A virtual necessity in more sophisticated airplanes, flight directors make hand-flying any airplane much easier. Most come in a package with an autopilot; few airplanes have a flight director with no autopilot. A flight director will tell of a straying from the desired condition before most pilots would catch on from using raw data, and it then tells how much attitude change is necessary to properly move the airplane to the selected condition. It is almost like having a flight instructor there, telling you when and how to move the controls.

Area Navigation and DME

DME, Loran, GPS and area navigation equipment add a great deal to an airplane's intelligence and flexibility in IFR operations. They also open up more instrument approaches; area navigation equipment can often be used for a straight-in approach where only a circling approach is available with a basic IFR package. The minimums are often lower on a VOR/DME or localizer/DME approach when compared with minimums without the DME.

En route, area-navigation gear makes possible direct routes (if the controllers approve, which they usually do), and when you get into the terminal area, you can have bearing and distance to the outer marker or the airport or any other point you might want. Sure, you can do without such capability, but it sure is nice. And the proliferation of area-navigation systems has brought the capability within reach of more pilots over the past few years.

The groundspeed readout from these systems can be very useful in catching erroneous wind aloft forecasts and choosing the best altitude for cruise. The ground track feature on most Loran and GPS units lets you tie down headings much more quickly. Most have a host of features that do nice things for the pilot.

Big Things

Deicing equipment and weather avoidance gear have long been available for light twins and have also come on strong for top-of-the-line singles. This is good. It recognizes the fact that pilots operate singles and twins in the same manner, and can put to good use the same equipment in both classes of airplanes. These items represent a large investment, and while many pilots believe they offer absolute answers to the ice and thunderstorm questions, they do not.

Deicing equipment is something to use while fleeing ice; weather avoidance gear is something to use in staying out of thunderstorms. I will say that after flying a P210 with deice plus airborne weather radar and a Stormscope, I became very attached to these devices. I won't say that they made possible a lot of trips that couldn't have been flown without them, but I will say that they were extremely helpful on a lot of flights.

Total Key

The airplane and each bit of equipment added to it come to a total, and there will always be compromises. Put in too much gear and the airplane might cost a fortune and weigh so much empty that the payload and/or range is on the short side of the average mission. Then the question becomes whether the heaviest and the most expensive item makes a contribution in proportion to its weight and cost. If it appears that the item in question makes possible one trip a year, or would result in your being able to conduct instrument operations to a couple of extra airports a year, is that worth the financial and weight compromises? Might the money be better spent on an airplane with more range, better climb and ceiling, or a higher cruising speed? After subjecting the heaviest and/or most expensive piece of gear to that test, go through it with some other items considered optional. There are plenty of choices. For a practical result, recognize that instrument flying introduces some factors that are not strong in VFR flying, and choose the machine for the mission on a methodical basis.

15. The Risks and Rewards

In aviation as in so many other things, a personal assessment of the risks involved has at times been based more on hearsay, guess, and assumption than on fact. This is both unfortunate and dangerous. It is unfortunate because in flying with unjustified hangups, we rob ourselves of utility, or at least we create unnecessary tension when doing certain things. It is dangerous because if we don't understand the real risks, we can hardly be expected to guard against them in an intelligent manner. A lot of pilots run high risks while going through a rather continuous version of building the levee on the other side of town from the river. They placate fears that have no basis in fact while ignoring the things that are proven killers.

What do I mean? The best illustration relates to the number of engines on an airplane. How many times have you heard people suggest that a person is crazy to fly IFR in a single-engine airplane? I have even seen newspaper articles—written by FAA employees—contending that single-engine IFR is not a wise practice. Such observations are based on ignorance of the actual risks, not on the experience of real people flying real airplanes.

The true illustration is found in accident reports. And as we examine accident statistics that cover three years, remember that singles are often flown by less experienced pilots, they often have less equipment, the airplanes average lower cruising speeds so range is more affected by winds aloft, and operational ceilings are often lower so more time is spent slogging along in clouds instead of flying on top. In spite of this, we'll find that there is no statistical risk that is unique to engine failure in single-engine airplanes. In fact, singles give a very good account in this area. I would hasten to add that engines can and do fail, though not very often, and there have been a few of those impossible ones where the engine failed when the airplane was over fog-covered mountains at night. Any pilot who flies a single in conditions like that is definitely accepting some extra risk, however slight.

Overview

Of the total events classified as accidents in general aviation, about 19 percent result in fatalities. Of the fatals, about 16 percent involve airplanes on IFR flight plans, which is half again as high a percentage as 15 or 20 years ago and an indicator of more IFR flying. Over half the accidents that occur on IFR flight plans involve fatalities, and two-thirds of these fatal IFR accidents occur in instrument meteorological conditions. So, while a high percentage of total accidents don't involve fatalities, a high percentage of IFR accidents do fall into this very serious column. In an average year, over half the IFR accidents are fatal. This clearly defines the risk management chore: identify the things that cause trouble and avoid them. If you trespass in IFR, there aren't many second chances.

Mechanical

Having started the discussion by saying that the number of engines on an airplane does not have a particular effect on risk, let's first look at the single-versus-twin picture. Remember, the comparison covers only IFR operations for a three-year period. Eight piston-engine twins were lost because of actual engine failures on IFR flights during this time period. One single was lost. If engine failures due to fuel exhaustion are included, we have to add three twins and no singles. So, for a three-year period, IFR flights, fatal accidents following engine failure, including fuel exhaustion, the score is TWINS: 11, SINGLES: 1. Remove the fuel exhaustion accidents and the score becomes TWINS: 8, SINGLES: 1. Now, you say, that doesn't mean a lot because twins fly IFR almost all the time and most singles seldom fly IFR. That still doesn't make up for the difference, because neither the FAA nor anyone else really knows with any accuracy how much the various configurations of aircraft use the system.

Flying magazine made a study of air route traffic control center records and found that of the piston-engine airplanes flying IFR on a "good weather" day, 27 percent were singles. The singles figure jumps to 36 percent on a "bad weather" day. So, while twins fly about twice as much as singles on an IFR day, they had eight times as many engine-failure-related accidents in a three-year period. And, incidentally, the veracity of the *Flying* study was more or less confirmed when the FAA administrator started using the figures in speeches, erroneously crediting them to an FAA study.

To find any IFR engine-failure advantage over singles, you have to go to turboprop twins. In the three-year period, there was one engine-failure-related turboprop fatal accident, the same as for singles. The turboprop fleet also flies about twice as much real IFR as the single fleet, so it has at least a 2:1 advantage. The jets do too: they seldom appear in the engine failure column.

When considering engines alone, only the piston twin seems to have had some unique IFR problems. Other airplanes are involved in engine-failure IFR accidents on a very occasional, random basis. The twin is there in numbers because the very marginal engine-out performance of most of them demands flawless judgment and flying technique after a failure. Unhappily, most general aviation pilots aren't up to the task.

The question must be taken past engines. To be realistic, it must be extended to systems—vacuum and electric. And, as you might expect, it's here that the single does show a weakness. In three years, nine singles were lost after the failure of a system. Four twins were lost in the same period, so the twin has a clear advantage. And when engine failures (other than fuel exhaustion) are combined with system failures, the score becomes TWINS: 12, SINGLES: 10.

Again, twins fly twice as much IFR, so when engines and systems are considered, twins do indeed have an advantage. I would add that these statistics are from a few years ago, before pilots started adding standby vacuum and redundant electrical power to singles. The improvements in those airplanes have probably improved the systems-related accident picture on singles, although they still do occur.

In the case of a system failure, the pilot of a single can still complete the flight safely, given good judgment and technique. Unhappily, some general aviation pilots aren't up to the task. Those are the same words I used to describe the twin problem after a failure, and I'm convinced that either the twin or the single could rival the turboprop and jet record if pilots were properly trained to begin with and if they maintained proficiency. The proliferation of dual systems for singles will come to affect the record, too, as airplanes with dual vacuum and/or electric systems become a substantial portion of the IFR fleet.

The strong relationship between systems failures and accidents was clearly demonstrated by the Cessna 210. In 1979, the airplane was certified with deicing equipment that was approved for flight into icing conditions. A high-capacity air pump was used to (1) create suction to drive the gyro instruments, and (2) provide pressure to operate the deice boots. The pump proved to have a very short service life. When a pump failed, the pilot had to revert to partial panel. With the autopilot installed on most of the airplanes, the total autopilot function also was lost. And the pump failure occasionally occurred at the time of deice boot cycling, which would usually occur in clouds.

At the time, the Federal Aviation regulations were not specific on the point of partial-panel flying, saying only that a pilot had to be competent in "simulated emergencies, including . . . equipment or instrument malfunctions" to get an instrument rating. The flight test guide said that the inspector or examiner "may simulate a partial or complete loss of flight instruments . . . ." There was thus no requirement, and while some examiners and inspectors demanded good partial-panel performance, others required very little in this area. Finally, there was no mention of partial panel in the recent-experience requirements.

Given a total lack of emphasis on the subject in training and proficiency, it's no wonder pilots did poorly at risk management in airplanes with a short service life on vacuum pumps.

An NTSB safety recommendation dealt with the subject and cited five accidents that occurred in just over a year. They are interesting because they defined a clear risk that wasn't effectively managed.

"On January 21, 1982, a Cessna Model P210N, N4947K, crashed in instrument meteorological conditions near Boise, Idaho. All four persons aboard the aircraft were killed. About 20 minutes after departing Boise, the pilot had indicated to the air traffic controller that he was 'losing his gyros,' and requested assistance in returning to Boise. Shortly thereafter, the aircraft broke up in flight. Examination of the pressure/vacuum pump revealed that the (frangible) plastic drive shaft had sheared.

"On November 20, 1981, a Cessna Model T210N, N4823C, crashed at Charleston, West Virginia. All three persons aboard, including two instrument-rated pilots, were killed. After indicating that he had experienced a complete loss of vacuum, the pilot had operated the aircraft in the emergency partial panel mode for about 20 minutes. However, during an attempted instrument landing system (ILS) approach, the aircraft struck a ridge at a steep angle of bank. Examination of the pressure/vacuum pump disclosed a sheared drive shaft.

"On September 25, 1981, a Cessna Model T210L, N94136, crashed at Big Timber, Montana, while on an instrument flight rules (IFR) flight plan; the pilot was killed. The aircraft was above the clouds at 19,000 feet when it was cleared to descend to 13,000 feet. The pilot lost control of the aircraft shortly after entering the clouds and the aircraft broke up in flight. The investigation disclosed that the pressure/vacuum pump shaft had sheared.

"On February 22, 1981, a Mooney Model M20F, N1919T, crashed at Montgomery Township, New Jersey; all four persons aboard were killed. The aircraft was on an IFR flight plan from Hilton Head, South Carolina, to Teterboro, New Jersey. Shortly before the accident, the aircraft had been flying above the clouds when the pilot reported a vacuum malfunction and inoperative attitude and directional gyros. The pilot continued to fly toward his planned destination and was subsequently cleared to descend into the clouds. Shortly thereafter, the aircraft crashed in a steep, high-speed, nose-down attitude.

"On December 2, 1980, a Cessna Model T210N, N4846C, crashed at Tazewell, Tennessee, killing all four persons aboard. The aircraft had departed Peachtree City, Georgia, on an IFR flight plan to Mansfield, Ohio. When the aircraft was at 12,000 feet, the pilot had called the Atlanta Air Traffic Control Center, saying '46C has lost vacuum, I would like to have immediate clearance back to Knoxville.' The pilot was cleared to proceed directly to Knoxville and to descend and maintain 8,000 feet. However, the pilot did not begin a descent until several minutes later, at which time the center asked if he needed special handling. The pilot declined and said '. . . everything's okay except for the vacuum.' Shortly after entering the clouds, with tops at approximately 10,000 feet, the pilot lost control of the aircraft. An examinaton of the wreckage revealed that the right wing and empennage had separated in flight. The examination also disclosed that the drive shaft of the pressure/vacuum pump had failed for unknown reasons."

There's no doubt that statistically, the risk in single-engine IFR after systems failures will show up to be rather high for that period—especially in Cessna 210s. But the reason is clear and the risk is manageable. Standby electric gyros and/or dual vacuum systems were subsequently fitted to many 210s, and there is now more emphasis on developing and maintaining proficiency at partial-panel flying. For this period there is little question that the primary mechanical relationship to serious IFR accidents—again, especially in Cesna 210s—had more to do with vacuum pumps than with the number of engines.

In examining the total of IFR accidents, it's clear that while mechanical problems are a factor, we shouldn't be obsessed with them. Good maintenance, thorough training, and conscientious work on maintaining proficiency will give a pilot the necessary ability to keep running the store while handling any glitches that might arise. Context: less than 15 percent of the fatal IFR accidents relate to mechanical failures; only a half a percent of the fatals in a three-year period were related to a mechanical failure of the engine on a single.

While on the subject of mechanical problems, it is fact that the more complex the airplane, the more likely a mechanical problem with the engine is to be involved in a serious accident, IFR or VFR. Still, there are relatively few that are related to IFR in instrument meteorological conditions. There, even with dual systems, we find a lot of systems involvement.

Ice and Thunderstorms

Ice and thunderstorms appear as a big risk to many pilots. They are on the list, too, with each hazard accounting for about 10 percent of the IFR fatals, plus or minus a bit. In studying specifics, ice accidents are prevalent in January. A few are not serious, involving only a hard landing. The main damage is to the landing gear and supporting structures, and to the pilot's pride. There are a few cases of an airplane becoming iced to the point that it can't stay up, but this is not a common occurrence. More likely is the accident in which the pilot stalls a well-iced airplane while maneuvering for landing after successfully getting the airplane out of the icing condition. Or, in another scenario, the airplane winds up short of the runway.

In managing the risk of ice, we must consider the equipment solution: deice and anti-ice gear that is approved for flight into icing conditions. Buy deicing and the problem will go away. Does it work?

In the three-year period used as a basis for this discussion, there were nineteen fatal ice-related accidents. Twelve of the airplanes were twins; all the twins were types that have available deicing and anti-icing systems, though all the systems are not approved for flight in icing. Of the singles, only one (a Cessna 210) could have had deice gear. It's not likely that all the airplanes that could have had deicing equipment did indeed have it, but some are bound to have been so equipped. And the point has to be that buying deicing equipment does not in itself constitute any reduction of risk. It's only something to use while fleeing ice. I think I would rather fly on cloudy and cold days with a conservative pilot operating barefoot than with a daredevil wearing deice boots.

Thunder

Thunderstorms rank with ice, and the problem peaks in the summertime. May, June, July, and August usually appear as the primary months, though thunderstorm-related accidents can and do occur in any month. Singles appear to have a substantially greater involvement in thunderstorm accidents than do twins. In the three years, there were ten singles and seven twins on the list. We've established that twins probably fly twice as much IFR, so the single record is clearly worse.

This doesn't relate to airframe strength. Singles and twins are designed to the same requirements. The single, being smaller and lighter, might be harder to control in the turbulence of a thunderstorm and, if slower, it would remain in the storm for a longer period of time. I think, though, that this is a case where equipment does have a strong relationship to accident statistics. More twins than singles have weather avoidance gear, and when used properly—for avoidance rather than penetration of weather—these devices are very effective. More singles are being equipped with either airborne weather radar or a Stormscope. Every airplane can have one or the other, and many now have both. If the effort is put into both learning all about the weather avoidance device at hand, and then using the device only for avoidance, the record here should improve, although the Malibu problems related earlier in the book show that the potential relationship between the airplanes and turbulence is still a consideration.

Mr. or Ms. Clean

Virtually all the singles lost in thunderstorms are retractable-gear airplanes. True, most singles flown IFR are retractables. There are still a lot of Skylanes, Skyhawks, Cherokees, and Saratogas out there on an IFR day. The fact is, the thunderstorm-related risk does increase with aerodynamic cleanliness. If a pilot loses control of the aircraft, speed builds quickly, and the airplane moves into a flight regime where destructive flutter might occur or where it would take only light turbulence or the application of a few pounds of control pressure to overstress the airframe.

The lesson is clear: If you are flying a retractable in an area of turbulence and are the least suspicious of an upset, fly with the landing gear extended (observing the proper limiting speed for flight with the gear down) to minimize speed buildup in case of a loss of control. Also, if control is lost and the airspeed is building rapidly, close the throttle. If this is done in level flight, the nose will pitch down as the airplane tries to maintain a trim speed, but once an airplane is out of control in a spiraling dive, the decelerative effect of an idling engine will only help. Too, when the wings are rolled level from a high-speed spiral, the airplane's tendency is to zoom if in the same power/trim configuration as when it entered the spiral dive. Having the power off should help this.

The flying chore in turbulence is well defined when we consider that a loss of roll control almost always precedes (and leads to) a loss of pitch control in this type accident.

Using flaps to slow an airplane after an upset is not a proper thing to do in most airplanes. Extension of flaps lowers the limit-load factor (the number of *g*s the airframe will withstand) on most airplanes, and all available airframe strength is nice to have during a recovery.

Having said all this, it must also be said that the chances of a successful recovery from a spiral dive are not good. The dynamics of this maneuver are almost overwhelming, and when an average retractable gear single or light twin is in a fully developed spiral dive, the airspeed is likely 300 knots or more and the rate of descent exceeds 15,000 feet per minute. The spiral dive has been described as a "vertical barrel roll," and it is deceptively easy to enter.

Only one mistake is required after the beginning of a loss of roll control. If, for example, the airplane has reached a 45-degree bank angle and the airspeed, rate of descent, and angle of bank are increasing and the pilot addresses the airspeed and vertical speed instead of the bank angle, school is likely out. Pulling back on the wheel will only serve to tighten the spiral and allow the bank angle to increase even more.

Eventually, the airplane will reach a nose-down, steep-bank-angle equilibrium and accelerate to a terminal velocity. The *g*-force builds to over five. As a tribute to airframe strength, many airframes do not fail in the spiral itself. They get to the ground whole and they can literally disappear into the ground if it is at all soft. In some cases—one of the Malibus discussed earlier could have been an example—the airplane might exit the clouds intact and the pilot might dismantle it in an overly enthusiastic recovery attempt. Experimentation with spiral dives in a simulator led me to believe that, like so many other things, avoiding the event is the only sure way for it not to affect your life. To help minimize loss-of-control risk, proficient pilots seek plenty of unusual-attitude recovery practice, both full and partial panel.

A little aerobatic training doesn't hurt, either. It will show how the airspeed increases when the nose is down and how to roll an airplane back upright from an inverted position. Some pilots shy away from aerobatic training because they don't want to become aerobats. That isn't the point. If nothing else, let the instructor put the airplane in the most unusual of attitudes and then teach you how to manage the airplane in a recovery from that attitude. I would hasten to add that aerobatic training is a speciality, so seek out an instructor who works in this field.

Not all turbulence-related accidents occur in or around thunderstorms. There's an occasional airframe failure in turbulence over mountains. Here the preventive action is airspeed control. Maneuvering speed is *the* speed.

Routine

With those things behind us, IFR accidents take on a predictable sameness that is discouraging, and the record is quite bad. Because all the FAA numbers on hours flown are approximate and subject to any number of errors as well as a lot of interpolation, I shy away from any exact comparison, but the accident rate in retractables and light twins flying IFR in instrument meterorological conditions appears to be at least twice as bad as the general accident rate—and it is possibly much worse than that.

Over 60 percent of these accidents are related to nothing other than poor flying technique, lousy judgment, and botched procedures. Time after time, we find that the pilot flew a perfectly good airplane into the whole world. No contest.

An Aztec hit a 50-foot tree on the third attempt at a night VOR approach in below-minimum weather conditions.

A Cessna 210 descended below the decision height and hit terrain.

A Mooney descended below the minimum descent altitude and hit trees two miles short of the runway at night.

An Aztec flew into a lake on a night approach.

An Aero Commander hit a tree when below the minimum descent altitude on a night approach.

A P210 crashed 1,250 feet left of the localizer and 3,250 feet past the approach end of the runway on a second attempt at a night ILS approach in dense fog.

A Travel Air crashed three miles from the airport on an ILS approach at night—on the localizer but quite below the glideslope.

A Mooney missed the approach and then flew into terrain on an improperly excuted missed approach at night.

A DC-3 hit a tower two miles from the runway. The weather was below minimums for the night approach.

A Cherokee hit a mile short of the runway on a night ILS approach in minimum conditions.

A Cessna 172 went below minimum descent altitude and hit, one-and-a-half miles from the runway, at night.

A Beech Sport hit trees three miles from the airport on a localizer approach at night.

A Skymaster crashed after letting down at an airport where there was no published approach. You guessed it: at night.

A King Air went below minimum descent altitude and hit trees one-and-a-half miles from the end of the runway at night.

A Merlin flew into the ground a half-mile from the runway on a night, circling approach.

A Baron descended from the assigned altitude and flew into terrain for undetermined reasons.

A Duke flew into the ground two miles short of the runway while attempting an approach in below-minimum conditions at night.

A Piper Arrow flew into the ground short of the runway while attempting an approach in below-minimum conditions at night.

A twin Cessna pilot flew into the ground on the third try at an ILS approach.

An Aztec pilot descended below the minimum descent altitude and flew into the ground on a night approach.

A Baron descended below minimums on an ILS, hit the glideslope shack, and crashed.

A Beech Sierra flew into a hill while below minimum descent altitude on approach.

A Cessna 210 crashed out of a rapid descent and steep right turn as the pilot maneuvered for a second attempt at a night ILS approach in below minimum weather conditions.

A Bonanza flew into a mountain after the pilot became lost on an IFR flight.

A Bonanza pilot descended into water on final.

A Cessna 210 pilot crashed on the ILS final approach course.

A turboprop Commander descended into terrain while flying a homemade instrument approach.

A Commander 112 hit a mountain while descending at night.

A Bonanza descended into the ground on the second try at a below-minimums ILS approach.

A King Air pilot descended below the minimum altitude for the segment being flown and hit a radio tower.

A Cessna 402 pilot descended below the minimum en route altitude and hit terrain.

A Bonanza pilot flew into the ground on a night, circling approach.

Those are primarily approach accidents. Singles and piston twins had about equal amounts of this type accident, showing the risk to be twice as high in singles, again because they fly half as much IFR as twins. Turbine-powered airplanes, which fly more IFR than either singles or piston twins, had about half the involvement in approach accidents.

There is an extremely high incidence of nighttime being a factor in these accidents. If an exact figure on the accident rate per 100,000 hours in night IFR operations in general aviation could be calculated, this would undoubtedly be shown as an area of totally lousy risk management with the accidents happening mainly on approaches. In everything we do in general aviation, night IFR could probably be isolated as the most lethal activity.

A lot of the accidents occur after a first approach is missed. A surprising number occur on ILS precision approaches where vertical guidance is provided but apparently disregarded.

I think there is a direct relationship here to professionalism on the part of the pilot. The best record goes to the pilot who has the best training and who reduces IFR operation to a matter of precise flying and matching numbers on the panel with numbers on the chart. At the other end, flying the single, is the pilot who tends to have the least training, who tends to neglect proficiency flying, and who is probably a lot more prone to descend an extra hundred feet or so to have a look. The great number of night accidents is clear definition of when this reaches a dangerous peak. I dislike using the word *discipline*, but a lack of it is certainly evident when considering the risks taken by pilots on approach, especially at night.

It might be argued that general aviation pilots face more inherent risks on approach than airline pilots. More of our approaches are non-precision, without vertical guidance but, as shown by that list (which was picked at random), we don't do well on ILS approaches either.

The fact that we often fly approaches to airports without weather reporting is not a valid reason for a flight to be any riskier than one to the best-equipped airport in the world, either. If flown correctly, a non-precision approach keeps the airplane at a safe altitude until the pilot has the runway in sight. The fact that the pilot doesn't have access to a weather report makes no difference: either you see the runway from a safe altitude or you don't. It's all cut-and-dried, and the problem arises only when the pilot leaves the safe altitude without the runway in sight or leaves it from a position that precludes a normal landing.

Dropped Ball

Another frequent IFR occurrence is a loss of control for no apparent reason. The airplane hits the ground in an attitude that no pilot would intentionally fly. Thunderstorms are not involved, and there is no apparent mechanical failure. In some, there might well have been a failure that was undetected in the accident investigation, but that would be the exception rather than the rule and is certainly no explanation for any great number of the accidents. This is not related to amateur time in the clouds, either. Over half the accidents were in twins, and there's even an occasional turbine airplane on the list. All you can say is that the airplane got away from the pilot.

A lot of these accidents happen in the course of a missed approach. Things go okay until the approach is missed, then the airplane goes its own way. This could be related to autopilots—those associated with flight directors usually disconnect when a go-around is commanded—but I don't think the correlation can be made without doubt. It is something to consider when practicing, though; let the autopilot fly an approach and then fly a missed approach manually.

A more likely relationship is with the fact that pilots are often distracted during a missed approach. Instead of thinking about the number-one task at hand—controlling the airplane—a pilot instead may think about all the ramifications of missing the approach—such as "Where do I go now?"

Other losses of control could come simply from inattention to the airplane. An inadvertent disconnection of an autopilot could go unnoticed, or the pilot might become distracted by bookkeeping or other chores. Whatever, it's a rather odd cause for a substantial percentage of the IFR accidents, as well as proof that to be a successful pilot you have to pay attention 100 percent of the time.

Some IFR accidents occur during departure. These would include flying back into the ground after takeoff or flying into obstructions or terrain during climb.

No Reason

There are always a few cases in which IFR airplanes fly into the ground for no apparent reason. They just hit level, going fast. These usually happen at night, and there is often some suggestion of pilot fatigue in the findings. The message: remain on the ground when tired, regardless of the type of flight.

VFR airplanes also fly into the ground, but if a pilot must fly on, I'd suggest that possible fatigue is just one more reason to always operate on an IFR flight plan at night, regardless of weather. The demands of IFR can help keep a person more alert, and the requirement for communications can help keep a pilot from falling asleep at the wheel.

Tally

Having examined the bulk of the accidents, it is possible to examine the true risks involved in IFR flying. The myth that single-engine IFR carries with it some unique risk is not supported by fact. Systems are an identified problem but engines have not proven to be a great hazard, although they can and do quit, and occasionally a pilot will wind up in an extremely difficult situation because of an engine failure.

The myth that thunderstorms gobble up general aviation airplanes at a great rate is modified. Ten percent is a relatively small part of the total picture. This in no way minimizes the hazard of the beasts, but it does put the risk in perspective and gives some comfort to the IFR pilot who studiously attempts to avoid storms and who puts great effort into maintaining proficiency at flying in turbulence.

Ice is a problem of about the same magnitude as thunderstorms. A primary risk is in the approach phase of flight, especially at night, and this is best managed by simple discipline. The loss of control is prevented by paying attention.

"Hard" IFR?

In leaving the subject of risks, I would like to cast a harpoon at some terminology that has been floating around general aviation for years. Some say that they would not fly "hard" IFR or that they attach certain conditions to the machinery used to fly "hard" IFR.

This is pure fiction. All actual instrument flying is created equal. It is impossible to put a grade on an upcoming flight because of the basic limitations of information we receive in a preflight briefing. What might appear from the ground as "hard" weather could actually turn out to be a marshmallow. And what could appear easy from a distance can turn out to be wet and bumpy, or icy, when reached. The forecast 800-foot ceiling might indeed be 200 when you get there. The lowest approach I have flown in my life was to an airport where the ceiling was forecast to be 700 feet. When I got there, the runway visual range was precisely at the minimum value.

The situations and conditions that are found in instrument flying are dynamic, and they defy advance classification. When a pilot sets out to fly instruments, the risks are best managed by understanding, by flying with an open and disciplined mind, and by maintaining the ability to meet every challenge. It is fine to establish things you won't do—no turbulence, no flight over obscured mountains, no ceilings below 500 or however many feet you like, for example—but do be aware that the difference between forecast and reality might create a time when you have to perform to the limit of that instrument rating.

The Reward

How reliable does the light airplane become when operated IFR? What is the measure of the reward? It is not possible to put a set percentage on a higher degree of reliability, because a lot of factors can cause the figure to vary. Trying to operate IFR in the Rocky Mountains area in an airplane without turbocharging isn't something to bet on, for example. Too, some pilots are more reluctant than others. Some IFR operations lend themselves to cancellation because of airport location or configuration. Certainly you are going to miss approaches at an airport with a non-precision approach much more often than they might be missed at an airport with a full ILS. It is possible, however, to offer experience as a guideline to the reward that might be found.

My IFR flying started in 1955, and since that time I've completed a very high percentage of the planned trips on the prescribed day. Home base for most of the time I've flown IFR has been in the northeast, although my base was in Arkansas for about ten years.

In reviewing a year's worth of activity in the northeast, flying a Cessna 182 from an airport with a nonprecision approach, I found that 406 cross-country legs were planned. Of these, 384 were completed with little or no delay—meaning that I got where I was going at about the time I thought I would get there. Twenty flights were delayed substantially—I got where I was going on the day that I planned to get there, but I was very late. Two flights were scratched during the year. The number of outright cancellations in this year was a little below average. Looking at a lot of years of flying this and similar airplanes—without weather avoidance or deice gear—I found an average of four trips a year cancelled because of weather.

The reasons for cancellation were what you might expect. Looking at number of cancellations over 4 years, I found 15. I was based in Arkansas during this period, and thunderstorms were the primary cause of scratched flights. Eight of the 15 were prompted by either squall-line or widespread imbedded-thunderstorm situations. A couple of snowstorms are on the list, along with three below-minimum situations and an episode with a rough engine. High surface winds prompted one cancellation. (The winds also caused postponement of the meeting I was going to, so does that one really count?)

Almost all my trips are planned at least a week ahead of time, so you can't say that I must only plan trips when the weather is good. That's just not so.

In basing at an airport without an ILS, I have had numerous instances of landing at a nearby airport with an ILS, but I don't count this as a cancellation because I get where I am going—home—as scheduled, with only the minor inconvenience of having to hitch a ride to pick up my car or ride home in a taxi or rental car.

In recent times, I have had a P210, and for nine years I based it at an airport with an ILS. The airplane is equipped with deicing equipment and has both airborne weather radar and a Stormscope. At the three-year and 1,600-hour point on this airplane, I had cancelled only one trip because of weather. This came soon after I got the airplane, and the cancellation involved a line of thunderstorms. This was before the Stormscope was installed, I wasn't yet fully familiar with the radar in the airplane or with the airplane itself, and diverting instead of continuing seemed the best deal of all. In retrospect, it would still seem like the best deal.

In the eleven years after that, I flew the airplane 4,500 hours and had six outright weather cancellations. One each: blizzard, freezing rain, wind, ice, below minimums, and thunderstorms. A lot more trips than that were cancelled because either the airplane or I didn't feel well. I have flown out of the way many times to avoid weather in the P210, thus being late, and I've delayed trips for a little while, waiting for improvement. There have been several long trips where I was a day later than planned getting somewhere, but most of those were coast-to-coast.

The deicing gear has probably made possible a few dozen trips that I wouldn't have flown without it. In most cases, there wasn't a lot of ice actually there. Once, I diverted because of reported icing at lower levels. I don't think that I have averaged using the boots more than four or five times a year. That's not a lot but, on the other hand, one time pays for them if they are absolutely necessary.

Completing virtually all the trips in the P210 hasn't meant a lot of rough stuff, either. For over 1,000 hours I had a NASA flight recorder in the airplane that made a record of speed, altitude, and g-loading. The highest positive g-load recorded was well under three. In thinking back, I can't remember more than a few of what I'd call rough rides in the airplane. To me, a rough ride is what meets the definition of moderate turbulence—unsecured objects move about the cabin, and pilot and passengers would too, if they were not restrained with belts.

What would an average cancellation rate be when flying VFR? I'd guess at least 20 percent, so the IFR reward is great.

Honesty is the Policy

A pilot must be inwardly honest when making the decision to undertake or continue a flight. And a good grade on the decision comes from how you feel about the flight while en route or after landing. If there is any feeling that the things are (or were) chancy, that the completion was due even in small part to good fortune, or if you were nervous or ill at ease over the proceedings at any time, then the reward sought was excessive. Reaching the destination was simply not worth it.

I don't mean by this that you can't be conducting a good safe operation and still have moments of super-alertness when flying IFR. The greatest challenge in flying is to deliver the goods. The destination is straight ahead. Go that way; press on. Be challenged. Be alert. But also be ready to accept the evidence as conclusive when it stacks against going on to the destination. Part of such evidence is in what you see and hear; part of it is in how you feel.

A friend of mine told me of a flight that proved something about this to him. He was flying a light twin and was pressing hard to get home after being on the road for a week. The carrot was the warmth of family and home. The stick was a great collection of thunderstorms over the Appalachians. He kept on going toward the area of weather. The air traffic controller told him of the weather, and my friend asked for a vector through the best-looking area.

Mistake number one was on mental attitude. There is quite a difference between the "best-looking" or "lightest" area of weather return and a good place to fly. When fooling around with weather, these relative terms are often not acceptable. Had my friend asked if there was a good area to go through, the answer might well have been no. When he later related the flight, I got a strong feeling that he was apprehensive as he got close to the weather. Still, the potential reward outweighed the risk in his mind, and he plunged on.

Then came the first cell. He said that the airplane was ascending even with the throttles back. The rain was torrential and the turbulence almost unbelievable to him. The thought that this was a very hazardous situation surely crossed his mind, as did a wish that he had not proceeded. He hung on, though, emerging from the other side of the cell unharmed but well shaken.

The next question to the controller was whether there were any more cells ahead. There were a lot, and the pilot's mental conditioning was now such that the potential reward of getting on home wasn't worth the risk. That one sample had been convincing (like being clubbed), and he sought and found a storm-free path to an alternate airport, flew there, and landed. He had stepped across the line, and he knew it.

The Airlines

The air-carrier system does a magnificent job in the risk-and-reward business as it relates to IFR in general and thunderstorms in particular. The risk in their flying is very, very low, and the reward is very, very high. They seldom cancel for weather, but there is still a gray area in their thunderstorm operations, and it relates to all flying.

Thunderstorms don't often affect carrier operations, but carriers do lose airplanes to thunderstorms. It is, in fact, one of the larger identifiable risks in riding the airlines. If they lose one every five or six years, would the reduction in risk found in following absolute thunderstorm-avoidance precepts be worth the reduction in the reward of schedule reliability? If indeed the air carriers stayed five miles away from all observed thunderstorm cells and twenty miles away when severe weather is forecast and didn't fly at airports when a thunderstorm is reported, some slight element of risk would be removed, but there would be many days a year of schedule chaos at the major airports of our land.

Too, it must be considered that the elements are dynamic. Pilots and meteorologists can only make their best estimate as to the severity of a bit of weather and base the decisions on that estimate. In cases where air carrier airplanes have been lost in thunderstorm areas, the pilots certainly did not think that the existing weather conditions were too severe to fly through, and in terminal-area accidents other airplanes ahead of and behind one struck down by a storm often proceed unhindered.

If you think I'm suggesting that there is a slight amount of mystery found in seeking reward while dealing with risks posed by the elements, you are precisely correct. Nobody will ever know all there is to know about airplanes versus weather, and if we are going to fly when conditions are inclement we'll occasionally lose one—and that includes the best-trained air crews flying the best equipment. It is often impossible to explain this to a layman. People who aren't pilots often believe that something like a thunderstorm is a given force that can be fenced, isolated, and avoided.

Best Reward

IFR flying's best reward comes in benign weather situations. Here it is possible to plan a flight at a desired altitude and depart with knowledge that the flight can be flown at that altitude. That is in marked contrast to VFR flying, where available altitudes are often restricted by clouds.

IFR also offers a personal challenge and satisfaction that can only be considered a reward. To plan and conduct an IFR flight with precision is challenging and stimulating. From the first thought of weather when preparing for the flight to the personal debriefing that should be conducted after every flight, the operation is demanding.

Flying VFR, you reach an accommodation with gravity. Flying IFR, the accommodation is with gravity, the elements, and the system. The total reward is much greater utility in a flying operation that involves little inherent risk, especially when compared with scud-running in marginal VFR conditions. Once you learn to do it, it becomes an enjoyable exercise as well. If there is a dark side to the reward, it is found in how poorly we, as pilots, manage that inherent risk found in IFR flying.

16. Keeping It Together

Once a pilot gets an instrument rating, has available an airplane fit for the envisioned mission, and understands the risks, the task becomes one of keeping the act straight. The first and prime requirement for this is avoiding self-deception.

First, consider that there are days when some pilots should eschew instrument flying, and there are even some pilots who should abstain completely. IFR is both more demanding of perfection and less forgiving of error than VFR flying. If a pilot feels that instrument flying has had a best shot but that performance during IFR flights is in doubt from start to finish, then keeping body and soul together becomes a matter of sticking to VFR until obtaining more education. If that doesn't help, quit the IFR.

There's nothing to be ashamed of in acknowledging an IFR weakness. Instrument flying requires a rather unique blend of skills and disciplines that is so foreign to some people's psyche that there's just no way for them to be comfortable with the activity. The real ace is the relatively rare pilot who is smart enough to stay away from instrument flying after recognizing that he or she isn't adaptable.

For the great majority, the task is only one of learning about the activity and maintaining a good level of proficiency. Past the initial basic training, the best way to learn is by practicing, by doing, and by being critical of each performance. The latter is both effective and especially important. Any pilot can grade his or her own technique at instrument flying; anyone who can't is not really capable of the basic task.

Practice

Periodic practice is very necessary for every instrument pilot. It takes two forms. One involves the routine flying of an instrument flight. This can be skipped if a pilot is flying actual weather regularly. The other form involves the practice of things that are not routine. This is necessary for all instrument pilots.

If practice of the routine is necessary, it should simulate actual operations as nearly as possible. If the mission is two hours' hood practice, a flight plan should be filed and the flight should be conducted in the IFR system. The required safety pilot can meet the minimum requirements, but it is productive to take an instrument instructor along on occasional proficiency flights.

In two hours of practice it is easily possible to make a short cross-country and fly several of the variations on instrument approaches. An ILS, VOR, and NDB approach should be practiced. At least one circling approach is a good idea, and it is good to land out of some approaches and to execute a missed approach in others.

If a pilot maintains a basic level of currency, this type of practice flight can be made in actual instrument conditions when the opportunity presents itself. Go to the airport early on an IFR Sunday morning and work around the airports in the area, actual IFR. It saves money—you don't have to have a safety pilot—and it is a much more valuable experience than hood time. There is no question that staying current on approaches by flying actual approaches is by far the best way to do it.

In examining risk, we saw that the risk of IFR is managed poorly at night. Perhaps one reason is that most of us do not practice at night and don't often fly IFR at night. Where we can consider ourselves legally current at night if the three takeoffs and landings have been done, does this really make us current at night IFR approaches? I think not. The work load on a night IFR approach is extremely high and it is even higher on a missed approach. Most of us do this very infrequently in actual conditions and seldom practice the events. It is no wonder the record is bad and, really, we need to stay away from night IFR unless recent experience or practice has polished the ability to conduct this difficult operation.

The Grade

When examining the level of skill displayed during a routine flight (practice or otherwise), be especially critical. Routine flights are the ones during which everything works in your favor. If an ideal situation can't be handled with precise aplomb, look out when the weather or the machine starts to show a seamy side. Start at the beginning, with the preflight, and examine every action for any weakness. Remember never to leave with the thought that "it was okay because I made it." The alternative to making it is usually an infinite period of silence, so you'd better always "make it" by a very wide margin.

In studying accident reports, I often look at the pictures of shattered airplanes and try to imagine what was going on in the cockpit just a few seconds before the impact. In most IFR accidents, there was probably no apprehension. The pilot felt he was doing the correct thing. Trouble was, he hadn't maintained a critical curiosity about the situation and double-and-triple-checked everything. Or the pilot was not following the rule to the letter. When your grades aren't straight A's, probe for weakness.

Not Routine

I recall a routine flight that suddenly varied from the routine and gave me an interesting exercise in self-grading. At such times we need to be exceptionally critical of our performance and examine every aspect of the event.

I was flying a brand-new turbocharged airplane. The IFR clearance was to 14,000 feet, and during climb I was deviating around some rainshowers. I zigged when I should have zagged for one shower and wound up in some heavy rain and moderate turbulence. The rain started affecting the aircraft's static system. The airspeed, vertical speed, and altimeter were all showing signs of being bugged by water, so I selected the alternate static source.

Immediately after I selected the alternate source, the airspeed started increasing. Thinking that I was in an updraft, I reduced power a little. The airspeed kept increasing, and I became suspicious. It was well up into the yellow, yet there was no increase in sound level, the wings were level, and the airplane was in a normal attitude. There was also no sensation of an updraft. I know you can't fly by the seat of the pants, but there are certain feelings related to certain things, and it is hard not to be physically conscious of a strong updraft. The airspeed indication just had to be in error, but one doesn't take lightly any decision that an instrument is in error.

It was far too late for an A in the course when I related the airspeed problem with the alternate static source and returned to the primary source. This brought things back more nearly to normal. My grade dropped even more when I realized that I had subconsciously and continuously reduced the power as the airspeed increased and had slowed to a rather low actual airspeed in responding to the problem. On later investigation I found that the alternate static source in this airplane has been hooked up incorrectly and would cause erroneous indications on the pressure instruments every time it was selected.

Some years later when all the flap about Malibus was reported, I thought a lot more about this day. An iced pitot head would cause the same problem—the airspeed acts like an altimeter and increases as the airplane climbs—and I wondered how far I would have gone in reducing power and slowing down had I not figured out what was going on.

The general lesson was that when something goes haywire, go immediately to the last thing that was moved or changed and see if that isn't what caused the problem. Or, if something appears to be malfunctioning or incorrect, check everything that has a bearing on the recalcitrant item. That would make you turn on the pitot heat. The specific lesson in that example was that I had performed poorly in using curiosity to quickly isolate a glitch.

This example is illustrative of many situations in which we become mentally paralyzed. Watch for it in grading yourself. When it happens, a good scolding about the necessity for keeping the mind active is quite in order.

The Detail Work

Back to the practice of the routine: demand perfection in holding altitude and heading and in maintaining a proper airspeed. That is the basis of instrument flying, and if it is not done well, the rest of the operation will probably follow a rather shabby pattern. Don't be satisfied with anything less than the proper position for navigation needle, either. There is a proper reading for each gauge for each phase of flight. The needles have to be somewhere, and they might as well be in the proper place.

Nobody is perfect, and all pilots wander and stray from the straight-and-narrow. In grading your own performance, consider how often you stray, how long it takes you to catch the problem, and how quickly and smoothly you return the needles to the proper position.

The Harder Part

In practicing, take advantage of the opportunity to experience less-than-ideal conditions. Something like the turbulence on a hot and windy day is too good to pass up. Fly approaches. If you can do a good job of instrument flying in uncomfortable conditions like that, turbulence on actual IFR flights is likely to bring less of a tightening of the gut. The winter winds blowing over rough terrain also offer good opportunity for practicing instrument flying in turbulence. Imagine you are in the grip of a thunderstorm, relax, keep the wings level, and make peace with the machine.

Partial-panel practice is also essential, for it is the backup to the vacuum pump in some single-engine airplanes and to the vacuum pumps in twins, which have been known to lose both pumps. In a real situation this would be considered a semi-emergency. In other words, I'd ask for and accept special favors from a controller. But when practicing partial panel, do it as if this is the way it is always done. Accept nothing less on partial panel than the ability to fly an ILS approach to minimums. Accepting anything short of that dramatically increases the risk created by vacuum failure.

I occasionally give someone a biennial flight review and like to start instrument pilots out on partial panel and let them fly an ILS. If they get to the decision height with the ILS needles perfectly centered, we can land and go to lunch and talk about flying. The ride is over because if a pilot maintains proficiency at that task, everything else you might see is likely excellent.

Steep turns are good practice, for they teach discipline. Most of us don't do very well at 45-degree banked turns in clear weather; it is even more difficult IFR, because rolling into and out of turns can be spatially disorienting. Unusual attitudes are also good practice, but don't let just any old safety pilot put you into any unusual attitudes. Reserve the practice of these for flights with an instrument instructor.

Engine Out

In a single, practice an engine-out glide. In the unlikely event the engine should fail, you might as well know what it is like to fly instruments in a gliding airplane. Practice the procedures for maximum glide distance.

Practicing emergency procedures in a twin is rather up to the individual. My personal feeling is that I do not want to fly IFR in a twin unless I feel I have the capability of flying an ILS to minimums in the airplane with one engine feathered. The only way to know that is to practice with one engine at least throttled back to simulate zero-thrust. By so doing, some slight risk is accepted in the training environment to minimize risk in the actual environment. I am willing to do that as a favor to people who ride in airplanes with me. If there is a simulator available for your airplanes, or a generic twin simulator, you can and should practice a lot of these—at no risk.

As you work into and through a practice session, a good feeling comes as mistakes are made, analyzed, and corrected. It's almost like going to the doctor for a checkup. Put it all on the line. Hide nothing. Examine all the nooks and crannies. Don't do this just to satisfy the minimum requirements, either. Stay way ahead of the rules. Just as minimum altitudes represent the very lowest acceptable height above the ground, minimum requirements specify the lowest acceptable level of proficiency activity to satisfy the letter of the law.

Never fail to critique an instrument flight, practice or actual. Examine every part of the flight. If, for example, you are flying into a busy terminal and things seem not to go right, probe your mind after the flight for reasons.

Simulators

Flight simulators are valuable in any proficiency-maintenance program. The true simulators (those that match a given airplane) are limited to turbine airplanes, some piston twins, and a few singles. Even the less sophisticated simulators can be of substantial value to the single or light twin pilot. In the big simulators you can practice all the emergency situations and can do things that would be downright dangerous in the airplane. I really enjoy pushing myself to and then past the limit in these. It sharpens your mind and clearly defines the possible and the impossible. It also often shows that haste makes waste when dealing with an emergency situation. I've learned more than once that a moment of careful thought followed by deliberate action is better than a split-second burst of brilliance.

One of the most challenging and interesting things aeronautical I have done was fly a session in the Concorde simulator, climaxing with a two-engine out approach, which was not exactly the easiest thing to do. I made it, though.

With the simpler simulators, you have neither the realism nor the matching of hardware and characteristics. You do have a basic airplane and can practice much of what goes on in actual IFR flying. A good instructor can overload you in one of these, too, and you can explore the outer limits of your capability.

When you fly any kind of simulator, follow the procedures applicable to the airplane. Don't just turn it on and start flying approaches. The value comes from going through all the motions of an IFR flight.

Total

In the final analysis, instrument flying is a large part of the total when the transportation capability of pilot and airplane is considered. It has been said that a pilot without instrument capability is only half a pilot. That is very true, and only true if the purpose of flying is to get somewhere on a reasonable schedule. In the history of general aviation, IFR flying by non-professional pilots started almost exactly when the airplane started being considered something other than a toy. Since then, everything has worked for the better. Avionics equipment has become more capable at lower relative costs, airplanes have become more reliable, facilities have become very much better, and, above all, the user has been getting more value from flying.

Epilogue

Some of the principles of instrument flying are worth reviewing over and over again. I list some of these here. The list is not offered as a complete one; rather, it is something for you to contemplate and expand to suit your need.

• Don't overcomplicate instrument flying. While it is different and challenging and is not for everyone, it shouldn't be considered exceptionally difficult.

• Recognize that the basics are the cornerstone of IFR flying. Just as you can't fly at all if you can't take off and land, you can't fly IFR if you can't maintain the desired heading, airspeed and altitude, or rate of climb or descent.

• After the basics are mastered, strive for excellence in the application of these basics to navigation and aircraft handling during difficult times.

• Be wary of absolute pronouncements about the effect of controls, such as: "The elevators control altitude." In truth, moving one control always affects more than one instrument. If you must think in terms of what controls what, think of the pilot as controlling the whole airplane. There are times when a pilot might forget that simple fact, but the airplane always remembers.

• Don't forget the importance of always knowing your position in space, especially in relation to the terrain. Immediately preceding an IFR accident, the answer to the simple question "Is this a safe altitude for this position?" is usually no. Continually ask that question about altitude. If the answer is not an unqualified yes, better get with making it so.

• Remember that IFR is a precise business. Numbers on charts mean exactly what they say. Minimums are the absolutely lowest safe altitudes at which you may fly without visual reference. When flying an instrument approach, be aware that this has proven to be the most lethal phase of IFR flight—especially at night. Never ever leave the minimum descent altitude or the decision height unless the runway is in sight and you are in a position to make a normal landing. The rules aren't quite that strict, but do yourself a favor and settle for nothing less than the runway itself.

• Recognize that the required meteorological knowledge for issuance of an instrument rating is sketchy, even though it might not seem so at first. The IFR pilot must continually study weather, and any time you feel that an FSS briefer knows more about meteorology than you do, it is time for you to really hit the books. It is your responsibility.

• Beware of the biggies—ice and thunderstorms. Study, understand, be curious, and never fail to respect their destructive powers. Never procrastinate when dealing with either. Remember that avoidance is the only policy, but do not give up if avoidance efforts fail and you wind up in thunderstorm or icing conditions. Failure is not automatic unless the pilot accepts it as such.

• Options are a big thing in IFR flying. Never intentionally operate without an option. The key is in always being able to say "If Plan A doesn't work, I can revert to Plan B."

Index

Accidents, 198-212
  on approach, 209-210, 212
  from engine failures, 199-200
  fatigue and, 211
  flaps and, 206
  from ice, 204, 212
  loss of control and, 205-207, 210-212
  on missed approaches, 209-210
  at night, 209
  poor technique and, 207-210
  power and, 205-206
  in retractables, 205
  in singles vs. twins, 198-200, 204, 209
  from system failures, 200-204
  from thunderstorms, 204, 211
  true risks of, 211-212
  from vacuum pump failure, 200-204
ADF
  groundspeed calculations with, 62-63
  localizer and, 19-20
  thunderstorm static on, 105-106
Air Force, U.S., 6
Airframe strength, 102-103
Airlines, 216-217
Airplanes, 180-197
  climbing and ceiling capabilities in, 183-186
  descent capability in, 191-192
  endurance of, 181-185
  fuel injection in, 192
  handling qualities of, 186-187
  maneuvering speed in, 189-191
  microphone switches in, 193-194
  panel in, 193-194
  redundant systems for, 159-160, 194
  ride quality in, 188-189
  special instrumentation for, 194
  speed capabilities of, 181-184
  total equipment on, 197
  twins vs. singles, 166-169, 184-186,
      198-200, 204, 209
  warning systems on, 193-194
  see also specific airplanes
Airspeed, 181-184
  in approaches, 33, 38, 176-177
  bank angle and, 16-17
  closure rates and, 139-140
  controller interest in, 176-177
  descent capability and, 191-192
  ice and, 118-119
  maneuvering speed vs., 189-191
  in middle altitudes, 139, 147-149
  power vs. elevators for control of, 9-10
  stall and, 29
  thunderstorms and, 96, 101-103
  in turbocharged airplanes, 148-149
Air traffic control system, 178-179
  see also Controllers
Altimeters, 17
  in approaches, 38
Altitude, 137-138
  controller interpretation of, 176-177
  ice and, 117-118

minimums in, 173
power vs. elevators for control of, 9-10
thunderstorms and, 97-98
see also High altitudes; Middle-altitude flying
Antennas, 193
Approaches, 31-41, 70-71
  ADF, 71
  airplane type and, 38
  airspeed in, 33, 38, 176-177
  altimeter in, 38-39
  artificial horizon in, 36
  autopilots in, 194-195
  bearings for, 71
  circling, 130-131
  daytime vs. nighttime, 126-127
  descent in, 71-74
  engine failure and, 167
  final heading in, 36-37
  final landing checklist in, 74-75
  glideslopes in, see Glideslopes
  gross corrections necessary in, 41
  ground-controlled, 171
  in-range checklist for, 74
  jet wake in, 73
  judging slope for, 129-130
  landing gear in, 74
  letdown in, 40-41
  localizer course in, 19-20, 35-38, 40
  maintaining heading in, 34-37
  MDA or DH in, 38, 40, 42, 71, 74-75,
    130-131
  missed, decision for, 38; *see also* Missed
    approaches
  MVA in, 72
  navigational-system failures and, 164
  navigation needle in, 36-37
  at night, 127-134
  nonradar, 71-72
  obstacles and, 71-72
  organization in, 73-75
  outer marker, inbound, 35-36
  oxygen used for, 73, 132
  partial-panel flying in, 19-21
  power settings for, 10, 34
  preparation for, 132-133
  with radar, 71-72
  radio procedures in, 32
  risks in, 209-210, 212
  runway visibility lost in, 131-132
  sample, 75-77
  slowing down in, 31-32
  system for, 33-34
  visual illusions in, 39
  visual part of, 42
  VOR/DME, 71, 196

weather emergencies and, 169-170
wind in, 35-36
Approach lights, 128
Approach plates, 54-56, 59, 70-71, 137
Artificial horizons, 3, 9
  in ILS approaches, 36
  in initial climb, 4-6
  vacuum pump failure and, 13
ATIS (automatic terminal information
  service), 69-70
Attitude, 6
  missed approaches and, 39
  turn coordinator as reference for, 15-16
Autopilots, 8, 85, 194-195
  autopilot limitations, 23
  flight directors for, 195-196
  vacuum pump failure and, 13
Aviation Weather, 96
AWOS, 70
Aztec, 1-2

Bank-attitude, 15-17
  determination of, 16-17
  instrument changes with, 17-18
  primary tasks for, 16
  in standard-rate turns, 16
Baron, 186
Basic maneuvers, 8-10
  fixation in, 9
  power vs. elevator in, 9-10
  touch in, 8-9
Batteries, 164-165
Beech Sundowner, 186
Beginning flying IFR, 43-45
  experience in, 46-47
  familiarity with environment and, 46
  as normal, 47
  picking weather in, 47
  relaxed atmosphere needed for, 45-46
  solo flight as help in, 47
Bonanza, 186

Cancellations, 213-214
Cardinal RG, 33, 154, 184
Cessna 182, 213-214
Cessna 210, 33, 187, 201-209
Cessna P210 Centurion, 75-77, 103, 122,
  139-160, 188, 214
Cessnas, fixed-gear, 119
Cessna Skyhawk, 33
Cherokee, 5
Clouds, 62
  cumulus, 114-115
  stratocumulus, 113
  stratus, 112

see also Thunderstorms
Cockpit voice-recorders, 99-100
Comanche, Twin, 33
Communications, 32
    audio quality in, 67
    brevity in, 64-67
    call signs in, 64-65
    difficulties with, 80-81
    dry snow and, 116-117
    on ground, 179
    managing thought processes in, 66
    nonroutine, 65-66
    weather information procedures in, 105-106
Compass, in VOR tracking, 18-19
Computers, air traffic control, 178-179
Controllers, 63-67, 79-80, 85-86, 176-179
    airspeed and, 176-177
    altitude and, 177
    attitude of, 177-178
    clearance changes by, 80
    engine loss and, 166-167
    in ice conditions, 124-125
    minimum fuel notification for, 163
    nonroutine communication and, 65-66
    observation of, 176-177
    partial-panel flying and, 12-13, 15
    pilot conflict with, 176
    regional phraseology of, 65-66
    strike by (1981), 177
    traffic called by, 64
    weather information from, 103-106, 110
Control touch, 8-9
Cross-checking. *See* Scanning
Cruise climb
    clouds in, 62
    temperature checks in, 61
    winds in, 61-62

Deicing equipment, 121-122, 196-197
Descent, 71-75
    airspeed and, 191-192
    deceleration during, 25-26
DG, 13, 18-19, 33
DH, 38, 40, 42, 71, 74, 130-131
DME, 196
    groundspeed calculations and, 62-63, 151
DUAT, 51

Elevators, 10
    Mach tuck and, 30
    use of, 10
Emergencies and glitches, 161-171
    communications difficulties, 162
    electrical system failures, 164-165
    engine loss in singles, 166-167

engine loss in twins, 167-168
    immediate action needed for, 161-162
    low fuel, 163-164
    navigational gear failure, 164
    non-safety-threatening situations, 161-162
    weather and, 169-170
Engine failure, 166-168

FAA (Federal Aviation Administration), 174
    on ice, 123
    on scanning, 6
Federal Aviation Regulations, 139, 173-174, 200
First flights. *See* Beginning flying IFR
Fixation, 9
Flight directors, 195-196
Flight plans, 50-51
    alternates in, 69
Flight recorders, 95, 99-100
Flying, 200
FSS (Flight Service Stations), 15, 50, 88, 104,
    174-175
Fuel, 53-54
    calculations for, 54
    extra allowance in, 54
    groundspeed and, 54, 63
    landing gear and, 163-164
    minimum amount of, 53-54, 163-164
    night flying and, 137
    tank-switching and, 166
    in turbocharged airplanes, 149-150
    wind and, 53, 63-64
Fuel injection, 192
Fuel selectors, 74, 137

Glideslopes, 40-41
    jet wake and, 73
    night approaches with, 128-130
    on partial panel, 20-21
    visual approaches vs., 42
Goldwater, Barry, 154
Groundspeed
    ADF and, 63
    fuel and, 63, 53
    in-flight calculations for, 63
    turbocharging and, 149
    VOR cross bearings for, 63

Hail, 109
Hand-flying, importance of, 8
High altitudes
    Mach tuck at, 30
    turbulence and, 31

Ice, 111-125
    accidents from, 204, 212

airspeed and, 119
altitudes choices in, 117-121
boots for, 121-123
cold fronts and, 114
controllers and, 124
in cumulus clouds, 114-115
deicing equipment for, 121-122
in high country, 120-121
at higher altitudes, 153-154
landing with, 111, 120
noise from, 119
possible encounters with, 117-120
in precipitation, 116-117
quick reaction needed for, 125
respect for, 111-112
rime, 112
rules for, 173-174
in stratocumulus clouds, 113
in stratus clouds, 112
supercooling and, 112
surface temperatures and, 123
temperature information and, 118-119
visibility and, 123
IFR rating, 3
perfection as goal with, 220-221
pilot weaknesses and, 218
practice with, 44-45, 218-223
self-criticism and, 218-223
in training vs. actual situations, 43-44,
    46-47, 172-173
In-flight planning
alternates in, 68-70
approach information in, 69-70
approach planning during, 70-73
ATIS in, 69
cloud check in, 62
communication during, 64-68
cruise climb in, 61
groundspeed calculations in, 62-63
plans changed during, 68-70, 215
routine in, 62-63
takeoff in, 60-61
takeoff roll checks in, 60
temperature check in, 61
traffic in, 64
weather checks in, 63, 68
wind check in, 61, 63, 68, 139
Initial climb
acceleration error in, 5
artificial horizon in, 5-6
attitude in, 6
heading in, 7
scanning in, 6
Instructors, 11

Jeppesen (manual), 55, 58
Jet aircraft, Mach tuck and, 30
Jet streams, 109, 139-140, 149

"Leans," 81-83
Learjets, 30, 186
Lindbergh, Charles, 1
Localizers, 19-21, 35-36, 38
ADF and, 19-21
Lockheed Electra, 99

Mach tuck, 30-31
MDA, 39, 40, 71, 74-75, 130-131
Mechanical flying, 4
Microphone switches, 193-194
Middle-altitude flying, 139-160
climbing and descent time in, 149-150
example of, 155-157
icing and, 153-154
machinery and, 140
navigation in, 152
physiological factors and, 154-155
redundant equipment and, 159-160
speed and, 139-140, 147-148
speed limit regulations and, 139
weather and, 153-154
wind in, 147-148
Missed approaches, 38-40, 75-76
accidents on, 210-211
advantages of, 38-40
climb power needed in, 38-40
pitch attitude in, 40
turns in, 70-71
MVA (minimum vectoring altitude), 71-72

National Transportation Safety Board, 99-100
on IFR-approach accidents, 42
National Weather Service
convective sigmets of, 89, 109-110
on wind changes, 148
Natural flying, 3-4
Navigation
dry snow and, 116-117
equipment failure and, 163
in middle altitudes, 152
see also specific systems
Night flying, 126-138
accidents in, 207-209
approach lights in, 128
circling approaches in, 130-131
fuel and, 136-137
height judgment in, 127
ILS approaches in, 128
lights in, 134
night vision and, 131-132

nonprecision approaches in, 128-134
oxygen and, 132
precipitation and, 127
preflight planning for, 135-136
takeoffs in, 134-135
thunderstorms in, 134
visual approach slope indicators in, 128
visual miscues in, 127-128
weather and, 136-137

Oxygen, 73, 132, 154-155, 184

Partial-panel flying, 12-24
ADF in, 19-21
approaches in, 19-20
controller notified in, 12-14
dead instruments covered in, 14-15
experimenting with, 17
glideslope and, 20-21
maneuvering in, 13-14
navigating in, 17-20
pitch in, 17
plans changed in, 13-14
practice for, 222-223
rate of turn in, 15-16
regulations on, 200-204
scan patterns in, 15-16
in single-engine airplanes, 12
tracking in, 18-19
vacuum-source failure and, 13-14
VOR in, 18
Passengers, 57
Peripheral vision, 7-8
Piper Malibu, 140-142
Piper Pacer, 180-181
Piper Warrior, 186-187
Pitch attitude, 17, 29-31
Mach tuck in, 30
stall and, 29
trim maintenance and, 30
in turbulence, 31
Power
basic settings for, 10
use of, 9-10
Practice, 45, 218-224
criticism of, 218-223
of engine-out, 223
in less-than-ideal conditions, 222-223
perfection in, 221-222
simulators for, 223-224
Preflight planning, 48-59
airplane check in, 55-56
approach plate in, 54-55, 59
checklists in, 56-57
clearance in, 58-59

flight log in, 54-55
flight plan in, 50-52
fueling in, 53-54
go/no-go decision in, 51-52, 215-216
grades for flights and, 48
ice in, 122-123
importance of, 48
machine and, 49
for night-flying, 135-136
object of, 57-58
on-board arrangements in, 56-57
passengers in, 57
pilot's condition in, 49-50
route surveyed in, 55-56
for second leg, 59
SID in, 55
start/continue decision and, 52-53
takeoff and, 59
telephone briefing in, 50-51
weather in, 50

Radar, traffic, 105-106
Radar, weather, 103-105, 110
Rainfall levels, 106-107
Range, 181-185
Rate instruments, 6
Reagan, Ronald, 177
Retractables, 10
Rewards, 213-215
RNAV equipment, 196
Rocky Mountains, 120-121
Rudders, 187-188

Scanning (cross-checking), 6-8
changes in, 7-8
patterns of, 15-16
Self-deception, 218
Shoulder harnesses, 167
SID (Standard Instrument Department), 55
Skyhawk, 63, 182, 184-185
Stabilizers
Mach tuck and, 30, 31
Stall, 29
Static wicks, 193
Stormscopes, 88-89, 103-105, 110, 204-205
Stress, 78-87
anticipation and prevention, 84-85
attention diversion and, 81-83
beginning of flight and, 79
changes in clearance and, 79-80
communications as cause of, 80-81
confusion as cause of, 83-84
glitches and, 79-80
leans and, 81-83
learning from, 86-87

planning and, 78-79
single pilot and, 85-86
turbulence as cause of, 81
visual cues and, 81-83

Takeoff
checks during roll for, 60-61
flaps in, 60-61
at night, 134-135
from VFR airports, 179
Thunderstorms, 88-110. 216
accidents caused by, 204-205, 211-212
airframe strength and, 101-102, 108
altitude and, 97-98
avoidance of, 88-89, 109
calculations for, 90-91
climax of, 91-92
drafts in, 89-90, 92, 94-97
electrical activity of, 89
forecasts of, 88-89
formation of, 90-94, 108-109
freezing level and, 91
hail in, 109
jet stream and, 109
life cycle of cells in, 91-92
movement of, 108-109
new cell generation in, 108-109
at night, 134
precipitation and, 89-90
rapid development of, 108, 110
rate of climb and, 93
requirements for, 90
rules on, 173-174
speed and, 96-97, 102-103
tornadoes and, 94-96
turbulence and, 89-94
turning in, 99-102
visibility and, 99
warm fronts and, 98
wind shear and, 93-94, 97-98
Thunderstorms and Airplanes (Collins),
Traffic, 64
airspeed and, 176-177
Traffic radar, 104-105
Turbocharged airplanes, 149-150, 183-184,
185-186
airspeed and, 147-149
engine temperatures in, 153
fuel in, 149-151
wind and, 140, 146-149
Turbulence, 26-28
airspeed in, 189-191
fuel used in, 149-151
in high-altitude upsets, 31-31
lateral stability in, 188

overcontrolling during, 26-28
pausing at neutral in, 27-28
peripheral vision in, 6-7
pitch in, 29
power adjustments in, 30-31
primary factors in, 26
relaxation in, 26-27
speed in, 29-30
stress from, 81
wind changes indicated by, 147-149
Turn coordinators
misleading information from, 17
as primary attitude reference, 16
Turn indicators, 17
navigating with, 19-21
see also specific instruments
Turns
bank angle and, 15-16
leans in, 82-83
Twin Comanche, 33

Vacuum-source failure, 13-14
VASI (visual approach slope indicator), 128
Vectoring
around weather, 104-105
Vertical speed indicator, 18
VOR, 18-19, 152, 163
approaches with, 164, 196
preflight check of, 49
Vortacs, 86, 152

Wake turbulence, 73
Warning systems, 193
Weather
from ATIS, 69-70
controllers' help with, 103-106, 110
emergencies in, 169-171
in-flight planning and, 62-64, 68
middle-altitude flying and, 153-154
night flying and, 136-137
vectoring around, 105, 107
see also specific conditions
Weather avoidance gear, 196-197
Weather radar, 103-105, 110, 204-205
West Virginia, 182-183
Winds
in cruise climb, 61-62
fuel and, 53, 63-64
in middle altitudes, 146-147
turbulence as change indicator for, 147-149
Wind shear, 29, 31, 41-42, 69
overcontrolling in, 28
in thunderstorms, 93-94, 97-98
World Aeronautical Charts, 72